The Great Murdering-Heir Case

The Great Murdering-Heir Case

A Biography of *Riggs v. Palmer*

WILLIAM B. MEYER

SUNY PRESS

For information, contact State University of New York Press, Albany, NY
www.sunypress.edu

Library of Congress Cataloging-in-Publication Data

Name: Meyer, William B., author.
Title: The great murdering-heir case : a biography of Riggs v Palmer /
    William B. Meyer.
Description: Albany, NY : State University of New York Press, [2024] |
    Includes bibliographical references and index.
Identifiers: LCCN 2023022984 | ISBN 9781438496344 (hardcover : alk. paper) |
    ISBN 9781438496368 (ebook) | ISBN 9781438496351 (pbk. : alk. paper)
Subjects: LCSH: Palmer, Francis B., –1882—Will. | Inheritance and
    succession—United States—History. | Disinheritance—United
    States—History. | Murder—Law and legislation—United States—History.
    | Decedents' estates—United States—History. | Inheritance and
    succession—United States—Case studies. | Disinheritance—United
    States—Case studies. | Legal maxims—Case studies. | LCGFT: Court
    decisions and opinions.
Classification: LCC KF759.P35 M49 2024 | DDC 346.7305/2—dc23/eng/20231003
LC record available at https://lccn.loc.gov/2023022984

10 9 8 7 6 5 4 3 2 1

In memory of Andrei V. Bell

Contents

Acknowledgments

I am indebted to Colgate University for a sabbatical leave during which much of the research for this book was conducted; to the New York State Archives for access to the records of the Elmira Reformatory; to Wallace and Jacqueline D. Philips for information on the Palmer family; and to Jeff Staiger for correspondence and encouragement while the book was being written. Two anonymous reviewers provided many helpful comments and suggestions on the manuscript, as did a third on an earlier draft. I am grateful to Richard Carlin, acquisitions editor for the State University of New York Press, and to Susan Geraghty, Aimee Harrison, Céline Parent, and the staff of the press for their work in producing the book. Material that previously appeared in my article "The Background to *Riggs v. Palmer*," *American Journal of Legal History* 60, no. 1 (March 2020): 48–75, is reprinted by permission of Oxford University Press.

Introduction

One April day in 1882, Francis Palmer, a sixty-five-year-old farmer of St. Lawrence County, New York, died suddenly after taking a drink from a bottle of rum that turned out to have been poisoned with strychnine. Suspicion quickly centered on Francis's grandson Elmer, an orphan who was named as the chief beneficiary in the dead man's will. In November, a jury convicted Elmer of second-degree murder in his grandfather's death. Francis's two daughters then appealed to the courts to prevent their nephew from receiving his legacy. As Elmer's lawyers pointed out in reply, no clause in the New York statutes that governed bequests expressly forbade murderers to inherit from their victims. First a court-appointed referee and then a three-judge panel of the New York Supreme Court dismissed the challenge. In 1889, however, the state's highest court, though with two of its seven judges dissenting, reversed the earlier decisions and declared Elmer ineligible to profit from his crime. The Court of Appeals' decision in *Riggs v. Palmer* has been a focus of analysis and discussion ever since.

In a precedent-based legal system, certain decisions attain the standing of what are called leading cases: ones that either first or best stated the grounds for some principle of importance and are routinely cited as authority for it. Standing out from the gigantic and ever-accumulating mass of decided cases, they exercise a commanding influence. From 1870 onward, the judicial opinions in leading cases began to dominate the education of budding American practitioners as the Harvard Law School, soon followed by others, made their close reading the core of its curriculum.

Riggs v. Palmer fits the bill of a leading case twice over. In a narrow though contentious corner of the law of inheritance, it is by far the most

1

celebrated of American "murdering-heir" decisions, ones addressing the right to benefit from the estate of a person whom one has unlawfully killed. But the chief reasons for the fame and influence it has enjoyed lie elsewhere. In another legal domain as broad as the first is restricted, it has served as a kind of meta-leading case for what it seems to say about some of the most general issues in the philosophy and practice of law itself. How much latitude can courts claim in interpreting, and even in improving, the language of legislative statutes? What role should broad principles play vis-à-vis explicit, hard-and-fast rules in resolving legal disputes? How are we to understand the phenomenon of judges disagreeing with one another about what the law requires? What influence ought precedents from the law of one country to have on that of another? What is, and is not, law itself?

Over the course of the twentieth century, the majority opinion in the case acquired some distinguished and influential admirers whose advocacy helped make it the admired touchstone that it is today. One of the most renowned of American judges, Benjamin N. Cardozo, extolled it in 1921 as a model of the art of appellate judging in cases that ordinary legal methods could not satisfactorily resolve. One of the most influential American legal scholars of the mid-century years, Henry M. Hart Jr. of the Harvard Law School, enshrined *Riggs* as an exemplary decision in his widely used, co-authored textbook *The Legal Process* (last revision, 1958), which gave its name to the philosophy and methodology that dominated the American profession in the post-World War II decades. The legal theorist Ronald Dworkin's invocation of *Riggs* as a paradigm of judicial craft, in a series of discussions beginning in 1967, has kept it an inescapable presence in the subsequent literature on the philosophy of law.[1] Advocates of jurisprudential approaches as opposed to each other as natural law and pragmatism cite *Riggs* in their support. Ubiquitous in the upper atmosphere of legal theorizing, it is no less so in the down-to-earth setting of the first-year law school class, where professors use it to introduce some of the challenges of legal reasoning and—it is presumed—the way the best judges respond to them. It is likely that few students receive an American JD degree without being exposed to at least the majority opinion and to something of what has been written or said about it.

Riggs is, then, a very familiar case. Even thirty-five years ago, one commentator described it as already a "too familiar" case.[2] Often called a jurisprudential *chestnut*, a word the Oxford English Dictionary defines as "[a] story that has been told before . . . anything trite, stale, or too often repeated," it has even been promoted, or demoted, to the rank of an "*über-chestnut*."[3] It would be easy to suppose that by now it has been scrutinized and debated well past the point of diminishing returns.

But anyone who presumes to offer the public an entire book on the case must think otherwise. The mountain of commentary *Riggs* has generated rests on a precariously narrow base. Much of the material available for making sense of it has never been exploited. Almost all of the commentators have depended for their understanding on the published appellate decision of the Court of Appeals: its statement of the facts plus the majority and dissenting opinions, along with some assumptions that some of them have supposed (not altogether correctly) that they could infer from that record. When law-school professors ask students to analyze the case, it is on the basis of the same materials. Even the few writers who have argued that a better knowledge of its historical background and context makes for a better understanding of the decision have looked almost exclusively to sources of the same kind—other appellate-court opinions from the same era—to provide that context and understanding. A broader historical dimension to the case has similarly been disregarded: that of how the underlying assumptions about law that later generations of readers have brought to it have evolved. Legal argument tends to assume most questions it addresses, and the right answers to them, to be timeless and unchanging. Advocates and judges discuss the reasoning and the outcome of cases decided a century ago or more as if they were the work of yesterday.

This approach is the conventional one in Anglo-American legal practice and scholarship. The rationale for it is simple: what the opinions in leading cases say and how they justify it, not anything lying beyond their text, is what makes them relevant for law today and defining what the courts can be expected to do. It is thus appropriate that analysis and argument focus almost exclusively on their wording and reasoning. So long as they have not been repudiated by later decisions, they remain controlling precedents when similar factual situations appear in court again. The same assumptions guide the education of those being socialized into the profession through the case method. "Historical background, social context, the identity of the parties, pre-trial skirmishing, and the vagaries of litigation would only distract students from the task of extracting general principles from court opinions."[4] Therefore, "legal analysts exclude insofar as possible events external to their narrowly defined system."[5] In practice and education alike, appellate opinions will need, at most, to be supplemented by sources of a closely related kind: statutes, legal codes, and secondary printed works such as treatises that seek to shape the mass of case decisions into coherent form.

Riggs offers a particularly attractive opportunity for comparing these usual narrow limits of attention with the much broader inquiry suggested by two other approaches. The first of them goes most often by the name of *legal archaeology*. Studies of this sort share an expansive view of the sources that it may be useful or appropriate to explore when trying to understand how a leading case or a doctrine that it supports came about. "Legal archaeology," according to Debora Threedy, one of its leading advocates and practitioners, "begins where most legal scholarship ends: with a reported case decision."[6] In the words of A. W. Brian Simpson, in whose work the term *legal archaeology* first appeared (he credited its coinage to his colleague Peter Fitzpatrick):

> It is no more than common sense to appreciate that it is misguided, if other relevant materials exist, to rely upon law reports alone to tell us what happened in the case, how the dispute arose, what the persons involved conceived the dispute to be about, how it came to be litigated, how it came to be decided the way it was, much less what the consequences of the decision were to the people involved, or to others indirectly affected by the decision.

Legal cases, he suggested, are "fragments of antiquity," and "we need, like archaeologists, gently to free these fragments from the overburden of legal dogmatics, and try, by relating them to other evidence, which has to be sought outside the law library, to make sense of them as events in history and incidents in the evolution of the law."[7] As historical research, the approach needs no defense. Its justification as law lies in the degree to which the materials it explores may make for a better understanding of the origins and proper reach of particular precedents than an approach eschewing them does.

A second and kindred approach is that of the *case biography*. As personal biographies trace the interactions of individuals, once they have come into being, with the world that surrounds them over the course of their life span, case biography explores "the way in which cases develop, and live on in the world of lawyers after the specific disputes that gave rise to them are resolved." The two scholars who offered this definition continued: "The case biography method anticipates that our understanding of legal decisions and law-making processes will become richer when they are located not only in social, political, and doctrinal contexts, but also when considered over time."[8] Though they are fixed at the moment they are issued, what the words of a court opinion mean can change, sometimes quite drastically, as the setting in which they survive and persist does.

The distinction between legal archaeology and case biography should not be given too much weight; their differences are minor and chiefly ones of emphasis. Studies identified with the former approach tend to focus more on the ancestry, conception, gestation, and birth of an appellate-court decision, so to speak, and case biographies give more sustained attention to its postnatal experiences.[9] But there is no antagonism between the two methods, and much overlap in practice; few studies can be exclusively assigned to one category or the other. What they have in common is much more important than anything that sets them apart. What distinguishes both of them from conventional legal discourse is the attention they pay to sources and contexts that it neglects or ignores.

Can these two approaches contribute anything that changes how *Riggs v. Palmer* looks as law? They can indeed. Previous discussions have not even fully exploited the resources of printed American appellate-court records. Details gleaned from these and from sources less often employed in legal scholarship, ones documenting Elmer Palmer's crime and punishment and the milieu in which the case arose and was debated, highlight neglected but crucial aspects of the decision and of the presuppositions of American law in that era.

Among other things, they suggest a novel interpretation of what the five judges who denied Elmer his inheritance were doing: not obeying the imperatives of the law as generally understood at the time, but bending them under the pressure of facts quite specific to the record. Though the Court of Appeals decision fails to say so, and most later commentators have been unaware of the fact, Elmer Palmer was sentenced upon his conviction not to the usual penalty of life in prison, but to New York State's recently established Elmira Reformatory, from which he had been paroled in 1886 and discharged the next year. Other neglected facts of the case unearthed by such legal archaeology bolster the supposition that the key to the outcome is to be found here: that the judges found it intolerable that having been set free so quickly, he should also enjoy the gains he had killed to obtain. Their assertion that existing law forbade him to do so was a kind of counterfeit coin that needed only to be good enough to pass in the single transaction for which it was produced. It might happen with a skillfully counterfeited coin that the internal evidence of its metallic composition or the accuracy of its design would pass the usual tests and leave its genuineness unchallenged, and only external evidence, such as the prior history and associations of the forger, would establish it for what it was. And so it might be too with the internal evidence of an opinion and the circumstances of its production.

Similarly, a long-term case biography shows how eventful and uneven was *Riggs*'s path to the classic status that it now enjoys, in particular how disreputable it was in its youth and adolescence. For its first thirty years, it was dismissed as untenable by most American state courts and leading legal scholars. To see how strongly it was criticized and how little it was followed in its own time, and why, is to recognize how little the New York decision itself can merely be taken as what it claimed to be: an application of the law's unchallengeable imperatives. And to see how attitudes toward it metamorphosed gradually from contempt to reverence is to recognize the need for something more than a strictly internal analysis of its reasoning if we are to understand how it could have represented quite different things to readers holding different assumptions.

These discoveries about *Riggs* put in question most of what has subsequently been said or supposed about the larger rationale, meaning, and importance of the decision. It suggests that twentieth- and twenty-first century readers have taken it far more seriously than its authors or its earliest readers did. Modern interpreters of the case have accepted at face value, and analyzed as good legal authority, assertions that were highly dubious in their own day and that were most likely made only as a show of justification for an urgently desired but, at the time, doctrinally indefensible result. The principles that the court invoked did not dictate the outcome of the case. The outcome, rather, dictated the selection of principles, which were discarded once they had served their purpose. This account transforms the majority opinion from a paradigmatic leading case luminous with universal significance into a unique, historically specific, and rather freakish response to an exceptionally provoking situation, one that eventually gained its present stature because unforeseen developments in the law happened to make reasoning that was unsound in 1889 valid in later times.

That is not to say that its story has no general lessons to offer, for it does. But they are not to be found where they have usually been sought. What they illuminate is not so much the reasoning judges use, and ought to use, to decide difficult cases, as it is the limits and the dangers of presentist and purely opinion-based legal research and reasoning, of what Simpson called "the deeply anti-empirical tradition of the world of academic law and legal theory."[10] Justice Oliver Wendell Holmes wrote in 1921 of a key issue in a case he was deciding: "Upon this point a page of history is worth a volume of logic."[11] A volume of history sets *Riggs* in a new light. In doing so, it illustrates what a more historical approach can contribute to legal studies generally.

This book begins with the story of the Palmer murder itself: the rural setting in northern New York State, the crime, the investigation, the trial, the verdict, and the sentence. The evidence presented to the jury left little doubt that Elmer Palmer had poisoned his grandfather. Yet several subtle but serious legal missteps in his trial would likely have overturned his conviction for second-degree murder on appeal, had not his exceptionally light sentence of indeterminate confinement to the state reformatory (from which he was released after four years) instead of life in state prison made an appeal unadvisable. That lenient punishment was a crucial factor in what followed.

Dismayed by the prospect of Elmer, upon his release, taking possession of the farm he had killed to inherit, his two aunts, Francis Palmer's daughters, appealed to the New York courts to stop him. Chapter 2 traces what happened: how the chance interest of a leading lawyer strengthened the case they were able to present; how the judges at the first two levels where the suit was heard nonetheless upheld Elmer's right under the law to inherit; and what arguments, in 1889, the judges of a divided New York Court of Appeals presented for and against its decision reversing the lower courts. The chapter then looks at similar cases that were decided over the next several decades in other American states. An overwhelming majority of their courts rejected *Riggs* as a precedent, as did the leading legal scholars of the time. Chapter 3 explores their reasons for doing so. Some rested on then-prevalent beliefs about law and about the role of the courts that made them unwilling to follow New York's lead. Some practical concerns about what would happen if they stepped in to amend the law strengthened these misgivings.

Chapter 4 explores the question that then arises: given the strength of the legal objections to the *Riggs* doctrine at the time, why did a majority of the New York Court of Appeals act as it did? I propose an answer, that it discarded accepted legal principles in order to prevent an unworthy and only lightly chastised heir from profiting from murder, and I offer such tests of this hypothesis as are possible with the surviving evidence. This chapter also examines the third way through such cases that the court found and adopted in 1896. Seemingly forced to choose between letting a murderer inherit and twisting the law, it avoided both and reached a desirable result by valid means through the use of its equity powers. Yet that solution to the murdering-heir problem, the most satisfactory in many ways, was nevertheless largely disregarded by later judges and commentators.

The next chapter traces, through the work of its most influential advocates, *Riggs*'s resurrection in twentieth-century American law. How has it been transformed from an aberrant and generally scorned decision to an admired model of how judges do and ought to decide? Not, of course, because the text of the decision itself has changed by so much as a single letter or punctuation mark. Rather, it has offered proponents of an overlapping variety of jurisprudential positions an attractive and appealingly venerable model for the kinds of action they have advocated, becoming with time and repetition a classic decision more taken as given than questioned and critically analyzed.

Chapter 6 juxtaposes *Riggs* with some other decisions that have been studied through the methods of legal archaeology and case biography to illustrate the insights that such inquiry can offer. It can expose important gaps in the relevant factual record in a case as presented in a court's opinion and shed new light on the actual situation that it confronted. Using contextual materials, it can do much to explain decisions that on strictly doctrinal grounds appear surprising and difficult to account for. And it can add depth to our understanding of changes in legal doctrine by relating them to broader changes in society beyond the courtroom that normally go unmentioned in the opinions that judges write.

Finally, a brief epilogue returns to *Riggs*'s origins and traces the main characters (family members, lawyers, judges) in the original case through their subsequent lives, concluding with Elmer Palmer himself.

In a way, this book is an investigation of a historical mystery. The uncertainty, however, does not lie where one might first expect it to. There has never been much doubt about whether Francis Palmer was poisoned, or by whom, or (though later discussion, as we will see, has confused what was originally clear) for what ends. There has long been mystery, not always recognized, about why the New York Court of Appeals ruled as it did; why the courts of other states either chose or (as most of them did) refused to follow its lead; why another and more satisfactory solution to the dilemma of the murdering-heir cases was so rarely taken; and how and why *Riggs* became the classic case that it did. I offer new evidence bearing on those puzzles and propose some answers to clear them up. But the verdict rests with the reader.

To read this book does not require a knowledge of technical legal terms. Phraseology matters, though, and a few points call for explanation at the outset. Like many earlier writers, I have called *Riggs* a "murdering-heir" case, and the words make too convenient an umbrella label to forego. In its strict legal use, however, the word *heir* refers only to a recipient of property from the estate of one who has died intestate, that is, without leaving a will. Such property descends, or is distributed, according to the rules followed in a particular jurisdiction for its allocation among particular survivors. One who benefits through a provision in a will is not an heir, but rather a *devisee*, if the bequest consists of real (i.e., landed) property, or a *legatee*, if it consists of personal (i.e., other than "real") property. If one uses the terms in these ways, Elmer Palmer was not his grandfather's heir but rather, under the latter's will, his devisee and his legatee. Ordinary usage, however, collapses all of these terms into the single one of *heir*, which embraces the others. In this book, I follow ordinary usage. Where the distinction is a significant one, as it sometimes is, I refer to an heir in the narrow sense as either a *legal heir* or an *heir at law*. Where I do not specify otherwise, I have likewise used the term *legacy* indiscriminately to refer to bequests, devises, and legacies in the technical meanings of those terms, and *inherit* to refer to the acquisition of property whether by descent (as the legally designated next of kin), by devise, or by legacy. Similarly, in using the term *murdering heirs* I do not necessarily exclude ones who were accused or legally adjudged guilty only of some lesser degree of homicide. Most of the cases I discuss did involve murder in the technical as well as the broad sense of the term, but some did not. The text makes it clear where they did not and where the distinction mattered.

Chapter 1

Crime and Punishment

The brick farmhouse where Francis Palmer lived, and inside which he took his final gasping breaths in April 1882, still stands, though it is much altered both externally and internally. It is no longer a farmhouse, however, and almost all of the land around it has gone back to forest. Agriculture is far from being the principal livelihood in St. Lawrence County, New York, today as it was then. The road that runs in front of the house is paved, and all of the traffic on it is motorized. But there is little traffic, and the town of Hopkinton—not a clustered settlement, but a territorial division in New York and New England equivalent to what is called a township elsewhere—has fewer residents now than it had in the late nineteenth century. The town of Stockholm, into which the road crosses just north of the Palmer property, is only slightly more populous than it was in 1880. During the same span of time, the national population has grown more than six-and-a-half-fold.

Remote and sparsely settled, St. Lawrence County has never borne much resemblance to the metropolis it shares a state government with. It may seem an improbable locale for a murder; it is a widespread assumption of modern times that homicide is a characteristically urban crime. But it was an assumption that knowledgeable observers in the late nineteenth century did not share. City life, many of them supposed, had a civilizing, moralizing, and restraining effect; rural dwellers were more ungoverned and more disposed to impetuous acts of violence. The great French sociologist Émile Durkheim declared flatly in the 1890s that homicide was more prevalent in the countryside than in the city.[1] Modern research has shown that murder rates declined rather than rose in the major American cities as they grew during the nineteenth century, and that throughout the nineteenth and well into the twentieth, New York City's homicide rate was lower than that of the country as a whole—though it then became much higher.[2] A study of murders in Massachusetts in the decades after the Civil War found them disproportionately common in the thinly populated western counties of the state. Its author suggested isolation and remoteness, the absence of policing, and the outmigration of the most ambitious and successful residents as possible reasons.[3]

The Place and the People

The setting of the Palmer story remains rural, and the seasons today too are much as they were in the 1880s. The winters are long, cold, and snowy in what has come to be called the North Country of New York State, the region lying between the Canadian boundary and the central belt traversed first by the Erie Canal and then by the railroads and highways. But Francis Palmer and most of his neighbors came from Vermont. The severe winters were nothing new to them, and the terrain of far upstate New York—which has also remained largely unchanged—was distinctly appealing. The flat or rolling slopes of the plain country north of the Adirondacks were a welcome change from the steep hills they had left, easier to farm and to travel. In the pioneer settlement of New York in the late eighteenth and early nineteenth centuries, natives of the Green Mountain State found the North Country so appealing that it came to be called *Little Vermont*.[4]

St. Lawrence County's three thousand square miles of land surface made it the largest county in New York and larger than either Delaware or Rhode Island. Its northern and northwestern edges faced Canada across the river that carries the waters of the Great Lakes to the ocean. These townships drew and held the earliest and densest occupation. Towards the south and southeast, population gradually thinned, farm values declined, and crop and pastureland gave way to wilderness as the soil deteriorated and the gradients steepened. Hopkinton and Stockholm, twenty miles from the St. Lawrence as the crow flies, lay in a middle zone where the land was fertile and the terrain still subdued. Rural though the Palmers' neighborhood was, there were many other farms and several hamlets within a few miles. The closest railroad depot, in the north part of

Stockholm, lay five or six miles away; the closest incorporated village, Potsdam, about ten miles to the east-northeast.

The Palmers were relative latecomers to the area. At the time of the 1850 federal census, thirty-three-year-old Francis B. Palmer lived and farmed in the town of Lincoln in Addison County, in western Vermont, south of Lake Champlain. With him resided his widowed mother Dorothea; his wife, Phoebe or Phebe, a year Francis's senior; their son Byron, aged eight; and their two daughters, Cecelia and Lorette, six and three years old, respectively.[5] The next federal census, taken in July of 1860, found the family (without Dorothea, who had died in the interim) on a farm covering about one hundred thirty acres, owned by Francis, in Hopkinton.[6]

Whether they moved directly from Vermont is unclear. Francis was thought by some of his new neighbors to have lived for a time in the West, probably Illinois. If he had, it could have been before his marriage, or it could have been in the 1850s, before the family established itself permanently in New York. Vermont throughout the nineteenth century lost far more residents to other states than it gained from them. By the 1850s, most of the outward movement was to the western states.[7] In any event, 1860 found Francis and his family permanently established in Hopkinton.

The Palmer farm was, by local standards, of more than middling size but not exceptionally large. Its operations, like those of most in its vicinity, were conducted chiefly by the family itself, with occasional hired help. It produced mostly the staples of the grain, livestock, and dairy agriculture of the nineteenth-century Northeast: wheat, corn, potatoes, and barley for household consumption and for sale, and grass and hay for the livestock (several horses, some sheep for wool, a small herd of milch cows, and a few pigs for meat). Most of the milk from the cows was turned into cheese or butter. Several dozen acres of woodland provided fuel, timber, and, in the spring, maple sap for boiling into sugar. In 1870, the cash value of the farm's output amounted to $1,363, according to the federal agricultural census of that year, and that of the farm itself—land, brick house, barn, a few smaller structures, tools, and livestock—to about $7,000.[8]

Unfortunately, though New York State conducted censuses of its own intermediate between the decennial federal ones, the individual-level records for St. Lawrence County for 1855, 1865, and 1875, which might add some useful information on the household, have been lost. Nonetheless, the landmark events in the family's history are matters of record.

All three of Francis's children were married during the 1860s: Cecelia to John Preston of Ferrisburgh, Vermont, in Addison County, and Lorette to Philo Riggs of Stockholm, both farmers; Byron to Susan Nichols of Stockholm, a farmer's daughter.[9] While his sisters moved in with their husbands, Byron brought his wife to live in his parents' household. They enlarged it on May 21, 1865, with the birth of a son, Elmer Ellsworth Palmer, named evidently—as were many male infants in the northern states in those years—for the handsome and charismatic Union hero Colonel Elmer Ellsworth, killed in a minor action in the opening days of the Civil War. The young Elmer and his mother remained on the farm with Elmer's grandfather after Byron's death from consumption in June of 1874.[10] As he grew up, Elmer learned the skills of farming by doing them and attended the local common school for a few months each winter.

Francis appears to have been fond of his young grandson, or else he regarded the fatherless boy as more in need of support than his two now-married daughters. In August of 1880, his wife having died a year or so earlier, he had a will drawn up by a lawyer in the nearby hamlet of Nicholville. It left fifty dollars each to Cecelia and Lorette and the rest of the property to then-fifteen-year-old Elmer, making him responsible for Susan Palmer's support for the remainder of her life. If Elmer survived Francis but died himself before reaching the age of twenty-one, the estate, which would have been held in trust for him, was to go to his two aunts, subject to the same condition.[11] When Susan Palmer died on December 5, 1881, a victim of typhoid fever, the orphaned Elmer inherited directly from his parents a parcel of land of about a dozen acres split off from the larger farm, including a small dwelling that was occasionally rented out, plus some other odds and ends of property. Worth something more than a thousand dollars in all, this legacy remained in trust until he reached adulthood.[12]

The shrunken household gained a new member on March 16, 1882, when Francis married Eliza Bresee, a Stockholm widow in her mid-forties and mother of six grown or teenage children. Of French-Canadian ancestry and birth, she had married her first husband, Peter, a Vermont native, in Canada, whence they had moved to Stockholm in the early or mid-1870s. Peter had died several years later. Eliza's second courtship was a somewhat eccentric one. Francis proposed marriage to her the first time they met, and she accepted on their second meeting.[13] They signed a prenuptial agreement on the day of the wedding, which came less than a month after their paths had first crossed. It provided that in the event that Francis predeceased her, Eliza was to be, as Susan was to have been, supported from the proceeds of the farm by Elmer (or, if he too died first, by the residuary legatees, his aunts), but she was to have no other claims on the estate. Francis signed the agreement with his name, and Eliza with an X mark; she had never learned to write.[14]

Shortly thereafter, Francis, Eliza, and Elmer were joined in the brick farmhouse by Willis Doud, a boy about a year Elmer's junior whom Francis employed and boarded as a hired hand, paying him wages of fourteen and a half dollars a month. Willis's father, Martin Doud, handicapped by the loss of one arm, received some support from the county for his disability. The Doud family lived otherwise on what a small farm in Stockholm yielded them—a cash income in 1880 of around $450—plus remittances from some of the ten children who were old enough to work for neighboring families.[15] Willis was considered slow but reliable. During his first weeks on the farm, he did jobs mostly in the sugarhouse and the barn.[16]

It was not the only connection between the Palmer and Doud families. Around the same time, Elmer met Willis's younger sister Myrtie, who had just begun working for his aunt Lorette Riggs in Stockholm. Promptly smitten, he proposed marriage and gave Myrtie, among several presents of lesser value, what he asked her to regard as an engagement ring. An evidently susceptible young man, he had done the same not long before, much to his grandfather's displeasure, with a Hopkinton girl, Nellie Conlin, whose sister Emma had worked for five weeks at the Palmer farm around the time of Susan's fatal illness late in 1881. Francis had broken up that courtship and gone and retrieved the ring from Nellie; he was not happy to see the story repeating itself. His relations with his forceful, even domineering grandfather strained, Elmer spoke to Eliza about getting away for a while, either to visit his Preston relatives in Vermont or (more vaguely) to go out west. To Willis, as would come out in due course, he expressed his unhappiness much more bluntly. So stood matters on the farm in late April 1882, with Francis a month and a half short of his sixty-sixth birthday and Elmer less than a month short of his seventeenth.[17]

Death in the Afternoon

Before breakfast on the morning of April 25, a Tuesday, Francis—as he not uncommonly did—took a swallow of picra, an herbal purgative, and chased it with a mouthful from the bottle of rum he kept handy in the farmhouse pantry. Around nine o'clock, he and Eliza drove off to pay a visit a few miles away in Stockholm. Leaving Elmer and Willis to do some chores around the farm, mostly woodchopping, and to have a lunch that Eliza had prepared for them, the newlywed couple enjoyed the meal of "potato, meat, maple molasses, fried cake, and tea" to which they were treated by their host.[18] At three in the afternoon, Martin Doud, Willis's father, showed up at the farm to buy some seed wheat from Francis, hoping to use Willis's promised wages as credit for the purchase. He waited for the Palmers to return, which they did shortly after four.

As the two men discussed their business, Martin, who was recovering from a cold, fell into a fit of coughing. Francis offered him a drink from his rum bottle. When Martin complained that the liquor tasted very bitter, Francis took a large swallow of it, and, agreeing with his visitor's assessment, asked Elmer angrily if he had done something to the bottle. Elmer denied having touched it, and he underlined his reply by having a drink from it himself. After Francis and Martin had gone to the barn to begin measuring the wheat, the former soon showed signs of discomfort that quickly turned into acute distress, shortness of breath, and the stiffening of some muscles and violent spasms in others. Martin and Eliza helped him into the house, first onto a chair and then onto a sofa, and Elmer bridled a horse and rode away to fetch help from Nicholville, five or six miles away. By the time he returned with a doctor, Francis was dead, having expired only about forty minutes after taking his dram. Martin and Elmer both showed similar though less severe symptoms of twitching, spasms, and irregular breathing, for which they were given treatment, and which eventually passed off.

The manner of Francis's death immediately aroused suspicion. Poisoning was and remains a relatively uncommon means of homicide in the United States. Yet three sensational cases and four trials over the past decade involving deaths from one particular poison had familiarized the medical and legal communities and the general public of New York State's northern fringe with their characteristic features. One evening in January of 1872, in the midst of his own crowded barroom, a hotelkeeper named Almon Farnsworth of the town of Hermon in St. Lawrence County poured himself a glass from a full pitcher of beer, drank it, fell into a fit, and died within an hour. The beer in the pitcher had been heavily laced with strychnine, a deadly vegetable substance that was readily available and widely used at the time for killing small-animal pests. One man was indicted and tried for murder in Farnsworth's death in August of the same year and acquitted. Three others were then brought to trial in April 1874 on the same charge, with the same result, and the crime remained unsolved.[19]

In 1879, a nineteen-year-old woman named Lillian Manchester died in convulsions while staying with her mother in the small city of Watertown, in neighboring Jefferson County. She was pregnant, it turned out, and the medical evidence pointed to a dose of strychnine as the cause of death. She had worked on and off as a servant in the household of a married farmer, Wesley White, and there was abundant evidence of a liaison between them, including a meeting in a Watertown hotel just hours before Lillian's death. The prosecution maintained that having attempted and failed to procure an abortion, White had then bought strychnine and either administered it to Lilian without her knowledge or had given it to her as a means of committing suicide. Opting for the latter version of events, the jury convicted White of manslaughter, for which he received a sentence of fifteen years in prison.[20]

Also in 1879, David Merrihew, who resided with his married brother Charles on a farm in Lewis County, adjoining St. Lawrence to the south, fell ill and died under circumstances that provoked suspicion once Charles himself soon began to display similar symptoms. Charles's wife Harriet and a ne'er-do-well cousin of the two brothers who had been living with them, Winthrop Merrihew, were indicted for causing David's death through poisoning by strychnine. The charges against Winthrop were eventually dismissed, but Harriet was convicted of second-degree murder and sentenced to life in prison.[21]

Making a Stockholm farmhouse not far from the Palmers' their base of operations, the St. Lawrence County coroner, William C. Smith, and the district attorney, Lewis C. Lang, convened an inquest the morning after Francis's death that went on for several days. Smith supervised a postmortem examination of the body and extracted vital organs for later testing. Several physicians identified Francis's symptoms as those of poisoning by strychnine, which the dead man had used for killing foxes and had stored in a trunk in his bedroom secured by a rudimentary lock.

The district attorney kept Elmer and Willis separate, and they made statements pointing fingers of blame at each other. Each alleged, Willis in more detail, that the other had repeatedly spoken of his intent to do away with Francis, or words to that effect: Elmer, to obtain his inheritance and marry Willis's sister Myrtie, and Willis, supposedly, out of resentment of harsh treatment by his employer. Elmer claimed that Willis knew about Francis's supply of strychnine; had at one point during the day borrowed his set of keys and disappeared briefly into the house; and had later commented that he had given Francis a dose that would finish him off.[22] Willis, for his part, asserted that Elmer had, in front of him, poured some white powder into the rum bottle and remarked—as if he had tried it before—that he was giving his grandfather "another dose."[23] Each maintained that he had not taken the other's threats or actions seriously enough to pass them along to anyone else. Elmer also asserted that there had been some quarrels between Francis and Eliza since she had moved to the farm, while denying that he had been on bad terms with either.

Having elicited their stories, District Attorney Lang then arranged for Elmer and Willis to be briefly together—alone, they thought—in an upstairs room of the house being used for the inquest. He urged Willis, the more suggestible and compliant of the two, to try to strike up a conversation. Lang had posted two men in the room hiding under a bed to monitor what was said. The young suspects, the listeners reported, had begun by talking about sheep. Willis had then said, more or less, to Elmer: "the old man dropped off pretty suddenly," and then "if you hadn't put in so much, he would have been longer dying, and if father hadn't drunk any and you hadn't drunk any it would have been all right, wouldn't it?" According to one of the eavesdroppers, Elmer had answered "Yes"; the other could not remember for sure if he had replied, but he had in any case not denied or contradicted what Willis had said. Willis, both of the witnesses added, had then commented that the lawyers were very sharp, and Elmer had replied that when taken to Canton—the St. Lawrence county seat, where the jail and courthouse were—the two of them would have to swallow a bushel of razors apiece to be equally sharp.[24]

With this testimony and the rest of the evidence before them, the coroner's jury ruled on Friday afternoon that Francis had died from the effects of strychnine, administered by Elmer and Willis with intent to kill. Both were placed under arrest and transferred to the Canton jail.

A reporter who visited them in early May found them lodged separately: Willis in a cell with several other prisoners, Elmer by himself. Willis "seems very glad to have people call on him but is not very talkative. His looks and acts show very clearly that he is far below the average as to mental abilities. He passes most of his time in sleep." The reporter found Elmer reading a Bible in his solitary cell. "He is very talkative and looks considerably younger than he really is (he is 17 years old). He is quite bright looking and is very fond of visitors."[25] Another reporter failed to see Elmer, who was feeling unwell that day and had gone to bed early, but he recorded his impressions of Willis, who "does not seem to be very bright, and does not realize the position he is in." He "willingly told his version of the affair," essentially the same one he had given previously. Asked why he had not warned Francis about the powder he had seen Elmer pour into the bottle, he replied that he had meant to but had forgotten.[26]

Though minors in law where civil rights and privileges were concerned, both Elmer and Willis were old enough to be regarded in the New York State of their day as adults in criminal matters and liable to indictment for first-degree murder. The coroner's jury had thought both Elmer and Willis responsible for Francis's death. From further questioning and observation, District Attorney Lang reached a different conclusion: that Willis was as innocent, in both senses of the word, as he appeared to be, and that his involvement had been no more culpable than that of a slow-to-comprehend and slow-to-react onlooker. For when the case went to the grand jury in mid-May, Elmer alone was indicted, on the charge of murdering Francis. He pleaded not guilty at his arraignment on the nineteenth, his lawyer requesting a postponement of the trial until the fall to prepare his defense. No indictment was sought or returned against Willis, who was released on bond to appear as a witness at the trial.[27]

Elmer spent the summer and early fall in the Canton jail. He shared it for much of the time with only one other inmate, a man accused of stealing a watch, who eventually pleaded guilty and was sentenced to six months in prison.[28] While he waited, the lawyers for each side assembled their roster of witnesses and arguments. Elmer and his initial counsel, W. M. Hawkins of Potsdam, had secured for his defense the services of another lawyer, Pardon C. Williams of Watertown, a leading trial advocate and former district attorney of Jefferson County, who appeared at the arraignment. Williams had a good deal of experience in similar cases, much of it from the other side. A couple of years earlier, he had been engaged to help the Lewis County authorities with the Merrihew poisoning trial, and he conducted much of the prosecution.[29] In June of 1882, he was similarly engaged, this time in his own county, in helping prosecute a Sackets Harbor shopkeeper named William Stokes for the alleged murder of his wife by poisoning (by mercury, rather than strychnine).[30]

The Trial

Amid the final days of a fiercely fought state election campaign, Elmer's trial opened at two o'clock on October 31, 1882, in Canton. Spectators eager to see the principals and hear the details filled every available seat. Presiding was Judge Joseph Potter, a sixty-year-old justice of the New York Supreme Court and former county court judge from the village of Whitehall in Washington County, on the shore of Lake Champlain in northeastern New York. Leslie W. Russell, a St. Lawrence County lawyer who had been elected the state's attorney general on the Republican ticket the previous fall, had announced his plans to conduct the prosecution. In the end, though, other business kept him away, and Lang, then in his first year as district attorney, and an assistant, Ledyard P. Hale, represented the state.

Seated with his lawyers, Williams and Hawkins, Elmer Palmer impressed a reporter as "of medium height and strong build; and with a face not lacking in intelligence, yet indicating a dullness of moral sensibility. His brown hair, recently trimmed, is carefully combed from his broad, square, and somewhat sloping forehead, and his small gray eyes are usually cast towards the ground. He sits with his head erect, and with an air of stolid indifference, and showing at no time any signs of emotion."[31] Another described him as "a robust-looking boy, somewhat pale, apparently from his long confinement . . . his countenance betrays little anxiety."[32] Observers would note his composed and seemingly detached demeanor during most of the trial. While the audience waited for the judge to enter, "two or three autograph hunters were seen hovering around Palmer, but Lawyer Williams drove them off, saying that his client wasn't Guiteau and didn't care to be immortalized in that way."[33] (The accused assassin of President James Garfield, while on trial for murder earlier that year, had passed much of his time both in and out of court signing cards that he distributed as souvenirs.[34])

It took the afternoon and evening of the trial's first day and the morning of the second to assemble a jury. The opposing counsel and the judge ran through nearly eighty prospective members before finding twelve they accepted. Many were disqualified because of opinions they said they had formed about Elmer's guilt or innocence, others for their professed reservations about the death penalty that state law automatically imposed for first-degree murder, the crime specified in the indictment. A reporter thought it "really wonderful how many men are conscientiously opposed to capital punishment when sitting upon a jury for a week will conflict with their business interests," though it was not ordinarily a controversial matter in the county.[35] Ten of the twelve men who finally made it onto the jury, like the deceased and the defendant and most of the county's adult males, were farmers by occupation, their principal chores of the year now completed. The other two were processors of farm produce: a butcher and the owner-operator of a small gristmill. None was from Ogdensburg, St. Lawrence County's only incorporated city (with a population a little more than ten thousand).

On November 1, District Attorney Lang made an opening statement briefly laying out the prosecution's case. He then proceeded systematically through the evidence for the state, first calling Eliza Palmer and Martin Doud to describe the events of the day of Francis's death. Five physicians, beginning with the Dr. Matthews whom Elmer had fetched from Nicholville, testified that Francis's symptoms matched those of strychnine poisoning and that substantial traces of the poison had been found in his body and in what was left of the contents of the rum bottle. The two planted eavesdroppers repeated what they had heard of the defendant's conversation with Willis. A witness who had spoken with Elmer at the time of the inquest quoted him as admitting that he had understood in advance that Willis had poisoned the rum. When riding to Nicholville for a doctor, Elmer had paused long enough to tell a passerby that his grandfather was sick, had always been expected to die of heart disease, and apparently was dying now.

Three younger members of the Doud family also took the stand. The most important testimony of the trial came from Willis, who repeated essentially what he had said at the inquest. Two and a half hours of cross-examination by Williams did not significantly shake his account: that he had heard Elmer speak of giving Francis a fatal dose and had seen him pour a white powder into the rum. Willard Doud, Willis's twin, remembered having heard Elmer say once that he intended to put his grandfather out of the way. Their sister Myrtie, aged fourteen, recalled the contents of a letter Elmer had written her before Francis's death and that she had later burned. He had told her that he would "dress her in gold," that he would be able to marry her soon, as "the old folks would be gone before long," and that he had already made arrangements to rent out the farm for four hundred dollars a year. Two naïve and ingenuous letters Myrtie had written to Elmer while he was in jail were read out in court. They suggested, though Myrtie denied it on the stand, that the two were on familiar and affectionate terms. One of them began:

FRIEND ELMER:—You wanted me to write to you if I wasn't mad at you, and I ain't mad. I am stopping at Philo's now but don't know how long I will stay here. I went home to-day. I have got that ring and won't I keep it till I see you again? I want you to write soon and let me know, and don't you tell Lorett what I write. I like her but I don't want Lorett to know what I write to you all the same. I had a good time to-day. Lorett wants to get the ring, but I shan't give it up until you tell me to. You let me take it, and I won't let anyone have it, will I? . . .

The second letter repeated Myrtie's affirmations about the ring, and both trailed off into a medley of local and domestic trivia ("You wanted to know if Philo had swore about frosted cake any time since you have been here. No he hasn't.") before ending, as the first letter did: "I can't stop to write any more now, and I want you to write soon, and so good by, from MYRTIE," and as the second did, "Write soon Elmer. From MYRTIE."[36]

Over the defense's objections, the statement Elmer had made at the inquest in April was read into the record. At the trial, the testimony that had preceded it threw it into glaring relief as an attempt to cast suspicion in every direction but his own. Acknowledging only that his grandfather disliked his attentions to Myrtie Doud and had made him promise to be more steady in his behavior, Elmer had denied having had any serious differences with Francis or with Eliza. There had, he asserted, been some recent trouble between the newlyweds. Francis once "told me that she told him to start a fire or she would start him and drew a stick of wood to him . . . they didn't speak much that day." He had pointed a much more direct finger at Willis. The hired boy, Elmer had claimed at the inquest, knew of and apparently had access to the strychnine, had meddled with the rum bottle the day of Francis's death, had "spat about some work" with his employer, and had "threaten[ed] several times he would put him out of the way."[37] Elmer had recalled, for good measure, having often heard his grandfather say he was sick of living and was going to do away with himself; and added that Francis suffered from fainting spells. He had maintained, finally, that the swallow he himself took from the rum bottle

Tuesday afternoon had all but emptied it and that the bottle he was shown at the inquest was considerably fuller than it had been before, implying that someone had later tampered with it.

Throughout the trial, Lang sought to bring out, and Williams to downplay, evidence of friction between Francis and Elmer. On cross-examination, Williams drew from Emma Conlin—whom the state had called to attest to having heard Elmer speak of his expectation of inheriting the farm—a denial that she had heard grandfather and grandson quarrel during the five weeks she lived at the Palmers'. Several witnesses described minor disputes they had overheard between the two, though none had taken them seriously at the time. Francis had reproved Elmer once for driving the team of horses badly, once for staying out too late, and on a couple of occasions for squandering too much of his inheritance from his parents on buying things (the purchases amounted to a musical horn, a revolver, a deck of cards, a box of cigars, and an autograph album and a silk handkerchief for Myrtie Doud). Evidence that there had been more serious quarrels over Elmer's neighborhood romances, of which Francis strongly disapproved and which he intervened to break up, came from Emma Conlin, Nellie's sister, and from Eliza. Both Eliza and Willis had heard Francis once or twice threaten to revoke Elmer's inheritance if the young man did not mend his ways of spending and courting.

It was then the turn of the defense. Elmer chose not to take the witness stand. A dozen witnesses asserted that his reputation in the neighborhood had always been good or at least that they had never heard of anything to his discredit. They included his maternal grandfather, Chauncy Nichols of Stockholm, but not his aunts Cecelia Preston or Lorette Riggs, though both sat by his side during parts of the trial. The teacher whose school he had attended for two months the previous winter described him as "an exemplary pupil" and her best scholar of the term.[38] One of the character witnesses, Henry McIntyre, the husband of Elmer's maternal aunt (another daughter of Chauncy Nichols), had something else to contribute. Eliza Palmer, a few days after Francis's death, had destroyed in the stove the half-empty bottle of picra from which Francis had drunk a swallow Tuesday morning. McIntyre testified to hearing Eliza say in his presence (though she denied any memory of it when recalled to the stand) that the fumes from the burning nostrum had made her feel sick. Williams also had several witnesses testify to the value of the land Elmer had inherited from his parents, apparently to show that he had resources of his own apart from his expectations from Francis. If his full legal access to them awaited his coming of age, still several years distant, the same would have been true of anything he could expect from his grandfather's will.

While putting Elmer's local reputation on display, Williams did all that he could to darken Francis's image in the jury's eyes. He asked, but was not allowed, to question on that subject the most prominent of the character witnesses, Jonah Sanford of Hopkinton, a former state legislator and chairman of the county board of supervisors. He was permitted only to draw from Chauncy Nichols the statement that he had not been on good terms with Elmer's other grandfather. (Elmer's family on his mother's—the Nichols's—side had "some religious relations," a later document recorded, but on his father's—and presumably his paternal grandfather's—it was "irreligious."[39])

More sensationally, Williams asked also to introduce evidence that Francis was believed locally to have "used poison upon animals, upon his neighbor's cattle, procuring the death of his wife, the death of his son's wife (the mother of the prisoner), the death of one person in Vermont, and of two old people—a man and wife, whose property he received under an agreement to support them, somewhere in the West."[40] Precisely what basis Williams had for this line of attack cannot now be identified. Nothing he may have had to support it has survived in the record. Yet it seems unlikely that he had no grounds for it at all and was merely counting on Judge Potter to block the line of questioning, as Potter in fact did, leaving the insinuation to do its work. At any rate, the request made in open court may have done something to paint Francis before the jurors, psychologically if not logically, as a sinister character who either had deserved what he had gotten or had made a disastrously bad model for his young and impressionable grandson.

Williams apparently also scented a prime opportunity to have any conviction that might ensue overturned on appeal, though it was one that events never put to the test. He had objected unsuccessfully to the introduction of Elmer's statement as "obtained from him through the influence of promises or threats, or both."[41] He now elicited from several witnesses, Jonah Sanford among them, an account of something that had happened at the inquest: District Attorney Lang, according to their testimony, had either told Elmer directly or said audibly in his presence that although he was not obliged to answer any questions that could incriminate him, he would do better to answer, because a refusal would be taken as an admission of guilt. By the law of the day, such silence could not and would not have been so interpreted. In 1869, the New York legislature changed an age-old provision of the common law and gave accused persons the right to testify in their own defense. Recognizing that such persons might now feel pressured to take the stand as they had not been before, it added a clause to safeguard their interests: "the neglect or refusal of any such person to testify shall not create any presumption against him."[42]

Lang's threat to Elmer was thus a legally hollow one, but it became significant for the fact of having been made.[43] American courts at the time consistently held any statements by a defendant, whether under arrest or during preliminary investigations, that had been uttered under the influence either of threats or of promises of lenient treatment to be inadmissible as evidence. A simple admonition to tell the truth did not fall under the prohibition. What Lang had said, however, if the witnesses were to be believed (and their assertions remained uncontradicted), plainly crossed the line.[44] The statement that Elmer had then made at the inquest, and that Lang introduced at the trial, ought not to have been admitted. That the district attorney should have taken the risk of using the statement suggests either inexperience or a lack of confidence in his chances with the jury without it.

Local interest in the case had by no means flagged as the testimony came to an end. The final arguments by the two sides attracted more would-be spectators than the courtroom could hold, even though "[c]hairs and settees were placed in the aisles and every window was crowded as full as the benches."[45] Summing up first, on Wednesday the eighth of November, following an election-day recess, Williams proposed that the death was most likely no homicide at all, but rather an accident. Having established that Francis kept and used strychnine for other purposes, had had some nagging concerns about his health, particularly his heart, and had regularly taken doses of an array of elixirs that he mixed himself, Williams proposed that he had in some way poisoned his rum bottle by mistake, or that the contents of the burned bottle of picra or another nostrum had been to blame. Willis and Elmer, Williams suggested, had both panicked after Francis's sudden and surprising death and the suspicions it aroused. Each had made up a story on the spur of the moment directing blame toward the other, and all of the Douds had then put their heads together and coordinated their testimony to support Willis, as Elmer's counsel had repeatedly insinuated when cross-examining them.

But not relying solely on the accident theory, Williams spent eight hours, interrupted only by a midday break, sowing doubts with a lavish hand throughout the whole of the prosecution case, disputing every element of it short of the fact of Francis's death itself. He queried the competence and experience of the medical authorities who had testified and the reliability of the chemical tests they had used. He cited details from the recent White, Merrihew, and Stokes trials to illustrate the uncertainties and fallibility of scientific evidence in poisoning cases. He challenged the accuracy of the prosecution witnesses' memories, highlighting some discrepancies between the accounts of the two posted eavesdroppers, and he condemned the propriety of the trick played to elicit information from Elmer and Willis.[46] He emphasized Elmer's confused and overwhelmed state of mind at the time of the inquest, with no member of his immediate family still alive to support and advise him, and faced with a district attorney determined to fasten Francis's death upon him and looking only for evidence that would help do so.

Williams emphasized, too, the presumption of the defendant's innocence, and he put much stress on the good character that the witnesses had ascribed to Elmer and the generally affectionate relations between the young man and his grandfather. He ridiculed the prosecution's attempt to paint Elmer as a dissolute spendthrift, cataloguing the modest array of items he had bought, and pointed out that Elmer, as a minor, would not for several years have been eligible to take control of the farm on Francis's death. He argued that a young man strongly attached and wishing to marry, as Elmer had been, was ennobled by his love and less likely than anyone else to commit a horrible crime to achieve his goal. The largely circumstantial evidence against Elmer, Williams urged, could be rearranged into a plausible case against Willis or even, though he emphasized he was not accusing her, against Eliza Palmer, who, he suggested, had both motive and opportunity to poison Francis just as her step-grandson had.

Appealing to the jury not to ruin his client's life on doubtful and inconclusive grounds, Williams concluded with another swipe at the dead man's character, invoking a conversation he had had with Chauncy Nichols outside the courtroom: "This boy has got another grandfather who is here waiting for your verdict." Williams pointed out. "He and the old man Palmer did not get along well together. He would have liked long years ago to have brought the boy away from under the old man," and he quoted Nichols as saying: "If I could have got him away, this never would have happened."[47] At the end, "hardly a dry eye could be seen in the vast audience and among the very few were those of the prisoner who although considerably affected did not break down."[48]

District Attorney Lang's final statement, which occupied all of Thursday's session, attracted an equally eager public. "As soon as the doors were opened a stampede took place for a few minutes. The crowd ardent to procure good places crowded and pushed in a frightful manner . . . and some of the window glass on either side of the entrance was broken in the rush."[49] Speaking for only six hours compared to Williams's eight, Lang cogently rebutted all the points raised for the defense. The evidence, he argued, pointed irresistibly to strychnine as the cause of death; the theory that Francis had poisoned himself by accident was wildly improbable; the picra bottle of which the defense had made so much could explain very little of what had happened, particularly the timing of Francis's death and the similar but milder symptoms both Martin and Elmer had displayed. Elmer knew of the will in his favor and was eager to inherit. Several witnesses had heard him declare he was going to poison his grandfather, and Willis Doud, his account unshaken by a thorough cross-examination, had seen him pour a white powder into the rum bottle and avow his murderous intentions in doing so. Francis, who knew his grandson better than anyone else did, had suspected him immediately on tasting the rum. Elmer had tried to throw suspicion onto Willis and Eliza at the inquest, and his conversation with Willis, reported by two witnesses, had amounted to an admission of guilt.

No more than his opponent had done did Lang omit a closing appeal to the emotions. "Too frequently does the 'old man' become a burden to the mind of a thankless posterity," he lamented in conclusion. In this case, "resentment, avarice, and precipitate heedless passion—infatuation" had intensified an heir's impatience to benefit. Francis had plainly been murdered, and the identity of his murderer lay beyond a reasonable doubt. Justice to the dead man as well as duty to society demanded that the crime not go unpunished. Lang called for a verdict upholding the demands "of law, of order, of morality," and representing "a beacon light of safety to our homes, and a warning against temptation in our households."[50]

In instructing the jurors on Friday morning, Judge Potter reviewed the evidence and explained the meaning of the various categories of homicide defined by the law. He emphasized the presence of deliberation and premeditation in the accused's actions as the key factors that separated first- from second-degree murder. Towards the end of his charge, he hinted at the verdict he thought most appropriate and offered a rationale for it. Willis Doud had testified that Elmer had drunk rum, fetched from a jug in the cellar, a number of times during the day. The jurors, Potter intimated, might decide that if he had indeed put the poison in his grandfather's bottle, with his faculties impaired by alcohol he had been acting on impulse rather than carrying out a deliberate and premeditated plan.

In offering this suggestion, Potter blandly disregarded the evidence that Elmer had been talking for some time, while fully sober, about doing what he now stood charged with doing; the fact that, if he had poisoned the bottle, he had left it that way for several hours before Francis drank from it; and the absence of any testimony that he had been truly drunk or even seriously befuddled by whatever he had consumed. Decisions in New York and other states indeed allowed juries to consider whether the accused was in such a state of mind as made it possible to form the intent that the law in some cases required for a verdict of guilty. The Penal Code enacted by the New York State Legislature in 1881 to take effect on May 1, 1882, a week after the Palmer murder, continued the established practice of permitting evidence of intoxication to be introduced when "purpose, motive or intent is a necessary element to constitute a particular species or degree of crime."[51] But the New York Court of Appeals had long since stated an exception for cases where, as evidently in Elmer's, the drinking had not preceded but had followed an intention to commit murder and been only a means for more surely putting it into effect: "For one to drink, that he may drown his conscience and the better nerve himself to commit a crime, is to aggravate his offence" rather than to palliate it, the court held.[52] Judges in other states entered the same caveat.[53] Williams had only followed the clear signals of the law in omitting to argue an invalid point on Elmer's behalf.

Potter did not acknowledge another objection to the verdict to which he was pointing. At the time, though New York's did not, the criminal statutes of a number of states, including the neighboring ones of Pennsylvania, New Jersey, and Connecticut, explicitly made any murder committed by poison (or "by lying in wait") first-degree murder, at least nominally withdrawing any discretion from the jury on the matter.[54] The rationale, one that would have applied in full to the Palmer case, was that no one could perform the sequence of actions necessarily involved in poisoning to kill without the elements of planning and forethought that defined murder in the first degree.

But though these other states merely spelled out what the legal standards necessarily implied in a case of poisoning, the wording of the law in New York made it easier for the verdict to be softened when other circumstances seemed to call for it. Harriet Merrihew had been convicted only of second-degree murder, though if she had poisoned her brother-in-law, and done it, as the prosecution alleged, through a series of doses given over the course of a week and a half, it could only have been with an ample measure of what the law called deliberation and premeditation. As the judge in that case later observed: "The verdict, I presume, was somewhat of a compromise," the jury regarding Harriet as weak-minded, under the influence of her supposed co-conspirator Winthrop Merrihew, and thus not entirely answerable for her actions or meriting the harshest penalty.[55] The jury in the Stokes poisoning trial in the summer of 1882 had similarly defied legal literalism with a verdict (later thrown out on appeal on other grounds) of second- rather than first-degree murder.[56]

The Palmer jurors, even more than the judge, seem to have understood their task to be that of deciding on the appropriate punishment for what they thought Elmer had probably done, not of determining the legal category that the evidence in the case best matched. The penalty, one of them later told a reporter, had been their main topic of deliberation. And they deliberated for quite some time. Beginning their task before noon on Friday, November 10, they took more than twelve hours to complete it. Partway through, they asked Judge Potter a question that a reporter called "a somewhat remarkable one in the light of the evidence": "If Willis Doud put the poison in the bottle, and Elmer Palmer simply knowing it said nothing, would Elmer be guilty of crime as an accomplice?"[57] (Potter's answer was no.) When they returned shortly before midnight, with most of the spectators long departed for the night, it was to declare Elmer guilty of first-degree manslaughter.

Under New York law, such a conviction would have meant a sentence of "imprisonment in a state prison . . . for a term not less than seven years."[58] (The Penal Code enacted in 1881 changed the punishment to from five to twenty years.[59]) Even more plainly than the verdict Potter had suggested in his jury charge, though, manslaughter of any degree was flatly inconsistent with the evidence. In a legally impermissible stretch of his authority, Potter declined to accept it. The rationale for his action was clear enough. According to New York law, manslaughter was homicide committed "without a design to effect death," but through culpable negligence or in the commission of a misdemeanor.[60] Yet it was clear and uncontested that either Elmer had poisoned his grandfather with the intention of killing him, or else he had not poisoned him at all and on the worst assumption had merely failed to prevent Willis from doing so.

Sent back to reconsider their verdict after a brief lecture on the law, the jury shortly returned to the courtroom to pronounce Elmer guilty of second-degree murder. Writing a few days later to correct a newspaper story that had their initial ballot standing at eleven for first-degree murder and one for manslaughter—something that, if it had happened, would make the manslaughter verdict they originally announced puzzling indeed—Lucius Crampton, a member of the panel, revealed that their initial opinions had been much more divided, with several jurors leaning at the start toward acquittal.[61]

If that were so, a recent action by the state's chief executive had perhaps kept Elmer from going free or at least from getting a hung jury and another trial, the strength of the evidence against him notwithstanding. In its annual session in the spring of 1882, the New York State Legislature passed a bill providing that in all cases where death was a possible penalty, the defense and not the prosecution was to have the privilege of summing up last. Governor Alonzo B. Cornell, considering whether to sign the bill, asked the advice of the state's attorney general, his fellow Republican Leslie W. Russell. Russell replied with a strong endorsement of the measure. In cases where the accused's life was at stake, he urged, no reasonable safeguard against an erroneous conviction ought to be withheld. The prosecution enjoyed, and would continue to enjoy, the right to the trial's opening statement, with all of its power to shape the jurors' first impressions. It was only fair and prudent to give the defense the opportunity to respond to any argument made in the final summation by the state that it could effectively contest. If the defense itself abused the privilege of going last by making outlandish and ungrounded assertions, Russell added, the judge could be relied upon to correct them in his subsequent charge to the jury.[62]

Having gotten Russell's favorable opinion of the bill, Cornell vetoed it anyway. He took the opportunity to read the legislators a little sermon on the dangers of coddling criminals further than he thought they had done already. "For many years," he asserted, "there has been a gradual tendency in legislation with regard to criminal law, to render conviction for grave offenses more difficult and uncertain. One impediment after another has been placed in the way by statutory enactment, until the conviction of a person indicted for crime has become almost a matter of surprise, when defended by able counsel. . . . Such tendencies to lessen the chances of conviction cannot fail to engender disregard and contempt of law, and embolden the dangerous classes to more reckless and defiant conduct." The rights of the accused, he continued, already enjoyed ample protection, including an appeal to executive clemency in cases of unjust conviction. The bill, Cornell concluded, "is certainly a step in the wrong direction. . . . It would be tantamount to a notice to criminals that their chances of escaping conviction were to be increased; and the effect in this respect could not be otherwise than unfortunate and injurious to the safety of life and property."[63]

The *Albany Law Journal*, which agreed with Russell's assessment, thought Cornell's picture of serious crime running rampant and unpunished wildly overblown and regretted that he had based his veto (which killed the measure, the legislature failing to override it) on such baseless assertions instead of addressing the central issue involved: "We should have liked to see some attempt to counter the proposition that on principle a man on trial for his life has a natural right to hear and answer the arguments and assertions of the public prosecutor."[64] Had Cornell signed the bill, it would have been law for the Palmer trial, and it might indeed have produced an instance of what the governor feared: a guilty prisoner "defended by able counsel" frustrating the demands of justice by throwing dust in the eyes of an inexperienced and unsophisticated jury without a chance for the prosecution to respond.

But if Elmer's luck was bad on this point, it did not entirely desert him. Had he been convicted of first-degree murder, it was either to Cornell—who was easily the New York governor of the period most reluctant to grant commutations and pardons—or to his just-elected successor, Grover Cleveland, who would prove nearly Cornell's equal in his aversion to softening the penalties of the law, that he would have had to appeal the mandatory sentence of death if the courts had upheld the verdict.[65] Even success in doing so would only have brought a reduction to the scarcely less appealing prospect of life in prison, and perhaps, after several decades of exemplary behavior, a pardon. Such was the fate that now seemed to confront him. As the court reassembled on November 11, Elmer entered looking "pale and anxious," though he was "soon seen chatting freely with his friends who were near him, and smiling."[66]

Williams made one more effort on his client's behalf. He argued that the jury's initial verdict of manslaughter constituted an implied acquittal on the more serious charge of murder. The judge, he continued, was not permitted to direct a verdict or, what amounted to the same thing, order the reconsideration of an acquittal in a criminal case, but could only accept the one rendered.[67] Thus the verdict of guilty for second-degree murder the jury had returned upon such reconsideration must be set aside and its original finding recorded. It was legally a solid claim.[68] On appeal, it would almost certainly have been upheld and the murder conviction overturned.[69]

Having denied Williams's motion, Judge Potter ran through the usual preliminaries to sentencing. He had Elmer state his name, age, place of residence, and occupation (farmer) and asked if he had anything to say on his own behalf (he did not). Assuring him, correctly enough, that on the evidence he could easily have been convicted of first-degree murder, Potter observed that under state law, a conviction for second-degree murder normally required a sentence of life in prison. He did not, however, impose it. Citing several mitigating factors, particularly Elmer's youth and otherwise good character and the possibility that he could still mend his ways, Potter opted for an alternative that had only a few years previously been made available and was at the time open to judges nowhere else in the country. He ordered Elmer committed to an indefinite term of confinement in the New York State Reformatory at Elmira.

The Sentence

By the late 1860s, some American theorists of penology had begun to assert that many convicted criminals could, with proper treatment, be rehabilitated rather than merely punished by their incarceration. The New York State Legislature responded by appropriating funds to construct in Elmira—a small city in the southern tier of upstate counties bordering on Pennsylvania—the first reformatory for adults established in the United States (and in 1882 still the only one in existence).[70] Acts passed in 1870 when its creation was authorized and then in 1877 once it had opened established the rules under which it was to operate. Judges could send "male criminals, between the ages of sixteen and thirty, and not known to have been previously sentenced to a State prison in this or any other State or country," to Elmira upon conviction for any crime punishable by such a sentence. A term in the reformatory was to have no fixed length but could not exceed the maximum provided by law for the offense in question. It "shall be terminated by the managers of the reformatory . . . when it shall appear to the said managers that there is a strong or reasonable probability that any prisoner will live and remain at liberty without violating the law, and that his release is not incompatible with the welfare of society"; when that point was reached, "then they shall issue to such prisoner an absolute release from imprisonment." The managers also had the power to free prisoners on parole on a trial basis, appointing appropriate persons to supervise them.[71]

In passing this sentence, Judge Potter emphasized to Elmer the extraordinary opportunity he was being given. Having escaped the life-long imprisonment to which he would otherwise have been doomed, he could cut short his incarceration by his own efforts and win his freedom by proving himself a steady and trustworthy member of society. For all the relief he must have felt as matters became clear, the young man, according to one journal, "lost a good deal of the composure that he has so well sustained during the trial and looked as though he for once realized the enormity of his crime." "At the close of the sentence," reported the same paper, "many rushed forward to shake hands with him and bid him a good bye."[72] Then, another recorded, "Elmer was taken back to the jail where he broke down and wept bitterly."[73]

Far from deploring the leniency of either the jury or the judge, the local press applauded both. Elmer's youth was surely a major factor.[74] His prepossessing and unthreatening appearance, his good local reputation as certified by his platoon of neighbors, some dislike or distrust of the victim or of Lang's investigative methods, and even some lingering doubts as to Elmer's guilt created by his lawyer's effective summing-up seem also to have contributed. He surely too benefited from his status as a native of the county and also as a racial insider, as an African- or Asian- or French-Canadian- or Irish-American or southern European accused of a similar crime in the same time and place would likely not have. The Canton *St. Lawrence Plaindealer* observed:

> General satisfaction is expressed with the result. Coupled with
> a prevalent belief in the guilt of the defendant, and the abhor-
> rence of the crime, is a prevailing sympathy for him, springing
> from a consideration of his youth and of the circumstances and
> influences under which his life has so far been spent, and the
> verdict and the sentence which have neither consigned him to
> the gallows nor to a hopeless confinement among older and

more hardened criminals, but which give him opportunity yet for reformation, with the hope of liberty to stimulate improvement, meet with approval.[75]

The reference to "the circumstances and influences under which his life has so far been spent" suggests that Williams's targeting of Francis's character during the trial had not been wasted effort. Other St. Lawrence County journals echoed the *Plaindealer*'s reaction: "there was so much in the prisoner's favor that a conviction was an exceedingly hard matter"; "The result, as well as the light sentence imposed upon the prisoner affords general surprise, and satisfaction, at the same time"; "The verdict was received with general satisfaction, Elmer having commanded the sympathy of all during the trial"; the sentence "will be generally approved by all familiar with the circumstances attending this sad tragedy."[76] Williams and Hawkins might have appealed on several grounds. Yet though Elmer's implied acquittal for murder by the jury's original verdict, if accepted on appeal, would have ensured him against anything worse than a conviction for manslaughter the second time around[77], there was little to be gained. Another conviction was probable, and the sentence might have been to prison rather than the reformatory. Elmer may also not have had sufficient money left to cover the costs of both an appeal and a second defense.

A week or two after the sentence, the culprit, in the custody of the county sheriff, departed Canton. During a stopover to change trains in Watertown, he met briefly at the station with Pardon C. Williams, who advised him to be a good boy and to make the most of the opportunity he had been given.[78] On November 23, 1882, he entered the massive brick-and-stone edifice of the reformatory on its hill overlooking the rest of Elmira. In accordance with the institution's procedure, he was interviewed, the details of his family and personal background were recorded, and his physical, mental, and moral characteristics were assessed. He was judged to be of a "low type physically," "but very strong and in good health" and "a very handy man," skilled at both farming and shoemaking. His past associations had been "bad," he was a "moderate drinker," and (in common with most of his fellow inmates) he displayed little or no moral "susceptibility" or "sensitivity." He possessed, however, what his interviewer classified as good intellectual capacity and a good common-school education, whereas a majority of those entering the institution were either illiterate or could merely read and write.[79]

Elmer then began the regimen of work and vocational training, seasoned with evening classes and recreational activities, that made up the program the reformatory's founder had designed. Zebulon Brockway, the institution's general superintendent and dominant figure, was a controversial figure in his own day and has remained so. He attracted much praise as a pioneer in rehabilitative penology, and Elmira soon became a model for similar reformatories in other states. He also began to draw criticism for his practices in running the institution, and later state investigations in 1893–1894 and 1899–1900 turned up much evidence of abusive and arbitrary treatment of inmates, leading to his retirement at the turn of the century. Brockway's reputation, and that of reformatory penology in general, suffered in the long term from the exaggerated expectations he had aroused, but he was handicapped too by being sent more prisoners than the facility was planned for or than it could adequately handle.[80]

For Elmer, all the same, the reformatory and the company into which he was thrown there undoubtedly formed a better environment than a conventional penitentiary would have made. A majority of his fellow prisoners were close to his own age. All of them were first-time offenders, and all but about five percent of them were confined for crimes against property, the rest for crimes against the person, most of which would have been ones much less serious, and none any more serious, than second-degree murder.[81] And if Elmer was fortunate in his new surroundings, compared to what they might have been, he was equally fortunate in the timing of his stay. One historian has pinpointed the years between 1880 and 1885 as the ones in which the Elmira plan had the best chance of rehabilitating the convicts entrusted to it, Brockway's system having by then been developed and fully launched, and the overcrowding that would soon afflict it having only begun to appear.[82]

That system, which its founder thought applicable to the majority of convicted criminals, whatever their crimes or backgrounds, relied principally on the incentives that it offered them to shorten their time in confinement, develop useful vocational skills and good habits, and return speedily to the outside world. It classified Elmira's inmates into three grades. All newcomers began in the second grade, and their performance was assessed every three months. If they behaved well and applied themselves to their tasks, within six months they could be promoted to the first grade, enjoying improved living conditions and other privileges as well as a speedier path to parole and release. Unsatisfactory behavior brought demotion to the third grade, and those who showed themselves incorrigible could be transferred to an ordinary prison to serve out their full sentence.[83]

Elmer, though judged somewhat averse to work on his initial review, was quickly promoted to the first grade, in the summer of 1883. He maintained this standing despite a number of minor lapses and a more serious one in 1885, when he fell briefly under suspicion of either planning to escape or helping others to try to.[84] In the fall of 1884, almost two years into his stay in the reformatory, his lawyer W. M. Hawkins visited him during a short sojourn in Elmira and found him "learning the moulder's trade" and "doing well, both in his studies and in his work." Zebulon Brockway assured Hawkins that he would be able to place Elmer "where he could earn good wages, if it was thought best to let him out."[85] His good record notwithstanding, he was held at Elmira for about twice the average span in those years, perhaps because of the unusual seriousness of the crime for which he had been committed.[86] But in late December of 1886, four years and a month after his admission, he was released on parole. And after receiving regular reports of satisfactory conduct, in June of 1887 the authorities issued him, now just twenty-two years old, an absolute discharge.[87]

Elmer might have been paroled to Hopkinton or to Stockholm, under the supervision of Chauncy Nichols or of one of Chauncy's four sons, his maternal uncles, living in the area, who were the only family members listed in his reformatory file (plus another Nichols who had moved to Wisconsin).[88] That something of the sort occurred is implied in an unsigned article published in the New York Sun in 1889, shortly after the Court of Appeals decision. "He returned to his home," this account ran, "but somehow his aunts Cecelia and Lorette did not like him, and he, therefore, stepped across the border and lived in Canada. Then his aunts, the children of Farmer Palmer, sued for the property which the young murderer was enjoying."[89] It is likewise suggested in the account of events by Leslie W. Russell, who represented Francis's daughters in the subsequent litigation. Russell implied in 1898 that Elmer upon his release had reappeared in Hopkinton. According to him, it was the outrage occasioned by "the freedom of the murderer within a few years, and his calm assumption of the possession of the murdered man's estate" that had prompted Cecelia Preston and Lorette Riggs to go to court to contest his right to the farm.[90]

If Elmer did return, though, he cannot have stayed long, for on March 16, 1887, (exactly five years, by an odd coincidence, from the day Francis and Eliza had wed), less than three months into his parole, he was married in London, Ontario, near and in which he would spend the rest of his life.[91] He was more likely released, not to St. Lawrence County but to Canada, according to standard reformatory procedure, under the supervision of a willing employer there, known to the Elmira authorities, who could employ his newly acquired skills as an iron molder: in his case, London's McClary Manufacturing Company, a firm specializing in cast-iron stoves and other metalware products, which the city directory published in the fall of 1887 listed as his place of work.[92] Possibly he returned to Hopkinton briefly sometime after his full discharge to explore the possibilities of resettling there or of renting out or selling the farm. But some obstacles to his doing so had already arisen. For, Russell's recollection notwithstanding, it was long before Elmer had left the reformatory, though not before his release under its rules and practices could be seen approaching, that his aunts took steps to deny their murdering nephew his legacies from their father's estate.

On May 3, 1882, a little more than a week after Francis's death, and with Elmer already in jail, the executor of Francis's will had applied to the St. Lawrence County Surrogate for permission to proceed. That officer postponed the matter several times, but on November 20, following Elmer's conviction and departure for the Elmira Reformatory, he reached a decision. Declaring that no one had put in an appearance at the scheduled hearing to challenge the will's provisions, he recorded and certified it and authorized the executor to carry out its provisions: the principal ones of which were the payment of small sums of money to Francis's two married daughters, and the transfer of the rest of Francis's estate to his grandson.[93]

The estate in question was, monetarily speaking, a modest one. It amounted, the courts would later specify, to about $5,500 in value, out of which attorneys' fees and the direct costs of a legal challenge would be expected to take a considerable bite. It was encumbered, too, by the obligation to provide Eliza Palmer her support for the rest of her life. Even so discounted, it might still have been worth suing for. But there seems little reason to doubt Russell's account of the main motive driving the two plaintiffs. Convinced, as well they might have been, of Elmer's guilt by the testimony and verdict at the trial, plus whatever insight into the matter their membership in the family afforded them, they could not have been happy at the prospect of his going free before long and claiming the farm he had murdered his grandfather, their father, to acquire. But they confronted a daunting obstacle: the apparent validity of the bequest, which infringed no prohibition stated in New York law.

Chapter 2

An Anomalous Decision

Launched in the fall of 1883, the action brought by Elmer's aunts took six years to wind its way through the state's legal system to its resolution in 1889 by the Court of Appeals, which overturned two earlier findings in Elmer's favor. Though conclusive for the case itself, that decision did not dictate how the courts of the other states hearing similar cases in the same period and for several decades afterwards would respond. Three decades later, only one other state, Missouri, had accepted it as good law, among more than a dozen that had at some level considered the matter. The rest dismissed the New York decision in *Riggs v. Palmer* as legally untenable.

The Road to *Riggs*

Cecelia Preston and Lorette Riggs began by consulting Carlton Elisha Sanford, an attorney practicing in the village of Potsdam. A close contemporary of theirs (he was Lorette's age), he too had grown up in Hopkinton, the son of the Palmers' neighbor and Elmer's character witness Jonah Sanford.[1] In late September 1883, he began an action in their names in the state Supreme Court. The complaint he filed asked that Cecelia and Lorette be declared the owners of the farm and the personal property left by Francis, subject to Eliza's rights during her lifetime, and that the administrator of the estate be temporarily enjoined from using any of the property for Elmer's benefit until a decision could be reached. Appended were copies of Francis's 1880 will and of his prenuptial agreement with Eliza, plus a surveyor's description of the boundaries of the farm.

Elmer, being still in law an "infant," and an incarcerated convict for good measure, responded through his court-appointed guardian, who, on his behalf, denied the central allegations of the complaint. So did Ira Dutton, the administrator of Francis's estate.[2] In October of 1884, Justice Potter of the Supreme Court, who had presided at the trial and to whom the matter came for decision, issued the temporary injunction that Sanford had requested. He further appointed the Canton attorney William H. Sawyer as referee, "to hear and determine the whole issues of this cause" and report to him on what ought to be done.[3]

Sawyer, fifty-eight years old, was a prominent and well-regarded figure in his profession who had, among other achievements, secured the acquittal of the defendants in the second Farnsworth poisoning trial.[4] He was also active in local and state Democratic Party politics. He had served for an interim year, by gubernatorial appointment, as a justice of the Supreme Court, though defeated for election to a full term in his strongly Republican judicial district. In 1878, he had fallen only a few votes short of winning the Democratic state convention's nomination for a vacant seat on the Court of Appeals. Their differing party allegiances notwithstanding, he had in earlier years maintained a law partnership with Leslie W. Russell (they had jointly and successfully defended the accused in the first Farnsworth trial).[5]

Russell now appeared before Sawyer in the summer of 1885, along with C. E. Sanford, to argue the case for Francis's daughters. Defeated in 1883 for re-election, the former state attorney general had, without cutting his ties to St. Lawrence County, begun to devote most of his time to a thriving legal practice in New York City, along with occasional ventures into state politics on the Republican side. The cases in the metropolis he was involved in during the 1880s included the contested estates of the "rich miser" James H. Paine and Cornelia Stewart, multimillionaire widow of the department-store magnate A. T. Stewart.[6] It cannot have been the financial rewards that attracted him to the Palmer will dispute. With a longstanding interest in the philosophy of law, a subject on which he had lectured at Canton's St. Lawrence University, Russell apparently saw an opportunity to raise issues that had not yet been passed upon by an American appeals court.[7] His contribution would prove crucial to shaping the outcome.

It did not, though, persuade the first person to pass on its merits, his onetime law partner. Sawyer heard evidence and arguments from both sides and announced his judgment in February 1886. His findings of fact were largely those that the plaintiffs had asked him to make. Elmer, he determined, had murdered Francis in order to obtain his legacy under Francis's will, and Francis "presumably would have altered his will in regard to him had he known or suspected Elmer's murderous intent." Sawyer's conclusions as to the law, however, were entirely in Elmer's favor. The inheritance of property in New York, he ruled, was governed entirely by statute, and "nothing remains to courts but to enforce the statutes as they are." Although the enacted legal codes of "some civilized countries" prohibited anyone who had killed or plotted to kill another from inheriting from the victim's estate—a point that Russell had raised—the relevant New York statutes included no such provision. Thus, as Francis's heir in every way stipulated by law, Elmer "is still entitled under the statutes of this State to take under his will and enjoy the fruits of his crime."[8] The clerk of the court recorded Sawyer's decision and notified the respondents that they were entitled to recover $270.50 in costs from the other side.[9]

Francis's daughters decided to contest the case further, and *Cecelia G. M. Preston and Lorette A. Riggs v. Elmer E. Palmer et al.* was argued before three justices of the appellate General Term of the New York Supreme Court on November 24, 1886.[10] As at the hearing before the referee, W. M. Hawkins, Elmer's cocounsel at the murder trial, appeared on his behalf. Russell again spoke for the plaintiffs. His brief restated the argument that the legal codes of many civil-law jurisdictions, in continental Europe and their North American colonial offshoots, explicitly blocked inheritance by murderers from their victims, attesting to a widespread and long-established sense of its unacceptability. He appealed as well to a recent decision by the United States Supreme Court in the case of *New York Mutual Life Insurance Co. v. Armstrong*. In the course of an opinion for a unanimous bench, Associate Justice Stephen Field observed that a man who had obtained a life insurance policy on another "forfeited all rights under it when, to secure its immediate payment, he murdered the assured. It would be a reproach to the jurisprudence of the country if one could recover insurance money payable on the death of a party whose life he had feloniously taken. As well might he recover insurance money upon a building that he had willfully fired."[11]

Hawkins might have argued, but did not, that Elmer's very conviction for second-degree rather than first-degree murder, as New York State defined those crimes, exonerated him of having poisoned his grandfather with the aim of inheriting his farm. For such an aim would necessarily have involved the elements of deliberation and premeditation, both of them inconsistent with the verdict that the jury had returned and that the judge had accepted. Either overlooking the point or fearing (or disdaining) to rely on such a technicality, he accepted Sawyer's finding of fact—that inheritance had indeed been the motive for the murder—and repeated instead the referee's conclusions as to the law.

Russell and Sanford were no more successful at this stage than they had been before. A unanimous decision in *Preston v. Palmer*, in an opinion written by Justice Judson S. Landon and filed in January 1887, upheld Sawyer's judgment as referee. Landon remarked that the insurance claim involved in the *Armstrong* case fell under the judge-made common law of contract and as such was open to invalidation on several well-established grounds. "But a will is not a contract. It is the designation in the forms prescribed by statute, by the testator, of the persons who shall enjoy his property after he is dead." There was nothing in the statute that authorized the courts to deprive Elmer of his capacity to inherit under a will that met all of the stated conditions. "The civil law," Landon continued, "and the law in those countries which derive their jurisprudence from it, as we are instructed by the diligence of counsel, holds otherwise," excluding murderers from inheriting from their victims. It held no authority in a New York court, though, which followed Anglo-American common law where statutes had not supplemented or displaced it, and where no such exception had been decreed. "Perhaps this case," Landon concluded, "will suggest to the law-makers the imposition of such incapacity in like cases. But as it has not been imposed by the legislature, we cannot declare it."[12]

Some changes in the cast of characters had taken place by the time of the ruling. Elmer, now legally an adult, had only just been paroled from the reformatory, but not yet formally discharged. Cecelia Preston had died at her home in Vermont on October 27, 1886, while the case was pending before the Supreme Court. She was survived by her husband, John Preston, and three children, Etta May (the oldest, born in 1878), Arthur, and Maude (six others had died earlier, four of them within a few days of one another in a diphtheria epidemic).[13] When the two families decided to take the matter to the one forum still open to them, the New York Court of Appeals, they had Lorette Riggs's husband Philo appointed guardian *ad litem* (for the purposes of the suit) of the rights in Francis's estate that the three young Prestons inherited from their mother.[14] Thus it was that *Preston v. Palmer* metamorphosed into *Philo Riggs, Guardian* ad litem *of Ettie* [sic] *M. Preston et al., infants, and Lorette A. Riggs v. Elmer*

E. Palmer et al., or, in short, *Riggs v. Palmer*, the name under which it would become famous.

Russell once more argued the case for the plaintiffs before the Court of Appeals, and Elmer was again represented by Hawkins.[15] Russell's lengthy, ambitious, and richly documented brief frankly admitted that the letter of the New York statutes did not support the claim his clients were making. He posed the question facing the Court of Appeals as: "whether the unwritten law, founded upon natural justice and public policy, is sufficient to prevent this murderer from reaping the benefits of his crime by the aid and protection of the law." Both the will itself and the statute of wills, he asserted, contained between the lines an implied exception, requiring no explicit statement, that covered such a case as this. The enacted legal codes of various civil-law jurisdictions denied murderers the right to inherit from their victims, attesting to the general rejection of such an outcome by much of the Western world.

That the judge-made common law, which held sway in Britain and the United States, likewise rejected it, Russell maintained, was shown by the time-honored status and currency among lawyers in both countries of several legal maxims—essentially, pithy proverbial formulas that purported to capture in a nutshell some principle of fundamental authority and applicability—that pointed the same way, one of them in particular: "No man shall take advantage of his own wrong" (in the original Latin, which Russell did not add, *Nullus commodum capere potest de injuria sua propria*). Sound public policy, finally, demanded that Elmer's legacy be invalidated, lest the message go forth that American courts would grant murders undertaken for profit their sought-after reward. Russell asserted again that the provisions of "the unwritten law" overruled anything in the written law that might seem to require that outcome. "It will not be assumed that the statute was intended to protect and cover a foul crime. If it were, the statute itself would be void." In conclusion, he depicted the awful consequences that upholding the lower court's decision would produce: "The devise and bequest sustained, Elmer will dispose of the property in the reckless way in which he used what he did have in his grandfather's life, even, perhaps, to clothing his possible mistress in gold, as he once said. . . ."[16]

The opposing brief, written by Hawkins and another Potsdam lawyer, John A. Vance, was shorter and less ambitious. Its authors wasted little flourish or ingenuity in elaborating an argument that they must have felt was unanswerable when simply stated. The provisions that Russell and Sanford cited from the codes of civil-law countries, it asserted, were irrelevant or even damaging to the appellants' case. Those countries had explicitly enacted such prohibitions, and New York, when it placed both criminal law and inheritance under statutory control, had not. Wills in New York were governed by legislative enactments; when the legislature took matters into its hands, it had superseded the provisions and maxims of the common law on the subject. Francis's will met all of the conditions for its validity set out in the statute. When Francis signed his will, he, "in effect, said thereby no matter when, where or by what means my death shall occur, my property, subject to such obligations as I may assume, and to the payment of legacies, shall pass to my grandson, Elmer E. Palmer. He accepted not only the probabilities, but also every possibility, as to the time and manner of his death."[17] The legislature had full control, not only of the conditions of inheritance, but those of punishment as well, and for the court to disinherit Elmer would be to usurp power by imposing on him a new and added penalty for his crime that the legislature had not decreed.

Hawkins and Vance also cited, but without discussing it, a decision—handed down so recently, in February of 1888, that they may only just have had time to insert their bare reference on discovering it—that at last offered a clearly apt American precedent for the Palmer will case, and one that fully supported their side of the argument.[18] In *Owens v. Owens*, the Supreme Court of North Carolina had unanimously held that a widow's statutory right to dower from her husband's estate, amounting to a third of its total value, was not affected by her having been convicted as an accessory before the fact to her husband's murder, so long as the law creating that right stated no such exception, as in this instance it did not. The judges observed that the legislators who had written the dower provision into law were free to amend it in order to close any loopholes that came to their attention. That they had once already amended its original wording, denying dower to a wife who had committed adultery and was not living with her husband at the time of his death, the North Carolina court added, was all the more reason to make any further alterations in the law their duty and not its own.[19]

The Court of Appeals Pronounces

Having considered the record and arguments in the case, the seven-member Court of Appeals, by a vote of five to two, reversed the earlier

New York judgments in a decision announced on October 9, 1889, declaring Elmer ineligible to inherit under Francis's will.[20] The majority opinion was written by Judge Robert Earl; Judges John Clinton Gray and George F. Danforth dissented, the former submitting his views in an opinion in which the latter joined. Earl and Gray both granted that under a literal reading of state law, there appeared to be no barrier to the legacy, but their reasoning diverged sharply from that point on.

Earl's majority opinion offered an impressive variety of rationales for the result it announced, presenting each of them as sufficient in itself, and with no apparent concern that the two principal ones contradicted each other. The first held that the legislators who had written the laws governing inheritance by wills had failed to provide for the case of a murdering heir only because it had not occurred to them that it might arise, or because their words had not conveyed precisely what they meant, and that they would certainly have made a ban explicit had they thought to do so. "If such a case had been present to their minds, and it had been supposed necessary to make some provision of law to meet it, it cannot be doubted that they would have provided for it. . . . The writers of laws do not always express their intention perfectly, but either exceed it or fall short of it," requiring judges in such cases to repair such verbal defects, infer what the legislators had wanted or would have wanted, and rule accordingly. The "rational interpretation" or the "equitable construction" of a statute by the courts involved discerning, behind the letter of its text, the actual wishes of those who had enacted it and avoiding absurd and unintended consequences that might follow from an excessively literal reading of its language. "What could be more inconceivable," Earl asked, "than to suppose that it was the legislative intention in the general laws passed for the orderly, peaceable and just devolution of property, that they should have operation in favor of one who murdered his ancestor that he might speedily come into the possession of his estate? Such an intention is inconceivable. We need not, therefore, be much troubled by the general language contained in the laws."[21]

Having supposed that the legislators had failed to say clearly what they really meant, Earl then attributed their silence to a quite different cause. His second argument, as Brian Leiter would point out in 2009, "simply abandons the first argument" the majority opinion made[22]; worse yet, the two arguments are actually in conflict with each other. The legislators had consciously and deliberately omitted to disqualify a murdering heir, Earl now asserted, because they knew that the case was already covered by the "general, fundamental maxims of the common law" enumerated in Russell and Sanford's brief, which they relied on the courts to apply, by which "[a]ll statutes are governed," and which ran, as he phrased them: "No one shall be permitted to profit by his own fraud, or to take advantage of his own wrong, or to found any claim upon his own iniquity, or to acquire property by his own crime." These maxims, Earl asserted, "have nowhere been superseded by statutes," nor could they be. The codes of civil-law countries, he observed, again drawing heavily on the appellants' brief, had similar origins. They had been "evolved from the general principles of natural law and justice by many generations of jurisconsults, philosophers and statesmen." That the Roman law and the codes of France and of French Canada established on these foundations explicitly held that "one cannot take property by inheritance or will from an ancestor or benefactor whom he has murdered" showed that to be their clear and unavoidable implication. New York's lawmakers, he reasoned, were aware of these basic principles and had supposed that they were "sufficient to regulate such a case and that a specific enactment for that purpose was not necessary."[23]

One might have expected Earl to support this claim by citing a string of cases in American or English law in which courts had overridden or amended the letter of a statute on the basis of any of these or other legal maxims. He cited none. Instead—sensing, perhaps, a need to bolster further his two rickety and mutually incompatible rationales for the outcome—Earl went on to sketch a third rationale, once again echoing the appellants' brief: one that, if the others were valid, was redundant, and that, if valid itself, made them redundant: that to allow Elmer to inherit would be "a reproach to the jurisprudence of our state, and an offense against public policy."[24]

As well as reversing *Preston v. Palmer*, Earl noted but simply and without much explanation dismissed as incorrect the other clearly relevant American precedent, *Owens*, which the brief for the respondents had called to the Court's attention. It was, he acknowledged, "a case quite like this," but he refused to follow it. "I am unwilling to assent to the doctrine of that case," Earl stated; "a widow should not, for the purpose of acquiring, as such, property rights, be permitted to allege a widowhood which she has wickedly and intentionally created." In his search for authorities to support his side of the argument, he leaned heavily instead on *Armstrong*, which the lower court had dismissed as beside the point when Russell cited it: insurance (governed by the judge-made common law of contract) and inheritance (governed in New York by statute) being legally distinct domains.[25]

Finding the facts of Elmer's crime sufficiently established both by his murder conviction and by the affirmation of his guilt in the referee's report, Earl concluded by announcing the decision of the Court: "that the devise and bequest in the will to Elmer be declared ineffective to pass the title to him; that by reason of the crime of murder committed upon the grandfather he is deprived of any interest in the estate left by him; that the plaintiffs are the true owners of the real and personal estate left by him. . . ."[26]

Judge Gray's dissenting opinion in *Riggs* is considerably more coherent. It dismissed as empty the argument that "the demands of public policy" justified a denial of Elmer's rights in his inheritance. Public policy, insofar as it could be known to the Court, was expressed and embodied in the wording of the laws passed by the policy-making branch, the legislature, and in their faithful enforcement by the judiciary and the other bodies of the government.[27] Gray agreed that Elmer had forfeited all moral claim on the estate. He denied, though, that the Court of Appeals had any authority to intervene on a point already fully preempted by statute. "We are bound by the rigid rules of law, which have been established by the legislature, and within the bounds of which the determination of this question is confined." The rules of inheritance were "matters of which the legislature has assumed the entire control, and has undertaken to regulate with comprehensive particularity . . . the legislature has, by its enactments, prescribed exactly when and how wills may be made, altered, and revoked . . . the very provision, defining the modes of alteration and revocation, implies a prohibition of alteration or revocation in any other way. The words of the section of the statute are: 'No will in writing, except in the cases hereinafter mentioned, nor any part thereof, shall be revoked or altered otherwise' etc."[28] A court that added a condition of its own to the list of those that the law enumerated as the sole ones applicable, Gray maintained, would be arrogating to itself the power to amend the legislature's work.

Gray further understood, as Justice Landon of the court below had understood and as Earl had not, that "[t]he appellants' argument is not helped by reference to those rules of the civil law, or to those laws of other governments, by which the heir or legatee is excluded from benefit under the testament, if he has been convicted of killing, or attempting to kill, the testator." For if in those countries murderers were forbidden to profit by inheritance from their crimes, it was not through the operation of some overarching unwritten law taken for granted in all civilized countries, as Russell and Earl had maintained. Rather, it was because the legislative power had enacted such a prohibition there, as it had not done in New York State. "In the absence of such legislation here," Gray concluded, "the courts are not empowered to institute such a system of remedial justice."[29] Echoing the lower court, Gray suggested that the remedy was a simple and readily available one: "the enactment of laws to meet such cases."[30]

He ended by highlighting an issue brushed aside by Judge Earl with a mere flat denial: whether the decision exceeded the Court's authority by adding to the punishment the trial judge had decreed under New York law for Elmer's offense, that of second-degree murder. His peroration ran:

> . . . to concede appellants' views would involve the imposition of an additional punishment or penalty upon the respondent. What power or warrant have the courts to add to the respondent's penalties by depriving him of property? The law has punished him for his crime, and we may not say that it was an insufficient punishment. In the trial and punishment of the respondent the law has vindicated itself for the outrage which he has committed, and further judicial utterance upon the subject of punishment or deprivation of rights is barred. We may not, in the language of the court in *People v. Thornton* (25 Hun, 456), "enhance the pains, penalties, and forfeitures provided by law for the punishment of crime."[31]

The Other States Respond

The Court of Appeals decision conclusively settled the disposition of Francis Palmer's farm and cash and, more generally, the law (for the time being, at any rate) of New York State. It settled very little as far as American law more generally was concerned. The courts of the other states were as free to follow or reject it as the Court of Appeals majority had felt free to reject the earlier precedent in *Owens* from North Carolina. Anyone who would celebrate the majority's reasoning in *Riggs* as a convincing statement—whether of the authority of overarching legal principles, or of the right and indeed obligation of the courts to interpret statutes to give them a more satisfactory meaning than their bare text seems to dictate—must reckon with an awkward fact: that so supposedly compelling an opinion persuaded the judges of so few other state courts in the several decades that followed.

There is a remarkable disparity between the respect and sometimes reverence accorded to *Riggs* in much of the modern literature on jurisprudence and the philosophy of law and its reception in its own day, when it commanded little esteem. Often analyzed as a touchstone of excellence in judicial reasoning, a quintessential or paradigmatic example of how judges decide or how they ought to, it was treated for years in discussions of inheritance as an eccentricity and an extravagance. Judge Earl's reasoning in *Riggs* carried the professional authority of the most highly regarded state court system in the country at the time. American appellate courts cited New York decisions more often, and by a considerable margin, than those of any other state, and far more than those of North Carolina, whose decision in *Owens* Earl had summarily rejected.[32] Yet even with this factor weighing in its favor, *Riggs* did not travel well. A heavy preponderance of American state courts in the late nineteenth and early twentieth centuries hearing analogous cases chose to follow North Carolina's lead instead. Most states, though not New York, eventually took the path that Judges Landon and Gray recommended and that Earl's decision would have made unnecessary. Their legislatures amended their laws to prohibit inheritance by a murderer.

The first parallel case decided by the courts following *Riggs* arose in Nebraska. Like several that followed, it involved a particularly repellent crime.[33] In April of 1886, an eleven-year-old girl, Maggie Shellenberger, was found dead, her throat cut, on the Otoe County farm where she lived with her father, Lee, her stepmother, Miranda, and her thirteen-year-old brother, Joseph Lee Shellenberger. Evidence pointed strongly to her father and Miranda as the perpetrators. The former was tried and convicted of first-degree murder and sentenced to death, though before the sentence could be carried out he was taken from jail by a mob on July 23, 1887, and lynched. On the death some years earlier of his first wife, Emma, Lee had inherited a life estate in a farm that she in turn had inherited from her father, a property that was then to pass to their two children, and it was apparently to gain title to Maggie's share of it that he had committed the murder. This share he had assigned in May 1886 as payment to the lawyers, Frank T. Ransom and John C. Watson, who defended him on the murder charge.

After Lee's death, Ransom and Watson claimed their fee. Joseph's guardian, O. P. Mason, a prominent attorney and former chief justice of the state, contested the claim on the grounds that by murdering Maggie, her father had forfeited any rights in her estate that he could pass on to someone else.[34] Unsuccessful in the Otoe County District Court, Mason appealed on Joseph's behalf to the Supreme Court of Nebraska. He made it his principal argument, much as Russell had done in New York, that the legal maxim denying the right to benefit from one's wrongful actions had an authority overriding any statutory provisions to the contrary. The court first upheld the challenge, adopting the then-fresh *Riggs* doctrine, on January 2, 1891.[35] It subsequently granted a rehearing and reversed itself, emphatically and explicitly rejecting *Riggs* in a unanimous decision issued in 1894.[36]

On January 11, 1889, Caroline Sharkey, a middle-aged widow, was found beaten to death, her head smashed in, in her farmhouse near the town of Eaton, Ohio. Her son and only child, Elmer, in his early twenties, who lived with her, was indicted and tried for her murder. Evidence at the trial indicated that, like Elmer Palmer, he had wanted to marry a young woman of the neighborhood and that his mother had threatened, if he did so, to leave his expected inheritance to someone else. He pleaded insanity, and his lawyers produced evidence of mental disturbances among ancestors and relatives on both sides of his family. Found guilty, he was awarded a second trial on appeal with a change of venue, and, found guilty again, was hanged on December 19, 1890.[37] Caroline had died without leaving a will. By Ohio law, her estate apparently descended to Elmer, her sole legal heir, who had claimed it and then mortgaged it to cover his legal costs. Caroline's surviving siblings and other relatives brought suit for title to the estate against the lawyer-mortgagees. They maintained that Elmer, by his actions, had forfeited his right to the inheritance, and they appealed for support to the *Riggs* decision.[38] The Court of Common Pleas ruled against them in an opinion that methodically examined and rejected their main contentions.[39] The Circuit Court of Preble County upheld the decision in 1892 in *Deem v. Millikin* in a full and elaborate opinion in favor of the mortgagees that similarly dismissed the doctrine put forward in *Riggs*. In 1895, the Ohio Supreme Court tersely affirmed the rulings and reasoning of the two lower courts.[40]

On the night of December 10, 1893, James Carpenter, of the small borough of Port Royal in south-central Pennsylvania, a blind man who in spite of his handicap had become a moderately successful dealer in poultry and eggs since settling in town five or six years earlier, was murdered in his office where he was working late: his throat savagely cut, and his body dragged and dumped into a creek a quarter of a mile away, where it was discovered the next morning. Suspicion fell on his only child, James, in his early twenties, who worked with his father in his business though they frequently quarreled, and on James Sr.'s estranged but still legal wife, Hetty Carpenter. Indicted on charges of first-degree murder, James Jr. and Hetty signed over as payment to their defense lawyers all but a small portion of the two-thousand-dollar estate that James Sr. had left and that, by the Pennsylvania laws of intestate inheritance, apparently fell in equal shares to them. The murder charge against Hetty was dropped, though she pleaded guilty to being an accessory after the fact. James Jr. was convicted, sentenced to death, and executed on June 14, 1894.[41] James Sr.'s brother sued, on his own behalf and that of the murder victim's other relatives, to overturn the auditor's award from the estate to the defense lawyers, on the same grounds alleged in the Shellenberger and Sharkey cases.[42] And the results were the same, James Jr.'s and Hetty's rights to inherit and convey the estate being upheld. Unsuccessful in the county court, the challenge was rebuffed again, and conclusively, in an 1895 decision by the Pennsylvania Supreme Court.[43]

The first case in the new century was also the first to arise in a state that had (in 1897) enacted a "slayer statute" to invalidate legacies and devises from victims' estates to their murderers. Charles Kuhn, an Iowa farmer in his early forties, died on September 4, 1900, after drinking a bottle of beer that turned out to have contained a fatal dose of strychnine. The state brought Kuhn's wife, Sarah, aged nineteen, to trial for his murder. Strong evidence of opportunity and of motive—she was unhappy in her marriage, Kuhn being considerably older and crippled, and had been keeping company with another man—proved sufficient for a conviction and a sentence of life in prison, upheld on appeal by the state's supreme court over a vigorous dissent.[44] Charles Kuhn Sr., the dead man's father, sought to prevent Sarah from claiming the one-third share of the estate that the language of the Iowa Code, which on this point specified no exception for murder, seemed to guarantee her as a widow. His lawyer argued on the basis of *Riggs* that the law did not permit her to profit thus by her wrongful actions. The challenge persuaded a lower court, which reasoned by analogy from the state's statute barring other forms of inheritance by a slayer, but the Iowa Supreme Court, in *Kuhn v. Kuhn* (1904) overturned its ruling in an opinion that accepted the essential reasoning of the *Riggs* dissent.[45]

The outcome was no different in the next case to arise. On March 13, 1903, Thornton Brant, a morose and unsuccessful drayman in the small Kansas city of Mankato, fell into a drink-fueled rage and fatally wounded his wife, Kate, with four blows to the head with a heavy carpenter's adze. Rejecting his plea of insanity, a jury found him guilty of first-degree murder.[46] Kate left no will, and under Kansas law her estate, worth a little more than a thousand dollars, apparently passed to her husband, who assigned it to the lawyer defending him at the trial. Kate's sister, Mollie McAllister, and her other siblings sued the administrator of the estate to prevent the transfer. Murderers, they asserted, could not inherit in law from their victims. The county court judge, however, dismissed their challenge, and so, unanimously, did the Kansas Supreme Court when the matter was appealed to and argued before it.[47]

In the next few years, Oklahoma and Texas followed these states in rejecting the New York precedent.[48] A 1908 case found the Minnesota Supreme Court so badly divided on a number of issues that it did not produce a clear decision, leaving the probate award that had been made to the convicted murderer in effect.[49] When a similar question came before it again two years later, it reached a more decisive result. This time, a majority lined up with the majority of the other states, accepting the gist of an opinion filed in the 1908 case, by the then-chief justice, that had explicitly rejected *Riggs*.[50]

The parade of courts dismissing the New York decision was continued by Illinois in October 1914, a quarter-century to the month after the Court of Appeals had handed down its decision. The case in question grew out of the goriest and most sensational of any of these crimes, which took place in the central-western part of the state in late September of 1912. The murder victims were Charles Pfanschmidt, a well-to-do farmer, his wife, Mathilda, their daughter, Blanche, and a young schoolteacher who boarded with them, Emma Kaempen. All had apparently been killed at night by blows of an axe in the farmhouse near Quincy where they lived, and the house had then been set on fire or had caught fire. The police arrested Blanche's brother and only sibling, twenty-year-old Ray Pfanschmidt, who at the time had been living and working at a construction site several miles away. He was convicted of first-degree murder at his first trial and sentenced to death. On appeal, the Illinois Supreme Court found the trial record riddled with legal errors; it overturned the verdict and ordered a new trial. Ray was retried and acquitted for one of the murders, tried and acquitted for another, and finally set free.[51] While his first appeal was pending, the Supreme Court ruled on a lawsuit contesting the probate award to Ray of his parents' property (much of which he had mortgaged to lawyers and detectives working in his defense) as their sole surviving heir at law. Though his eventual legal exoneration would have made an adverse ruling moot in his case, the Court, in *Wall v. Pfanschmidt*, found in his favor in any event, in a comprehensive opinion once more denying the validity of the arguments made in *Riggs*.[52]

During the same quarter-century, the highest court of only one state, Missouri, in its decision in *Perry v. Strawbridge* (1908), unambiguously followed *Riggs* in a parallel case.[53] And the Missouri decision might well not have been reached without the existence of the *Riggs* precedent to sustain it (moreover, as we will see, well before 1908, New York's Court of Appeals had itself abandoned the ground that the Missouri court followed Judge Earl in taking). In Tennessee in 1904, the court held (and not without a dissenting opinion), that a murderer was barred from inheriting as a matter of common law, the situation that then obtained in that state. It was a conclusion with which Judge Gray would not have disagreed. When the descent of property was governed by statute, however, the court continued (describing the situation in *Riggs* itself) "the weight of authority is against the New York court, and it may be conceded that the better legal reasoning is to be found in the opinions dissenting from the views of that court."[54]

Thus twenty-five years of judicial response to *Riggs* tended strongly against it. The highest courts of three additional states (Kentucky, Georgia, and West Virginia) fell into line with the consensus by 1920, while no others joined New York and Missouri.[55] In a case similar to *Owens* and *Kuhn*, Indiana's supreme bench held in 1914 that a woman convicted of manslaughter in the death of her husband was entitled to the widow's statutory allowance of $500 from the estate, though the state's slayer statute, passed in 1907, barred inheritance by "devise or descent" to anyone "who unlawfully causes the death of another and shall have been convicted thereof."[56] The earlier Texas decision was confirmed and extended in 1918 by another, holding that although the murderer could not collect as the beneficiary of a life insurance policy on the victim, her husband, she could receive the sum in question, after it had been paid instead to the victim's estate, via the statutes governing inheritance.[57] And a federal circuit court of appeals in 1920 refused to hold that a state slayer statute denying inheritance to one who had been convicted of the murder of the deceased blocked such inheritance when the conviction had been in the courts of another state, even though a similar statute existed in the latter as well.[58]

These cases presented a wide variety of legal situations. Some involved the rules governing the descent of property by persons who had died intestate, some the shares of spouses guaranteed by law, some the claims of lawyers or other persons to whom the inheritances had been deeded, some but not others a murder that had been shown to have been committed for the principal purpose of gaining the inheritance. Among them, only *Riggs* concerned inheritance by will. Yet, although one of the appellants' arguments had been specific to cases of that sort, involving the improbability that Francis or any testator would have bequeathed most of his estate to someone who murdered him had he been able to foresee that event, Judge Earl's central contentions fully covered the much broader range of questions arising elsewhere. So did those, supporting the opposite result, of the North Carolina Supreme Court in the statutory dower case of *Owens*. As that court had framed the issue: "in general terms, does any one, as a consequence of the unlawful taking of human life, become thereby disabled to take a part of the estate left by the deceased which the law gives him and gives him subject to no such condition?"[59] Its answer was no; Earl's in *Riggs* was yes. And although the state courts disagreeing with *Riggs* could easily on technical grounds have distinguished it as legally irrelevant to the cases they had on hand, most of them made no attempt to do so. Rather, they dismissed it as altogether wrong, as the New York Court of Appeals had dismissed rather than distinguishing *Owens*.

Some additional probate cases in the same years that never made it into the appellate law reports further highlight *Riggs*'s doctrinal freakishness, its isolation and anomalousness within the law of its day. The published reports of the California Supreme Court in the late nineteenth or early twentieth centuries contain no opinions dealing directly with the rights of murdering heirs. Yet the state's lower courts ruled at least twice on the question, and both times they rejected the doctrine from *Riggs* that they were asked to apply.

In 1897, a Solano County rancher named Frank Belew fatally poisoned his sister Susie and brother Louis, both of them childless and unmarried, with an arsenic-based remedy for rats and other pests. Frank and his two other brothers, Arthur and Thomas, were the victims' heirs at law, and his apparent motive was to obtain the third share of their estates to which the California rules of descent seemed to entitle him. He confessed to the crime and, after a failed defense of temporary insanity, he was convicted of first-degree murder and executed.[60] Thomas Belew brought suit in Superior Court to contest the award of a third of his deceased siblings' estates to Frank's children, who were his next of kin and heirs at law. Thomas based the challenge entirely on *Riggs* and the reasoning that it had offered: Frank, by his criminal deed, had forfeited his right to inherit from Susie and Louis regardless of what the statutes said. The judge dismissed the challenge in an opinion that waved aside the New York precedent as bad law.[61] Though newspaper reports indicated that Thomas Belew and his attorneys were considering an appeal, no such case ever reached the California Supreme Court, nor, though the murder and its legal aftermath were widely publicized, did the California Legislature then amend the laws to cover such cases.[62]

As a result, when a similar situation arose in the same state a few years later, a convicted murderer again was allowed to inherit from his victims. The crime in question paralleled in many ways the later Pfanschmidt killings in Illinois. On the evening of November 10, 1904, passersby saw a fire blazing in the house of the Weber family on a secluded lot in the small city of Auburn, California. When the flames were extinguished, searchers found inside the bodies of Julius Weber, his wife Mary, and their daughter Bertha, aged eighteen; their nine-year-old semi-invalid son Earl was still alive but died shortly after. All had suffered fatal gunshot wounds or blows. The only other member of the family, twenty-year-old Adolph Julius Weber, was visiting stores downtown at the time the fire was spotted. His behavior that evening, especially after the discovery of the bodies, struck observers as bizarre and unnatural, and he quickly became the prime suspect in the investigation. Brought to trial for murder early in 1905, Adolph successfully claimed his parents' estate, amounting to some seventy thousand dollars, and used most of it to pay for his legal representation and other expenses. He was convicted on strong circumstantial evidence and was hanged in September of 1906.[63] Again, another claimant mounted a challenge in the lower courts to Adolph's right to inherit; again, the challenge failed there and was not taken to the California Supreme Court.[64]

Other states furnish additional examples. A Massachusetts newspaper observed in 1869, apropos of a recent sensational homicide that had ended in a trial and a conviction, that under the law as it stood, "Deacon [Samuel M.] Andrews will receive the bequest of Holmes, whom he murdered." "This case," it added, recognizing the question as that could only be resolved by statutory change, "will probably lead to some legislation in regard to bequests to persons who take the lives of those who 'remember them in their wills.' "[65] A West Virginia man named Van Buren Baker was convicted in the late 1880s of murdering his wife and his mother-in-law, apparently with the direct motive of inheriting some of the latter's money through a bequest to him in the former's will, and was sentenced to life in prison. He had assigned his rights to his legacy, amounting to a thousand dollars, to his defense lawyers at the time of his trial. The lawyers sought to claim the money, and the executor of the slain wife's estate in 1892 purchased their rights at only a modest discount from face value, in effect admitting their validity, the recent New York decision in *Riggs*, of which the parties were aware, notwithstanding.[66] Several disappointed in-laws brought suit in 1900 in Indiana against Charles F. Dale, alleging that he had murdered several people, most recently his wife, in order to inherit from their estates. The courts rejected their contentions, finding that the allegations, even if true, formed no bar to the legacies as the law then stood.[67] Probate awards from their victims' estates in well-publicized cases in the early twentieth century to Ward E. Hedger in Wisconsin and J. Warren Jenkins in Wyoming, each convicted of murdering his wife, were not appealed to the highest courts of their states.[68] Those who had an interest in appealing apparently recognized the futility, as generally accepted law then stood, of doing so.

When the courts refused to interfere, a simple remedy existed, as Landon and Gray had pointed out in New York. If the legislators who had taken control of the law of inheritance wished murder to disqualify an heir, they had only to reword the statutes to say so. One state's lawmakers had already said so long before the Court of Appeals decided *Riggs*. The United States acquired the Louisiana Territory by purchase from France in 1803, and its southern part became first an American territory and then, in 1812, a state. Strongly attached to French traditions and practices, the Louisianians chose to adopt legal codes in the Continental fashion rather than the English-derived common law system of the other states. In 1808, they drew up a Civil Code for the Territory on existing French models, one that the state legislature redrafted and reenacted in 1825. Its provisions relating to inheritance echoed those of the continental *Code Napoléon*. They provided that the courts were to invalidate an inheritance on a finding of "unworthiness" in the heir. The unworthy included "[t]hose who are convicted of having killed, or attempted to kill the deceased; and in this respect they will not be the less unworthy, though they may have been pardoned after their conviction." The courts were similarly to invalidate a gift made to anyone other than an heir at law, during life or in a will, if "the donee has attempted to take the life of the donor," or on other grounds of "ingratitude."[69]

These provisions came into play in a sensational case that arose more or less contemporaneously with the Palmer murder and litigation in New York. Kate Townsend, the owner and proprietor of a lavishly furnished brothel in downtown New Orleans, had had a longstanding and turbulent relationship with a man named William Troisville Sykes. In November 1883, Townsend was found stabbed to death. Sykes immediately fell under suspicion, was arrested, and eventually confessed to the killing, but maintained that it had been done in self-defense when Townsend had flown at him in a rage and tried to stab him.[70] Acquitted by a sympathetic jury, he sought to claim Townsend's estate, amounting to some $200,000, her will, dated 1873, having named him sole beneficiary and executor. Hearing the case in 1886, a judge of the Civil District Court ruled that Sykes, by taking the life of the testator (the Civil Code stating no exception for self-defense), had, by his own admission, forfeited his claim to the legacy under the letter of the law.[71]

That Louisiana possessed and enforced such a provision at the time of *Riggs* casts a revealing sidelight on the New York majority opinion. Judge Earl, though he made much of the bar to murdering heirs in the legal codes of France and French Canada, oddly made no reference to the one that existed closer to home, in another American state. He cannot have been unaware of it, for Russell and Sanford cited it in their brief for the appellants.[72] His omission, therefore, was deliberate, and it was a confession of weakness in his argument. To have mentioned the law of Louisiana would have blunted his claim that the lawmakers of New York and the other states, relying on the maxim he invoked, had thought the matter already settled and any such enactment unnecessary. If those of one American state had already explicitly enacted such a provision, as indeed they had, the others might well have been left to do the same if they wished to.

And some legislatures took up that task after the judges called it to their attention, while others chose not to. Once North Carolina's appellate bench had ruled in *Owens*, the state legislature at its next session enacted a murder exception to a widow's right of dower.[73] Several state legislatures passed "slayer laws" or "slayer statutes," amending their inheritance procedures to exclude the murderer of the deceased, quite promptly following the rejection of *Riggs* by their courts, such as Tennessee in 1905, Kansas in

1907, and Wyoming in 1915.[74] Others enacted such a law in this era without the stimulus of any such recent decision or sensational case occurring within their borders, such as Iowa (1897) and Oregon (1917).[75] California's legislature passed a slayer law, in 1905, following and in consequence of the Weber murders, though it had not done so after the earlier Belew case.[76] In still other states, the legislature acted only after so long a delay that it could hardly be considered as responding to the court decision. Nebraska did not pass a slayer statute until 1913, almost twenty years after the final disposition of the Shellenberger estate, and Pennsylvania not until 1917, more than twenty years after *Carpenter*.[77] Ohio enacted its first such statute only in the early 1930s, while Illinois by the middle of that decade, more than twenty years after *Wall v. Pfanschmidt*, still lacked one.[78] In short, enough states acted promptly to put in doubt the notion that the legislature could not deal with the problem. Enough chose not to act to put in doubt Earl's assumption that no legislature could have intended such a loophole to exist.

Resolving the matter by statute, rather than leaving it to case law as New York had done, had two marked advantages. It set out in advance the general rules governing such situations, a much more efficient procedure than having them accumulate haphazardly and piecemeal as trial and appeals courts decided particular lawsuits at a heavy and unnecessary cost of time and effort. And it left the choice of the rules to the body generally recognized as the more legitimate maker of law, the elected legislature.

The statutes that the lawmakers opted to write, most of them covering inheritance both by will and by descent (most of them also barring insurance benefits to a killer), differed somewhat from state to state. Sections of two acts passed on June 7, 1917, essentially the work of a commission of leading lawyers who drafted language and submitted it to the legislature, together constituted Pennsylvania's slayer statute. The Intestate Act provided that: "No person who shall be finally adjudged guilty, either as principal or accessory, of murder of the first or second degree, shall be entitled to interest or to take any part of the real or personal estate of the person killed, as surviving spouse, heir, or next of kin to such person under the terms of this act." The Wills Act made the same provisions regarding inheritance by bequest.[79] Some other states extended the ban more widely to cover any unlawful or felonious killing, thus embracing manslaughter as well, and some more widely still, for having in any way caused the death of the victim. Virginia's statute went to the other extreme, specifying that only an heir who had killed for the express purpose of inheriting was to be excluded from doing so.[80] Unlike Pennsylvania, which barred inheritance by anyone who had been convicted or "finally adjudged" guilty of the required degree of homicide, some left the question of fact to be settled by separate civil inheritance proceedings. And some but not all of the statutes ordained who was to inherit in the killer's place: usually either whoever stood next in the statutory line of descent, or whoever would have inherited had the murderer predeceased the victim. If the result looked like a patchwork, such was unavoidable in a federal system where independent legislatures could write the laws of their states; rules laid down by each state's courts would probably have lacked uniformity too. If the statutes in turn gave rise to ambiguities that came to the appeals courts for solution, they forestalled many and probably most such suits by enunciating the rules that applied to the typical cases, and they could be, and were, amended as time went on.

In the long term, Judge Earl's failure to predict or to shape the course of events is clear. He had held that statutory language to bar inheritance by murderers from their victims was unnecessary, that the already-existing authority of the legal maxims he invoked made such an enactment redundant. But in 1936, the legal scholar John W. Wade found such statutory provisions on the books of half the states, plus the District of Columbia.[81] By the early twenty-first century, a murdering heir was disqualified by law in every American state, but in only three—New York, Missouri (which had declared in 1908 for the *Riggs* doctrine), and New Hampshire (which joined much later)—was the law solely of the *Riggs*-type judge-made sort.[82] The legislatures of the other forty-seven had barred such inheritance by enacting slayer statutes, of the sort that Justice Landon and Judge Gray had suggested and that Earl deemed superfluous.

Chapter 3

The Grounds for Rejection

That the courts of the other states hearing similar cases so strongly dissented from *Riggs* is an essential datum for understanding the New York court's ruling itself. Late nineteenth- and early twentieth-century American judges overwhelmingly disclaimed the authority that Earl and four of his colleagues asserted for them. They were not, they agreed, empowered to disinherit a murdering legatee when statutes governing the rules of inheritance and specifying the necessary conditions for a valid bequest made no provision for their doing so. Their opinions, standard legal treatises of the period, and some additional supporting materials suggest why they believed so.

The debate that surrounded *Riggs* was never about whether murderers should be allowed to inherit from their victims. Nobody believed that they should. It was, rather, about how and by whom they should be forbidden to inherit. The judges who rejected the New York decision, a hefty majority of those who took up the issue, were not concerned about the injustice that would be done to murdering heirs unpredictably deprived of the legacies they had killed to obtain. Their fears lay elsewhere. They were troubled, first and foremost, by the wider consequences of their being turned loose to decide cases as they saw fit, and thereby create law for future cases, on the authority either of an array of sweeping maxims about justice or of the freedom to reject as absurd any results they disliked. Either might set a dangerously expansive precedent in other and much more important fields for having judges alter the law that the legislature had made. Accepting *Riggs*, to its critics, did not chiefly mean denying murdering heirs their ill-gotten gains. To them it meant, far more consequentially, empowering courts to rewrite statutes according to their own tastes.

The Grounds for Rejection: Formalism?

Gray's dissent is sometimes disparaged or derided as a quintessential expression of "legal formalism." The characterization draws on some long-entrenched stereotypes. American courts in the late nineteenth and early twentieth centuries have often been supposed to have been in thrall to a vision of law as a seamless fabric woven of basic principles, timeless and immutable, of law as something objectively given and already existing that judges merely discern and declare in the cases that come before them: *finding* the law as expressed and exemplified in past decisions. Early twentieth-century critics who would come to be known as *Legal Realists* would contrast this supposed formalist orthodoxy to their own understanding of law as something that judges make, and remake, and should be honest about making, and that they make under the influence of a variety of motives, including their own emotional and ideological preconceptions as well as broader and historically varying considerations of social benefit. The leading realist Karl Llewellyn spoke disparagingly of "the conception of precedent as a static something, of movement as queer or improper or 'departure,' of those least happy days of our legal system, the 80s and 90s of the Nineteenth Century," and he saw it expressed in opinions that "run in deductive form with an air or expression of single-line inevitability."[1] Grant Gilmore in the 1970s influentially characterized the formalism of late-nineteenth-century American courts as having assumed "that the law is a closed, logical system. . . . The judicial function has nothing to do with the adaptation of rules of law to changing circumstances; it is restricted to the discovery of what the true rules of law are and indeed always have been."[2]

Yet it is not immediately clear that this picture of a reigning formalism in the post-Civil War decades, whatever the merits of that picture itself may be, has much to do with Gray's dissent. If formalism is to be identified with a belief in the law as fixed and certain, as underlain and unified by a coherent set of Platonic principles, few in number, highly abstract, and mutually coherent, then the majority opinion in *Riggs*, with its appeal to overarching legal maxims of a high degree of generality, expresses it much more clearly than the dissent does.[3] Such a view of law, indeed, sits more comfortably alongside a reverence for the common law of judicial precedent than does Gray's deference to the overriding authority of legislative statutes, which it is far less easy to suppose possess some organic unity. It was the dissent that insisted on deferring to the laws, whatever they might be, and however poorly they might cohere, that the legislature had made. And it was the majority opinion that opened the door, and the dissent that tried to close and lock it, to what critics then and later have most deplored about that era's "formalistic" jurisprudence: the invocation by judges of supposedly fundamental legal principles to invalidate statutory provisions that they did not like.

Its critics have sometimes defined formalism instead as a belief that right answers exist in legal cases that can be deduced with logical certainty, whether laid down as precedents in earlier cases or in the provisions of statutes. Such was the contrast Llewellyn drew between the *Formal Style* and its opposite, which he called the *Grand Style*, and which he supposed to have gone into eclipse after the middle of the nineteenth century and which he hoped to revive in the twentieth. This style, formalism's supposed antithesis, he defined as an intellectual flexibility that allows law to be adapted to the specifics of a case rather than be mindlessly and rigidly applied ready-made.[4] But again, the schema fails to make sense of *Riggs*. There is no more *Grand Style* flexibility in the majority opinion than there is in the dissent. Judge Earl conceded no doubt about what the applicable rules were and what they dictated, about what the right answer was, or about the court's duty to decide as it did. His words breathe no hint that the law permitted any other outcome than the one he announced.

The Grounds for Rejection: Judicial Legislation

The categories of formalism and realism are less useful in understanding *Riggs* and its contemporary critics than are that era's attitudes towards what could be called the making of law by judges. Those attitudes differed significantly depending on whether the subject was the common law, the interpretation of statutes, or the interpretation of constitutional provisions. One might strongly approve of the way that judges made rules in such traditionally common-law, precedent-governed fields as property, torts, contracts, legal procedure, and the conflict of laws, to the extent that they had not been displaced by statute. One might likewise acknowledge that in interpreting broadly worded clauses of constitutions, judges often had to exercise an analogous kind of creativity. Neither stance guaranteed similar approval when judges permitted themselves a similar freedom in dealing with legislative statutes in any domain that such statutes purported to cover. Here something close to a consensus did exist: that the legislature, when and where it chose to intervene and to express its wishes through laws that passed constitutional review, had an authority superior to that of the courts, which could only obey its commands when those commands were clearly expressed. If this was formalism of a kind—though diametrically opposed to another kind that saw the law's essence in the kinds of fundamental maxims enunciated in *Riggs*—it was one that enjoyed general support in the late nineteenth and early twentieth centuries.

Courts, on this view, could creatively develop the common law as they saw best. They could creatively interpret statutes only when some uncertainty in the statute's language obliged them to do so. The prominent Michigan judge and legal commentator Thomas McIntyre Cooley, writing in 1871, distinguished between two senses of the term "judge-made law," one of them denoting something he thought both useful and necessary and the other something he deeply deplored. The former involved "the law which becomes established by precedent" in the common-law domains governed by such past decisions. Judge-made law in the domains that had been taken over by enacted law was "that made by judicial decisions which construe away the meaning of statutes, or find meanings in them the legislature never held."[5] Decisions of this sort violated a principle that Cooley and most of his contemporaries held to be axiomatic in a democratic country, the subordination of judges to an elected legislature as makers of law whenever the latter chose, within its constitutional powers, to assert its authority.

Two American judges rarely accused, even by the realists, of a mechanical formalism stated the same principle in emphatic and memorable terms. United States Supreme Court Chief Justice John Marshall, in 1805, wrote: "Where a law is plain and unambiguous, whether it be expressed in general or limited terms, the legislature should be intended to mean what it has plainly expressed, and consequently no room is left for construction."[6] Associate Justice Oliver Wendell Holmes wrote early in the twentieth century that "when their task is to interpret and apply the words of a statute," judges might consider the desirability or otherwise of the statute's consequences "only when the meaning of the words used is open to reasonable doubt." Otherwise, they must and could only act according to those words' plain meaning.[7] Marshall construed the provisions of the federal Constitution with a particularly free and generous hand, but in his dealings with statutes he was much more restrained.

These were not permanent and timeless canons of jurisprudence, even in the United States. During the first half of the nineteenth century, Marshall's precepts and practices notwithstanding, many American appeals judges had felt themselves free, as had their English predecessors, to engage in a broad "rational interpretation" or "equitable construction" of statutory language—terms Earl himself used in *Riggs* to describe what he was doing—the better to carry out its apparent underlying purpose or policy. By 1889, though, a narrower conception of their proper role had come to prevail.[8] By characterizing the grounds of the decision as he did, Earl did nothing to make it more acceptable to the courts of other states. One of the two leading postbellum American treatises on statutory interpretation observed: "The rule is, as we shall constantly see, cardinal and universal, that if the statute is plain and unambiguous, there is no room for construction or interpretation."[9] What the other said was in no way different: "If a statute is plain, certain and unambiguous, so that no doubt arises from its own terms as to its scope and meaning, a bare reading suffices; then interpretation is needless."[10] What Earl had called rational interpretation or equitable construction, then, was permissible only when unclear language required it.

For most American courts, the results that followed in a case like *Riggs* from these principles—legislative supremacy and clear meaning— were inescapable. It is true, as many twentieth- and twenty-first-century commentators on statutory interpretation would emphasize, that words only have a clear and literal meaning in connection with the assumptions applied in reading them. But the same applies to the term *plain meaning* itself, and what the judges in 1889 and for some time thereafter understood the plain meaning of statutory language to mean was the statute read in the light of a particular set of assumptions that they generally shared. Judge Earl himself began by admitting that there was nothing uncertain in the language of the New York statute of wills or any ambiguity in what it instructed the courts to do. For most of his peers elsewhere, that concession was fatal to the rest of his argument, for only when such ambiguity existed did they acknowledge that the courts had room to intervene.

To reword what the statute called for in the way Earl had done struck judges in other states as an act of usurpation. *Riggs* was "judicial legislation,"[11] "legislation in disguise,"[12] trespassing on ground "which belongs to the law-making power alone."[13] The majority in *Riggs* presumed, unacceptably, "add to a clear and unambiguous statute an exception,"[14] "to ingraft an exception on the statute";[15] to read "into a plain statutory provision an exception which the Statute itself in no way suggests";[16] to amend statutory language in which there was "neither ambiguity nor room for construction."[17] "When the legislature, not transcending the limits of its power, speaks in clear language upon a question of policy, it becomes the judicial tribunals to remain silent."[18] "[T]he statute cannot be extended by implication beyond the fair and legitimate import of the words used therein."[19] "Under the rules for the interpretation of statutes the courts cannot read into a statute exceptions or limitations which depart from its plain meaning. . . . When the legislature has spoken in clear and unequivocal language, the courts are bound thereby."[20] There was "no justification to this court for assuming to supply legislation";[21] "the judgment of judicial officers as to when and in what cases the statutory heir is entitled to inherit would be substituted for a legislative determination of the question."[22] "The decision in *Riggs* is the manifest assertion of a wisdom believed to be superior to that of the legislature upon a question of policy."[23] "The right to determine what is the best policy for the people is in the legislature, and courts cannot assume that they have a wisdom superior to that of the legislature and proceed to inject into a statute a clause which, in their opinion, would be more in consonance with good morals or better accomplish justice than the rule declared by the legislature."[24]

Lower courts responded in similar terms. Judge A. J. Buckles, who in 1898 heard the Belew case in California, observed that *Riggs* "has been severely criticized by other courts of like jurisdiction on the grounds that the New York court construed something into the statute which plainly the Legislature did not intend to and had not put there," a criticism with which, he made it plain, he fully agreed. The Civil Code of California, he pointed out, laid down clear rules about who would succeed to the property of a person dying without a will. Those rules made no provision for disinheriting one who had murdered the deceased. Thus the plaintiff, Judge Buckles observed contemptuously, was asking him to amend the Code on his own authority to provide for such disinheritance, and that he declined to do: "having no legislative powers whatever, and not being concerned as to the policy of the law, this court is unable to reach out and corral some real or fancied 'legislative intent' which has been floating about for all these years since the adoption of the Codes, and inject it into this section, to change the meaning, which is now clear and well defined."[25]

Several of the state courts that rejected *Riggs* cited as an authoritative source for their doing so the opinion of Chief Justice Marshall in the case of *United States v. Wiltberger*, decided in 1820. It involved the appeal of the conviction for manslaughter in a federal court of Peter Wiltberger, master of the American merchant ship *Benjamin Rush*. On a trading voyage to China, the ship had been lying in a tidal river half a mile wide, its location fixed by the evidence at the trial as thirty-five miles above the river's mouth. Wiltberger exchanged some heated words on board with a seaman named Peters, and, finding his behavior insolent and menacing, and suspecting that some other sailors might join him in resistance or even mutiny, Wiltberger struck Peters first with his fist and then with an oak stave. Left unconscious by the blows, Peters died eighteen hours later.[26] Wiltberger was brought to trial in federal court on the ship's return, and on the facts of the case the jury found him guilty of manslaughter, subject to a query that they raised for further consideration: whether he was indeed liable to conviction and punishment by the courts of the United States under the terms of a congressional act of 1790 defining a variety of crimes against the United States and specifying their penalties.

The appeal turned on the interpretation of the statute's language relating to murder and manslaughter. Section 8 of the law provided for the punishment by the courts of the United States of murder and robbery when occurring in locations under American jurisdiction "on the high seas or in any river, haven, basin, or bay." The later Section 12 gave the courts the authority to punish manslaughter occurring "on the high seas." Yet even if it were assumed, in accord with prevailing usage, that a location on a river well inland could not be considered the high seas, counsel for the United States argued that a sensible interpretation of the law required that the wider range of places specified for murder and robbery be inferred as applying to manslaughter as well, as the lawmakers had surely intended.[27]

The Supreme Court ruled unanimously in Wiltberger's favor, overturning the manslaughter conviction. It invoked the plain-meaning rule: that when the language of a statute was clear, the courts had no power to add to or subtract from what it said. In his opinion, Marshall likewise appealed to the principle "that the power of punishment is vested in the legislative, not in the judicial department. It is the legislature, not the court, which is to define a crime and ordain its punishment." This rule he combined with that of *nulla poena sine lege*, "no punishment without a law": that is to say, death, corporal punishment, imprisonment, fine, forfeiture, or other penalties could be lawfully imposed only if the act for which the person was being punished had clearly been forbidden by the lawmaking power and its consequences spelled out. And such penalties were governed by yet one more principle that Marshall stated emphatically in his *Wiltberger* opinion: as he put it, "that penal laws are to be construed strictly." It was a rule that, as Marshall said, had a long history in the common law. In the twentieth century, it would come to be known as the *rule of lenity*. It held that genuine or reasonable doubts as to whether the language of a penal law—that is, one imposing a punishment as a consequence of violating it—covered the actions of an accused person were to be resolved in the defendant's favor. It reflected, in Marshall's words, "the tenderness of the law for the rights of individuals."[28]

This line of reasoning had obvious consequences for a case like the Palmer will dispute. Depriving Elmer of his expected legacy could be framed, as Judge Earl did frame it, not as a punishment or penalty at all, but as merely a clarification of the rules of inheritance. It did not take anything away from him, on this account of the matter; it merely denied that he had ever had a valid legal claim to it. But as Gray observed in his dissent, the very same foreign codes that the opinion cited as authority for its holding belied Earl's assertion, for they did represent the exclusion as a punishment.[29] Judge Buckles in California suggested, as Gray had done in New York, that "to give the interpretation sought by the objectors would add an additional punishment to the crime of murder not known to the laws of the State."[30] Defenders of *Riggs* could, of course, assert that it involved civil rather than criminal law, and thus did not entail any punishment, and in a technical sense the argument could be maintained. But to the skeptics, who predominated, it seemed plain that to deprive Elmer of a legacy to which the letter of the statute had entitled him because of a criminal act he had committed was, in substance, to expand the penalties for his crime beyond those that the legislature had specified for it.

Apart from begging the question of just what authority he had to declare Elmer's claim invalid, moreover, the framing that Judge Earl offered was correct only if it had previously been understood that a murdering heir did not inherit. If it had not been so understood, then a new and additional consequence of a crime was in fact being inflicted. And outside of Louisiana, where the matter was settled by the state's legal code, in no American state had it been held, prior to *Riggs*, that an otherwise valid claim to an inheritance could thus be lost. New York itself was no exception, as witness the referee's report and the Supreme Court's rulings in the Palmer will case. In other words, the rule that Judge Earl stated for the majority came into being only in 1889 and substantially postdated the actions to which he applied it. Though the federal Constitution barred states from enacting ex post facto laws, ones criminalizing actions that predated their passage, it has long been accepted that the rules that courts lay down in deciding cases apply retroactively, upon the fiction that when they do so they are always only declaring what the law already was. The courts held that power, though, on the understanding that they would not abuse it by applying genuinely new law to the actions of parties who had previously had no good reason to suppose it existed. That the rule in *Riggs* had previously existed, most of the judges before whom the question arose denied.[31]

The Grounds for Rejection: Lenity and Attainder

And the rule of lenity, one of unquestioned authority in this era, required that statutes having penal consequences be interpreted narrowly and strictly when doubt arose as to their reach. To read a statute as containing an entirely unexpressed exception carrying punitive consequences was to flout the rule egregiously. The exception the Court of Appeals read into the New York law of wills was penal if the loss of an inheritance that would otherwise have held good were seen as a punishment, which is how most *Riggs*-era courts outside New York indeed saw it. "It cannot be doubted that the statute is penal," the Iowa Supreme Court observed in 1904 of the state's slayer law. "It is not strictly a criminal statute, but so much in the nature of one that we have held that such statutes must be strictly construed."[32] In 1921, the Iowa courts reaffirmed that conclusion, and one year earlier, a federal circuit court of appeals characterized Oklahoma's slayer statute in the same terms.[33] The reasoning was simple: "divesting a person of rights otherwise accorded to him under the law," as the Supreme Court of Virginia stated the matter in 1951, inflicted a penalty on that person.[34]

When John W. Wade in 1936 drafted a model slayer statute for adoption by state legislatures, he included a section beginning with the words: "This Act shall not be considered penal in nature. . . ." Such laws, he explained, "have often been called penal and have consequently been subjected to a strict and narrow interpretation" by the courts applying them.[35] (He seems to have believed, or to have hoped, that courts that would have recognized his statute as penal could be persuaded that it was not by a simple assertion to that effect in its text.) Required to interpret penal statutes narrowly, all the more were courts considering the imposition of penal consequences bound to restraint when they lacked any explicit wording in any statute to back them up. In the words of a standard American treatise almost exactly contemporary with *Riggs*: "A penal statute cannot be extended by implication of construction. It cannot be made to embrace cases not within the letter, though within the reason and policy, of the law. . . . And as a general rule where a penalty is affixed by a statute to an act or omission, such penalty is the only punishment or loss occurred by the guilty party."[36] By this reasoning, that of most courts and commentators of the time, Judge Gray was correct in his dissent, and the Court of Appeals had, its own disclaimer notwithstanding, overstepped its authority and illegitimately added to Elmer's punishment.

Furthermore, if it was a punishment, then such a disinheritance could be seen as falling afoul of constitutional or statutory bans on *bills of attainder* and *corruption of blood*, two terms technically distinct but often used interchangeably. These categories of English law embraced, among other things, the inculpating of a particular individual under a law applying to nobody else and the forfeiture of a person's property and the loss of the power to bequeath it as the result of conviction for felony. They existed in a variety of forms until comprehensively abolished by the British Parliament in its Forfeitures Act in 1870.[37] The new United States had emphatically repudiated them much earlier, in the years following their declaration of independence. Sections of the federal constitution adopted in 1789 barred both Congress and the states from passing a bill of attainder, as they similarly prohibited ex post facto laws.

Many American states' constitutions or codes similarly and more specifically forbade forfeitures as a result of criminal convictions. Section 710 of the Penal Code enacted in 1881 by the New York State Legislature, for example, followed earlier enactments in declaring that: "A conviction of a person for any crime does not work a forfeiture of any property, real or personal, or of any right or interest therein."[38] If legislatures were barred from imposing forfeitures, courts were hardly allowed to inflict them, especially when, as in *Riggs*, they claimed the power to do so under legislation into which they had inferred a clause to that effect. Hence Judge Gray's protest against *Riggs* as effectively adding the penalty of forfeiture to Elmer's conviction for murder. The legal scholar Joel Prentiss Bishop wrote in 1872 that "if, under the authority of a general statute, a court should sentence one to be punished in excess of what the law provides for such acts as the indictment specifies," it would be "a judicial bill of attainder, even more odious in its nature than the particular thing which this provision of the Constitution forbids."[39]

The reply would again have been that nothing was forfeited because, by law, nothing had been inherited in the first place. Yet, as Justice Landon had noted in *Preston v. Palmer*, the law supposed an inheritance to take effect immediately on the death of the ancestor.[40] A revocation that in fact if not in law could only occur some time after the heir had come into possession, once that heir had been identified as the murderer, certainly looked like a forfeiture. Many of the state courts rejecting *Riggs* raised the issue in one form or another. The Illinois Supreme Court in 1914 saw the ban on forfeitures as one of several serious objections to following the New York doctrine.[41] So did the courts of Oklahoma and West Virginia, and so did the Nebraska county court judge who ruled on the first round of the Shellenberger inheritance case in 1888, before *Riggs* was announced.[42] The Pennsylvania Supreme Court in 1895 went farther than most, suggesting by the way it discussed the question that even a statute barring a murderer from inheriting might thus violate the state's constitution.[43]

No court ever overturned a slayer statute on such grounds. That fact, though, may reflect the very deference to legislative authority that the 1889 decision withheld. Not until 1918 did a state court explicitly uphold an enacted slayer law against constitutional challenge, and for a long time that decision stood alone.[44] As late as the 1940s, the supreme court of Georgia, which like New York had a statute of wills, but as yet no slayer clause or statute, treated the forfeiture argument as a serious obstacle to accepting *Riggs*. It quoted the relevant words of the Georgia Constitution, that "no conviction shall work corruption of blood, or forfeiture of estate," in order "to illustrate the policy of our law that, once the title to the property becomes vested in him, it could not be divested by reason of conviction of any crime." Only if the legislature explicitly changed the statute of wills to invalidate any succession to the victim's estate by the murderer, the court indicated, would it accept such a result as constitutional.[45]

Apart from any doubts that arose about the power of judges to disinherit murdering heirs, the ubiquity of bans on attainder and corruption of blood, as one of the early opinions rejecting *Riggs* pointed out, undermined Earl's argument that legislators could never have intended to leave such a loophole in the written law as Elmer Palmer was trying to squeeze through.[46] For it constituted a valid reason legislators might honestly have felt themselves barred from including such an exception in their statutes of wills. The lawmakers may reasonably have supposed, that is, that when both the letter and the spirit of a widely held doctrine apparently forbade them to deprive anyone of property when convicted of a crime, they were prohibited from doing just that: directly, of course, but also through any procedural subterfuge whereby the finding that the heir had killed the ancestor or testator was made in the civil proceedings concerned with the estate, disconnected technically from a criminal conviction. The judge in the principal Ohio case, *Deem v. Millikin*, wrote:

> . . . the lawmakers may have entertained the most serious doubt if they contemplated the change in the statute which we are now asked to make, whether it would not contravene the constitutional provision as to the corruption of blood. . . . Since the legislature did not undertake to create the supposed exception to the statute of descents, we are not required to determine whether it would have been repugnant to the constitutional provision referred to. But in the field of speculation to which *Riggs v. Palmer, supra*, invites, the provision suggests suitable reasons why a legislative body, careful to respect the letter and the spirit of the constitution, should hesitate to attach to felonies any of the consequences of corruption of blood.[47]

The Absurdity Rule

The rule that courts were bound to obey the plain meaning of a statute had, at the time, one generally acknowledged exception. In his *Riggs* opinion, Judge Earl invoked it in his support: that courts should avoid reading laws in ways that produced plainly absurd results. This *absurdity doctrine* partly underlay Earl's claim that the legislature simply had not considered the possibility of inheritance by the murderer and would never have intended such an outcome. He appealed to one of the doctrine's classic illustrations, a story from medieval Italy related by the seventeenth-century jurisprudential writer Samuel Pufendorf and then by Sir William

Blackstone in his classic *Commentaries on the Laws of England.* "There was a statute in Bologna," as Earl retold it, "that whoever drew blood in the streets should be severely punished, and yet it was held not to apply to the case of a barber [i.e., a "barber-surgeon"] who opened a vein in the street." "It is commanded in the Decalogue," he continued, "that no work shall be done upon the Sabbath, and yet, giving the command a rational interpretation founded upon its design, the Infallible Judge held that it did not prohibit works of necessity, charity or benevolence on that day."[48] A construction of the New York statutes that allowed murderers to inherit from their victims, he asserted, would be just such a one as the canon of avoiding absurd results, and a respect for the true intentions of the legislators, forbade.

But what Earl ignored was that the rule, in the examples he cited as well as in its other classic statements at that time, did not operate with equal force in both of two directions, in tightening and in loosening the law's severity. Consistently with the logic of the rule of lenity and the principle of *nulla poena*, it worked to limit but not to extend the scope of prohibitions and penalties. In the standard instances of the era, courts adopted it to prevent a person from being prosecuted for a crime or subjected to punishment as a result of an absurdly literal reading of the language of a statute. They did not adopt it, as Earl in *Riggs* asked them to do, to apply penalties to anyone whom only an absurdly literal reading seemed to exempt from their reach.

Chief Justice Marshall had explicitly rebuffed just such an invitation in *Wiltberger*. United States Attorney General William Wirt argued in that case that the federal statute of 1790 should be extended to cover the actions of the defendant on the grounds that a literal reading of its words that excluded them would produce an absurd result that the legislators had surely not intended.[49] Marshall admitted "the extreme improbability that Congress could have intended to make those differences with respect to place, which their words import."[50] He could see no good reason why Congress would have intentionally treated murder and robbery as punishable in such locations as a river or harbor, and manslaughter as not. He held, however, that its wording of the statute had in fact done so and that it was not for the court to expand the boundaries that the lawmakers' words had set for these crimes in order to suit its own views of what did or did not make good sense. However absurd it might seem to let him go free, the defendant was culpable only if the letter of the law clearly and unmistakably covered what he had done.

As historians of the absurdity principle in American law have established, judges and commentators typically identified a result as coming within its reach not by providing or employing a definition of absurdity, but by referring to several classical examples that illustrated it.[51] And the examples that served as the paradigmatic ones for courts in this period to rely on were indeed ones whose absurdity lay in the punishments they held a defendant liable to, but not—as in *Wiltberger*—in the ones they allowed a defendant to escape. Another influential decision by the United States Supreme Court, in *United States v. Kirby* (1868), which like Earl's opinion quoted the Bologna story as one of its touchstones for identifying absurdity in a result, did so to narrow rather than to enlarge the scope of the law. The court in *Kirby* held unanimously that a sheriff who had arrested a carrier of the US mail while at work, on a warrant for murder, was not guilty of violating a federal law punishing anyone who obstructed the operations of the postal service.[52] (Not surprisingly, the actual controversy between the parties, as David Achtenberg established in 1995 in an excellent piece of legal archaeology, was quite different from this caricature, but it was the caricature that formed the vehicle for the court's statement of the law.[53])

Only a few years after *Riggs*, the Supreme Court decided another case partly on the absurdity rationale, and once again it used the doctrine to limit the scope of a prohibition, not to extend one: it made no sense, it held, to read an act of Congress prohibiting the importation of foreign contract "labor" as applying to an English rector hired by a New York City Episcopal church.[54] For the legal scholar Ernst Freund of the University of Chicago, writing in 1917, a key difference separated *Holy Trinity*, which he accepted as sound, from *Riggs*, which he rejected. The New York decision had gone too far by using the absurdity rationale to impose a penalty, whereas *Holy Trinity* had used it, less objectionably, to withhold one.[55]

In the classic instances, moreover, what *absurdity* meant was somewhat different from what Earl saw in the letter of the law in the Palmer case. The canonical examples illustrated absurd meanings, created usually by the use of words that could signify multiple things. If inheritance by murderers from their victims was properly described as *absurd*, it was in a different sense, and one that cases like *Kirby* or *Holy Trinity* or the Bologna story did not involve: substantive and moral rather than semantic, better termed *unconscionable*, and understood to lie properly within the domain of the legislature rather than the courts. Earl's appeal to absurdity to justify the result in *Riggs* thus went beyond what the law of the time supported.

Additional Rationales: Public Policy and Legal Maxims

The courts of other states (again, Missouri alone excepted) found quite unpersuasive Earl's supplemental argument, raised in the briefs in many of the later cases, that the courts could declare the legacy void as "an offense against public policy."[56] Whatever basis the argument possessed lay, though Earl did not emphasize the point, in the common law of contract. It was an accepted rule that judges would refuse to enforce agreements made between private parties that in some way or another ran offensively contrary to a state's public policy. But in doing so, they normally inferred the character of public policy from the laws themselves. Earl's reasoning would have had them do something quite different, amending those very laws on the basis of their own understanding of what policy was sound and desirable. The Pennsylvania Supreme Court in 1895 asked rhetorically: "How can there be a public policy leading to one conclusion when there is a positive statute directing a precisely opposite conclusion? . . . when the imperative language of a statute prescribes that upon the death of a person his estate shall vest in his children, how can any doctrine, or principle, or other thing, called 'public policy,' take away the estate of a child, and give it to some other person? . . . There can be no public policy which contravenes the positive language of a statute."[57] Similarly, the Iowa court, nine years later, after reciting the gist of the argument Earl and the plaintiffs in *Kuhn* had made, responded: "But the public policy of a State is the law of that State as found in its Constitution, its statutory enactments, and its judicial records. . . . And when such policy, touching a particular subject, has been declared by statute, as in this case . . . the courts have no authority to say that the Legislature should have made it of wider application."[58]

Nor did Earl's use of legal maxims commend itself to most American judges. Russell and Sanford credited the master maxim underpinning their argument—*Nullus commodum capere potest de injuria sua propria*, "No man shall take advantage of his own wrong,"—to an English text, Herbert Broom's 1845 volume *A Selection of Legal Maxims*.[59] (They omitted mentioning that Broom listed it among ones that applied to cases arising under the common law of contract, not to ones governing other domains or the law generally.) Their brief, and Judge Earl's opinion, attributed to it a kind of overarching authority to which mere legislative statutes must bow. By failing to set any limits to the powers they thus invoked, they implied that the other maxims in Broom's or similar standard collections had the same authority. They thereby attributed to judges a license to range freely among the statutes, the book of maxims in hand, and correct them accordingly.

The possible breadth of that power can be suggested by two other maxims from the same volume's opening chapter: *Salus populi suprema lex*, which Broom translated "The good of the individual ought to yield to that of the community," and *Summa ratio est quæ pro religione facit*: "If ever the laws of God and man are at variance, the former are to be obeyed in derogation of the latter."[60] That judges had not merely the right, but the duty, to measure all enacted statutes against these and other highly general commands and bring them up to code where they fell short, was, however extravagant, the apparent message of the *Riggs* majority opinion. It was for the time an audacious assertion of judicial power. American courts in the early and mid-nineteenth century had used maxims liberally to shape the common law, though not to overturn statutes; by 1889, they did not.[61] Accepting Earl's reasoning, as the Minnesota Supreme Court summed up the matter in 1910, "would establish a rule of construction, the limits of which no one could foresee."[62] It would close a minor loophole in the law by empowering judges to strike down or amend statutes more or less as they liked.

Earl failed to cite any precedents for the use he made of his maxim or for the transcendent authority he attributed to it. A half-century later, he would have been in no better position. An article published in 1937 reviewing the role of maxims in Anglo-American law argued that they could occasionally be helpful servants but never legitimate masters in the resolution of cases, that "even those which are useful are dangerous and should not as a rule be employed as the vertebrae of an argument or judicial determination, but rather as an aid or support for other legal reasoning." In the actual practice of the courts, overwhelmingly "they merely lend apt expression to a result otherwise reached . . . to bolster or support a legal viewpoint rather than to decide a case."[63] *Riggs*, which had been an anomaly in this respect in 1889, remained one because of the unwillingness of other judges to follow its example.

Finally, the Nebraska Supreme Court in 1894 conclusively disposed of the use that Earl had made of the *Armstrong* case. It pointed out that the passage he (following Russell's brief) had quoted from the Supreme

Court's opinion was not an integral part of what that tribunal had decided. The question before that court had not in fact been whether a murderer could collect on an insurance policy on the life of the victim. The passage quoted was, in legal terms, *obiter dictum*: an incidental comment on a matter not crucial to the case being decided, and as such lacking the legal weight as a precedent that the core holding and the reasoning behind it possessed.[64]

The Grounds for Rejection: Legal Academia

Echoing its reception by the American courts, early comment on *Riggs* in the leading legal journals was mostly hostile. Its critics were more numerous and more eminent than its defenders. They included James Barr Ames, dean of the Harvard Law School, who wrote in 1897 that it was "impossible to justify the reasoning of the court" in *Riggs*, that it was "unsound in principle . . . and may be dismissed from further consideration." He asked rhetorically: "when the legislature has enacted that no will shall be revoked except in certain specified modes," as was the case in New York, "by what right can the court declare a will revoked by some other mode?"[65]

The future Harvard Law School dean Roscoe Pound in 1907 assailed *Riggs* as "the most conspicuous example in recent American case-law" of what he, following the English legal theorist John Austin, called 'spurious interpretation." Two situations, Pound observed, genuinely called for judicial interpretation: an unclear law or conflicting provisions of the laws. *Riggs*-like "spurious interpretation," as distinguished from the legitimate and valid kind, "puts a meaning into the text as a juggler puts coins, or what not, into a dummy's hair, to be pulled forth presently with an air of discovery." It overstepped the proper bounds of judicial authority. Pound granted that in an age when the law was still rudimentary, such a procedure on the part of judges had its usefulness in filling the gaps. But it was "an anachronism in an age of legislation," tending to frustrate the choices of the elected legislature, to discredit the law in the eyes of the public, and to open the door to the pressure of special interests and of preferences personal to the judges. *Riggs* itself, he noted with satisfaction, was "now generally repudiated."[66]

In an article on statutory interpretation published in 1917, another leading scholar, Ernst Freund, likewise summed up *Riggs* as a decision rejected by the great majority of American courts, and rightly so, attempting as it did "to read an unexpressed exception into a statute in order to carry into effect a theory of natural justice."[67] Accepting *Riggs*, to Freund and its other critics, did not chiefly mean denying murdering heirs their ill-gotten gains. It meant, far more consequentially and far less acceptably, empowering courts to rewrite statutes according to their own wishes.

The Grounds for Rejection: Practicality

Accepted legal doctrine thus offered little support for the conclusions announced by the *Riggs* majority. Thoughtful judges might also have recognized several good pragmatic or prudential reasons to shun the path that the New York Court of Appeals invited them to take, a path that would have led them onto terrain dotted with quicksands. Added to the procedural advantages of having matters settled by a slayer statute rather than by the accumulation of case law, and the way in which a decision contrary to *Riggs* might prompt the legislature to enact such a statute, these reasons added up to a compelling case in that era for appellate-court restraint.

Putting the *Riggs* doctrine into practice within the law of murdering heirs was bound eventually to raise some awkward questions. The New York courts themselves were soon made aware of one set of them, which had already troubled the Nebraska county court judge who heard the Shellenberger case in 1888. At just what point and by what specific procedure did a legacy to a murderer from a victim become invalid? Did the murderer have legal access to it before that point was reached? Judges in New York had to address the issue in a sensational case that pervaded the metropolis's newspapers during much of 1895 and 1896. A well-born but not well-off socialite, Mary Alice Almont Livingston Fleming, was indicted on a charge of first-degree murder, accused of having given her mother, Evalina Bliss, a fatal dose of arsenic in a bowl of clam chowder.[68] Fleming—a last name she had adopted for reasons of propriety, having never been married, though she was the mother of three children and expecting a fourth at the time of her arrest—was the daughter, born in 1861, of Evalina's first husband, the wealthy Robert Swift Livingston, who had died in 1870. In the disposition of Robert's estate, the court had placed a large sum of money in the hands of the New York City Chamberlain, to be turned over to Robert's then-underage daughter upon her mother's death. To hasten her receipt of this inheritance, the state alleged, Mary Alice had poisoned Evalina.

Facing trial and badly in need of funds for her defense, the accused petitioned to be given her legacy. Several other descendants of Robert Livingston challenged her claim, and they prevailed before both the New York Surrogate, acting on the report of a referee, and, on appeal, Justice Roger Pryor of the state Supreme Court.[69] Both jurists rested their decisions squarely on the Court of Appeals' reasoning in *Riggs v. Palmer*. The cases were not exactly parallel, for Mary Alice's inheritance did not come from the estate of her alleged victim. Yet they were close enough that the *Riggs* rule against profiting from one's wrongs could be held to apply, and in his opinion in the case, Pryor so applied it. If Fleming had indeed poisoned her mother, Pryor held, she had no legal right to receive and make use of any property that came to her through her criminal act. Her right to it, he continued, could be assessed only when the courts had determined whether she had in fact committed the crime alleged. Though that question would have to be heard separately and did not depend on the outcome of the murder trial, by the usual rules of legal procedure the criminal charges involved took precedence over the civil case and must be heard first. Pryor added, finally, that it was in Fleming's own interest that the civil action be postponed, for if she were found not entitled to the legacy according to the *Riggs* doctrine, that finding could not fail to prejudice the more serious outcome of the criminal case in her disfavor.

Fleming took the case to the Supreme Court's Appellate Division, five judges of which heard the case and, only days before her murder trial was scheduled to begin, unanimously reversed the lower-court rulings. Legally, ownership of the money in dispute passed to Fleming immediately upon her mother's death, the court ruled. (Justice Landon had said the same about Elmer's legacy in *Preston v. Palmer*.) It followed that "her right to enjoy presently that to which she has the clear legal title should not have been thus postponed." Even a conviction of murder, Justice George C. Barrett observed, would not settle the civil issue of her right to the inheritance. Still less, then, did a mere indictment for murder resolve it. And the concern that Pryor had expressed that a rejection of her claim might bias the outcome of the murder trial was baseless, for any evidence to that effect would be inadmissible. "This woman comes, and asks for what in law is her own," Barrett disapprovingly summed up the lower-court decisions. "The answer is, 'You have been accused of murder.' Upon that the court dismisses her from its presence until she shall have secured an acquittal. In our judgment, this was a denial of the justice to which, upon the record, she was entitled."[70]

The Supreme Court's decision was left in force when the case was not appealed further. Fleming used a substantial portion of her inheritance to fund a successful defense to the first-degree murder charge in the face of strong circumstantial evidence of her guilt.[71] An heir accused of murder, given the contested legacy without delay, could spend much or all of it on a legal defense, and if adjudged both criminally and civilly culpable, could then, at best, hand it on in a severely depleted condition to the heirs the courts deemed the legitimate ones. It was not an ideal outcome, but the alternative was even less appealing. If the legacy were withheld, the result might be a conviction that would not have taken place if the accused heir had possessed the resources to secure good legal representation in the criminal and the civil proceedings, and thereby perhaps an acquittal and a valid claim on the legacy after all. (It would also, in effect, have encouraged a practice that American courts have consistently disallowed, the use of contingency fees for lawyers in criminal cases, for a prospective heir charged with murder and bereft of other resources would have been able to hire counsel only on the chance of inheriting following an acquittal.) If the Illinois courts had denied Ray Pfanschmidt his inheritance, he could not, lacking other resources, have successfully defended himself against a prosecution so convinced of his guilt and determined to convict him that it tried him three times; nor could he have, as he did, successfully appealed his flawed first conviction to the state's supreme bench.[72] The decision of the court itself, in short, could help determine a result that would be used to justify the decision. And as illustrated in the Fleming case in New York, judges could and did disagree as to what the correct legal answer to the problem was. It is hardly surprising that most courts, when the legislature itself had remained silent on the question, sensed the quagmire into which Judge Earl was offering to lead them and declined to enter it.

There were other ways in which answering the question as Earl had done obliged judges to confront some further and awkward questions as well. The sweeping maxims his opinion cited did not, for example, specify what degree of homicide, or even what lesser forms of "wrong"—perhaps mere neglect or negligence—subjected unworthy heirs to the loss of their rights. Did manslaughter? Did involuntary manslaughter? Did even second-degree murder, which by its legal definition, if not always in reality, could not have been committed for the purpose of inheriting?

The questions arose in the first use made of *Riggs* by any American court. A Chicago woman, Lena or Maggie Schreiner, in June, 1888 poured kerosene over her husband Mathias as he lay in a drunken stupor outside their house and set him afire with a match. Charged with murder, she was sentenced to ten years in prison for the lesser offense of manslaughter on the testimony of a police captain that Mathias had repeatedly and brutally beaten her.[73] She transferred her rights in an insurance policy on her husband's life to her defense attorney. The benefit society refused to pay and Cook County Circuit Court Judge John P. Altgeld—later a famous radical governor of the state—upheld its action, citing the just-announced New York case in support.[74] An appeals court, however, reversed Altgeld's decision. Manslaughter, it held, legally meant an unintentional killing, and therefore it did not invalidate the society's contractual obligation to pay as deliberate murder would have done.[75]

Both the majority and a concurring opinion by the Minnesota Supreme Court in 1910 went still further. They held that even if the reasoning in *Riggs* (which they rejected) were accepted as good law, it should not apply to an heir convicted only of second-degree murder.[76] Such matters seemed to these and other judges to be better settled in each state by a comprehensive statute, one moreover expressing the judgment of the people's elected representatives, than in common-law fashion by a series of cases, each contributing only part of the answer like a piece in a very slowly cohering jigsaw puzzle that offered little guidance for a case arising in an as-yet uncompleted corner of it. In New York, it took a number of decisions, some of them inconsistent with others, over a number of decades for a pattern to emerge, one that remains unclear in some respects to this day. In the courts of Great Britain and the Commonwealth, the essence of *Riggs*—the disallowance of a murdering heir by judicial rather than legislative authority—has been followed since the late nineteenth century. A twenty-first century critic of the results has found the results too mechanical in their adherence to previous cases and has called for legislative intervention in the form of a statute to correct their inflexibility. Regarding precedent as establishing "a rigid rule" for them to follow, this critic observed, judges, often inappropriately, tended to treat manslaughter under all circumstances as requiring the same outcome as first-degree murder.[77]

Yet another crop of thorns could also sprout from the *Riggs* doctrine if it were allowed to take root, as Judge Gray warned in his dissent. If the courts chose, against a murdering heir, to disregard either the expressed wishes of the testator or the legal rules governing the descent of property, they would often then have to decide who did inherit among a number of possible candidates, scarcely an appropriate decision for judges to be making and one likely to leave one or more parties understandably feeling wronged. To side with the appellants in the Palmer case, Gray protested, "would involve the diversion by the court of the testator's estate into the hands of persons, whom, possibly enough, for all we know, the testator might not have chosen or desired as its recipients. Practically the court is asked to make another will for the testator. The laws do not warrant this judicial action, and mere presumption would not be strong enough to sustain it."[78]

To award the legacy to the deceased's next of kin, as was done in *Riggs*, would in some cases mean withholding it from the murderer's heirs, to whom it would presumably have descended in due course and who certainly could not themselves have been regarded as guilty parties appropriately visited by such a forfeiture. In the Belew case in California, which was argued after Frank Belew's execution, a ruling based on *Riggs* would have left the court with the additional task of deciding whether his children did or did not receive the third share of his victims' estates legally passing through him. Legislators who considered the question differed somewhat in their answers. Slayer statutes could stipulate that the inheritance in question should pass as if the murderer had predeceased the victim, or that it should go to the victim's legal next of kin: both reasonable expedients, but that could in some cases lead to different outcomes. The dissenter in the Tennessee case of *Box v. Lanier* objected to a decision that by judicial fiat diverted the estate from one blameless set of claimants—the children of the murderer, who had taken his own life—to another set; it was, he argued, "to visit upon the children the iniquities of the father, which human law does not do, whatever may be the rule of the divine law."[79]

Such dilemmas were most satisfactorily avoided by continuing to award the estate to, or through, a murdering heir legally designated to receive it until the legislature decided what should be done instead. They were also, once again, more efficiently settled by a comprehensive set of rules laid down in a statute than by the slow and erratic procedure of piecemeal trial and lawsuit laying down the rules one at a time, and in ways that judges considering later cases might find inapplicable to the particular circumstances at hand but nonetheless constraining as precedent. In Britain and its former colonies, according to a New Zealand legal scholar, the judges who in the absence of slayer statutes have taken upon themselves the disposal of such cases have found answering the question "Who then is entitled to the victim's property?" to be "very problematic," and "[t]heir solutions have not always been consistent or rational."[80]

One more prudential argument against the *Riggs* doctrine lay in some problems that it threatened to produce in many of the cases heard by other appeals courts, though they did not arise in the Palmer suit itself. Strictly applied, it dispossessed not merely the murdering heir, but also, by declaring his or her title void, any other party who had subsequently acquired all or part of the victim's estate through that heir. The county court judge in Nebraska who in 1888 rejected the challenge to Lee Shellenberger's right to inherit from his murdered daughter expressed particular concern about the havoc that a contrary decision might have made with the rights of those to whom such properties subsequently passed.[81] Courts had good reason to hesitate before subjecting third parties to such a loss, and might well have preferred to do so only on the express authority of a disinheriting statute. Of course, the rights of such parties, if they had been aware of the circumstances, would not have been a matter of concern had it been generally recognized at the time, as Judge Earl maintained it should have been, that the law allowed a murderer no claim on a victim's estate. Those who sought to acquire such rights from even a suspected or possible murderer would have done so at their own risk. But the very concern that most courts showed for the rights of such parties is evidence that they did not believe such an understanding to have existed.

The Influence of an Anomaly

By underlining the weakness of the majority's reasoning in *Riggs*, this overview of legal doctrine in the years surrounding it and its successors clarifies one more puzzle about this set of decisions. Before 1888, no reported case in an American state court of last resort directly addressed the issues they raised. A rash of such cases then occurred in relatively short order, beginning with *Owens* in North Carolina, continuing in the next year with *Riggs* in New York, and followed by the others noted above. Several writers have raised the question of why we see this sudden and unprecedented outbreak. As one of them observed: "Heirs must have been murdering all along in order to benefit under their victims' wills . . . but for some reason the courts that produced written records were not called upon to rule whether they could inherit under statutes or wills—at least until the 1880s."[82] The question is an important one, for different answers to it differ in their consequences for how we understand *Riggs* itself.

A number of reasons for this patterning of decisions have been suggested. The earliest of them is also the least satisfactory. Already in 1897, James Barr Ames merely attributed the sudden eruption of murdering-heir cases in the appellate courts to the workings of "a strange chance."[83] But to treat any regularity as merely the work of chance or randomness is not to offer an explanation of it, but rather to confess one's failure to explain or understand it.

Daniel A. Farber, in an article on *Riggs* and its legacies and implications, conjectured that in earlier times, the speed and severity of the criminal process in cases of murder, and especially murder for profit, would not have left the culprit alive and able to take part in an appeal by the time an estate was settled: "Maybe, in those days of swift and widespread capital punishment, murderers rarely lived long enough for anyone to worry much about whether they had been unjustly enriched."[84] Plausible at first glance, this turns out to be no answer at all. For one thing, Farber offered no independent evidence that there was an abrupt and significant slackening in the punishment of murderers across the United States beginning in the 1880s, as the hypothesis implies. For another, the first three cases following *Owens* and *Riggs* (in Nebraska, Ohio, and Pennsylvania) were decided after the murderer had been put to death and involved, as already noted, the property rights of the murderer's heirs. Even assuming for the sake of argument that murderers were on the whole being punished less severely, these kinds of situations would have arisen quite as readily before 1888 as they did afterwards.

The most original and ingenious theory, proposed by Kim Lane Scheppele, points to the changing status of a venerable legal fiction in these years as the underlying reason.[85] That a person sentenced to life in prison was henceforth regarded and treated as "civilly dead" just as if he or she were really dead had long been the law, both in New York and in the rest of the English common-law world. Such a person could no longer inherit property, and the property he or she possessed was distributed to the heirs at law or the legatees; the marriage of a civilly dead person was dissolved and the former spouse freed from the union. But in 1870, the common law was unsettled by the passage of the Forfeitures Act in England, which contained a number of explicit provisions regarding the legal status and rights of convicts while saying nothing about their right to inherit, thus placing the matter newly in doubt. And then in 1888, Scheppele argued, the New York Court of Appeals filled this doctrinal vacuum when it ruled in the case of *Avery v. Everett* that the consignment to civil death of a life convict did not impose the distribution of that person's property, nor, by implication, did it prevent that person from inheriting property or acquiring it by other means.

Scheppele noted that the only dissenter in *Avery* was Robert Earl, the author of the majority opinion in *Riggs*, and she suggested that the later case was Earl's way of recouping some of the ground he had unsuccessfully taken in 1888. Elmer Palmer, she argued, would under the previous doctrine have been unable to inherit from his grandfather, being civilly dead, and the doctrine announced in *Riggs* operated as a substitute means to that end. More generally, she hypothesized, it was the prevalence of the civil-death rule that accounted for the absence of *Riggs*-type cases in the pre-1888 American law reports: the question never arose because convicted murderers—typically sentenced either to death or to life in prison—were prevented as a matter of course from inheriting, whether from their victims or from anyone else. By the same line of reasoning, it was the rapid erosion of the civil death rule triggered by *Avery* in 1888 that for the first time made the rights of murdering heirs a genuine legal problem in the United States.

As an explanation even of the *Riggs* decision itself, though, the argument fails. Elmer would not in fact have been ineligible to inherit from his grandfather even under the old doctrine, and the judges of the Court of Appeals knew it, for as we have seen, he was not sentenced to the term of life in prison that would have rendered him civilly dead. (Scheppele erroneously assumed that he was.) His sentence was not life but rather an indeterminate one limited only by life as the maximum possible for his crime. Judge Earl himself in 1884 had ruled, in a classic application of the rule of lenity, that the New York Code's provisions for civil death, being, in his words, "highly penal," must be construed strictly, and it follows that Elmer would not have been regarded as a life convict subject to them. Moreover, the prisoner seeking relief in the 1884 case had been sentenced to serve his term in a country penitentiary, not in the state prison stipulated in the Code's civil death clause, and Earl held again that by the strict construction obligatory in penal cases, he had not incurred its penalties.[86] Neither, then, had Elmer, who had been sentenced not to a state prison but to the state reformatory. And Justice Landon, in his opinion in *Preston v. Palmer*, delivered prior to the Court of Appeals decision in

Avery, considered and explicitly rejected the argument that his civil status disqualified Elmer as a legatee. Even if his sentence rendered him civilly dead and incapable of inheriting, which Landon did not believe, "he did not become so until sentenced," whereas the legacy, if valid at all, came into effect immediately after Francis's death.[87] Nothing in the *Riggs* opinion that reversed Landon's decision disputed his reasoning on this point.

Other writers have suggested that no recorded cases arose until *Owens* and *Riggs* because for all of that time it was simply assumed by lawyers and judges that the legally designated heir or legatee, even a murdering one, received the legacy in question.[88] And this would seem to be the correct answer to the question, or at least the one most consistent with the available evidence. As already noted, in a number of cases, a probate award to a victim's convicted murderer was not challenged in the highest court of the state at all. And as John W. Wade pointed out in 1936, although there is no earlier American case in the appellate reports directly discussing the rights of a murdering heir, an opinion addressing other issues handed down in 1875 by the Tennessee Court of Chancery took it for granted that such an heir would inherit.[89] As we have seen, *Riggs* largely failed to convince the judges of other states. But as a citable precedent on their side of the argument, it did, for the first time, offer hopeful litigants elsewhere enough grounds for hope—delusive though it usually proved to be—to appeal the probate decisions to the higher courts.

This explanation, if it is the correct one, casts an additional shadow over the reasoning of the majority in *Riggs*. For if the case was truly as clear-cut as Judge Earl professed to think it—if the venerable legal maxims to which he ascribed such authority had always and everywhere prohibited murderers from inheriting from their victims, relentlessly overriding any statutes that held otherwise—it is more than surprising that prior to 1889, no one, including Referee Sawyer or Justice Landon and his two colleagues of the New York Supreme Court, had realized it, and that for three decades after *Riggs*, most American judges persisted in failing to realize it. If, on the other hand, in order to justify the majority's disposition of the case Earl wildly exaggerated the reach, currency, and potency of the maxims he cited, then what had happened before and happened subsequently is quite easy to understand.

What that explanation further suggests is that the rash of reported murdering-heir cases from the late 1880s onward can largely be attributed to the decision in *Riggs* itself. Hardly any of them, that is to say, would even have been brought to the attention of the appeals courts that ruled on them if the New York case had been decided as Judges Gray and Danforth urged, for there would have existed no accepted legal grounds on which a murderer's inheritance could be challenged. And the evidence on that point is largely in agreement. The brief filed by O. P. Mason in the first post-*Riggs* case outside of New York to reach a state's court of last resort, the Shellenberger suit in Nebraska, leaned so heavily on *Riggs* as to suggest that without the precedent that it offered, the appeal to the Supreme Court would never have had a serious chance.[90] All of the later challenges (almost all of them unsuccessful, as we have seen) likewise arose in a world in which the *Riggs* precedent existed (briefly bolstered by the Shellenberger decision, before it was reversed) and thus furnished a respectable legal basis, previously lacking, for an appeal.

That leaves only *Owens* and *Riggs* to explain. Although the law report in *Owens* makes no mention of it, other sources on the case suggest a strong reason why the legacy that came under challenge could have aroused such discontent as to be appealed to the highest courts despite a generally held presumption in its favor. Sarah Owens, a white woman, had been convicted of hiring several black men to murder her husband, something that in the post-Reconstruction South might well have seemed to many members of the race in power so shocking as to prompt a court challenge to her accepted legal rights of inheritance. (The challenge indeed succeeded at the trial level, but, as already noted, was rejected by the state's Supreme Court.) It was the interracial dimension of the case—the mere killing of one spouse by another being hardly unheard of—that a North Carolina newspaper apparently had in mind in commenting: "It was such an unnatural murder that it has attracted much attention."[91]

That anomalous character may equally explain why only in *Owens* among all of the earliest cases of record (those reaching the appeals level before 1900), the probate and/or lower court had ruled against the murdering claimant—a pattern that, in turn, strengthens the likelihood that the right of such a claimant to inherit had previously gone unquestioned at all levels of the legal system. In *Riggs* itself, both the referee and (unanimously) the General Term of the Supreme Court had rejected the challenge to Elmer's legacy. The Kuhn case in Iowa in 1904, the first after *Owens* where the lower courts denied such a claim, was also the first to take place in a state with a slayer statute, which, though the Supreme Court found it not applicable, had afforded some plausible grounds for the decision.

If the flurry of challenges that followed *Riggs* is to be attributed to no cause more profound and deep-seated than the New York decision itself, there remains the task of accounting for that decision: one that, when replaced in its historical context, looks much more surprising and much more incongruous than it did before. What explains its sudden appearance in a legal landscape that was, and for some decades remained, resolutely hostile to it? The next chapter considers that question and offers and tests possible answers to it.

Chapter 4

Explaining an Anomaly

The late nineteenth- and early twentieth-century judges across the United States who weighed the *Riggs* decision by and large did not consider it valid. In their eyes it was bad law, which is therefore what, in its historical context, it must be considered to have been. But neither can one simply dismiss the decision of the Court of Appeals in the Palmer case, a decision made by five distinguished and experienced judges, as a random aberration of judgment. Fortunately, there is no need to, for as it happens, a quite plausible hypothesis is available to reconcile these conflicting data. Elmer Palmer's case in New York was an exceptional one, presenting as it did the possibility that a convicted murderer could be set free after only a few years and take full possession of the fruits of his crime. It confronted the judges on the court, who enjoyed more freedom than those below to make new law, with no fear of being reviewed by a still higher court, with a remarkably provoking respondent whose claim they had to adjudicate. Their decision, though couched in impeccably general and abstract terms, may have been formulated first and foremost for the purpose of denying that claim.

Riggs: A "Soft Case"?

Any adequate explanation of why the decision in *Riggs* won the support of a substantial majority of the New York Court of Appeals must at the same time be able to account for its failure almost everywhere else—and vice versa. For the point could just as usefully be phrased the other way around. No explanation of the outcomes in other states is adequate that does not also explain the rather emphatic finding to the contrary in New York. The requirement that any hypothesis cover these two facts does much to narrow the range of possibilities. It casts serious doubt, for example, on any appeal to the psychology or preconceptions of a single judge in the exceptional case, New York's, as a sufficient explanation. For the result and the reasoning in *Riggs* gained the assent of five of them.

It is hardly plausible that the judges of the courts of last resort in New York, and also in Missouri (an odd pairing in itself) simply had moral sensibilities more finely tuned than those in the other states and were more deeply revolted by the prospect of murderers profiting from their crimes. All of the courts that refused to follow *Riggs* expressed their disgust at such an outcome and their wish that the law did not permit it. There is no reason to doubt their sincerity, particularly given the gruesome details of many of the cases. It is even less likely that the judges of these courts acted as they did because they sympathized with the murdering heirs and sought to protect their interests. A cynic might note that many of the cases involved the rights not of the murderer, who had signed them away, but of the lawyers to whom those rights had been assigned, and might suppose that the judges were looking after the interests of their fellow legal professionals. But that hypothesis fails to account for the same prevalent outcome in the cases that, like *Riggs* itself, determined whether the guilty heir himself or herself would benefit—including the first of them all, *Owens v. Owens* in North Carolina, an important precedent for every one that followed. Indeed, in the Illinois case (*Wall v. Pfanschmidt*), the court upheld the heir's claims against those of a lawyer whom survivors of the victims had hired to aid the prosecution, assigning to him the money they hoped to inherit on the accused murderer's conviction.

It is true, finally, that the judges of New York's Court of Appeals were elected rather than appointed. Were they attempting to curry popular favor in ruling as they did? Murderers are not an influential or a popular constituency, and rejecting their claims in a blast of righteous rhetoric would have cost judges nothing with the voters. But the explanation fails, because an elective judiciary in the late nineteenth- and early twentieth-century United States was the norm rather than an exception, and existed in all of the states that decided important murdering-heir cases: most of them in the murdering claimant's favor.[1]

What explanations, then, are possible? When the courts of state A reach one result and those of the rest of the country reach an opposing one, the reason for the difference could be that the bench of state A is in some way ideologically out of step with the others and predisposed toward legal doctrines that they reject. Perhaps *Riggs* was a case of this sort. Such divergences can and do occur; the supposed cause is not one merely invented out of thin air to explain this particular anomaly. That, however, is about all that can be said for it. For *Riggs* was a more surprising than characteristic decision for a court noted for its relative doctrinal conservatism to have handed down. The legal historian Peter Karsten's study of the jurisprudences of *heart* and *head* in American common law in the nineteenth century points up its oddity. Legal doctrines had a geographical pattern, and it was not one to which *Riggs* conformed. Karsten found judges in the Northeast, and New York within it, to have been notably more inclined than the rest of the country, and especially the less industrialized and less urbanized Plains and the South, to a traditionalistic approach that eschewed novel rulings and especially ones prompted by moral or emotional leanings.[2] The Court of Appeals, normally reluctant to explore and claim new ground, is an improbable pioneer of the theories *Riggs* introduced into American law, which, although presented as deductions from age-old principles, were revolutionary in their implications. "To nearly all who took an interest in the case the decision is more or less of a surprise," one New York State newspaper observed in 1889 after *Riggs* was announced. "There were but few lawyers who felt sure that a decision would be made like that handed down by the Court of Appeals last week."[3] It had evidently struck them as out of character.

Another possible explanation of a divergence between one state and the rest of the country is that there was some feature of the specific case argued in state A that was not present in the others, that was not an appropriate basis for distinguishing the case in the usual legal sense, but that nonetheless powerfully deflected the court toward the result it reached. And this is a far more promising possibility, for a candidate for such a role in *Riggs* is not hard to identify. It does not lie where one might first seek it, in the particularly outrageous character and circumstances of the crime in question. Murder is never calculated to ingratiate the person committing it to a court of law. Yet Elmer Palmer's actions, as murders and even as murders for profit go, were not extraordinarily shocking. What might well have seemed so, however, was the meager punishment they had earned him. Elmer had received what must have struck the appellate judges as a ludicrously light sentence for second-degree murder, most of the reasons (other than his youth) that had prompted the jury and judge to leniency having faded from view as the case moved from the trial courtroom to the Court of Appeals. He had been set free in his early twenties after four years of vocational training at public expense in the state reformatory. Having paid so small a price for his crime, he appeared to be seeking a reward for it by claiming the legacy that he had poisoned his grandfather to obtain. The possibility that the five judges in the majority found such effrontery more than they could stomach, and gave thwarting it priority over following the law, deserves consideration.

The American legal system normally establishes rules and precedents applying to future controversies only in the act of settling concrete ones that are brought before it in the present. Consequently, decisions carefully framed to make good general doctrine (by whatever standard) may work hardship or injustice for the particular parties involved in the case at hand. Conversely, decisions dictated by a sense of justice or of favor toward those parties can produce rules and precedents that are far from optimal for the typical case. The term *hard cases*, as in "hard cases make bad law," originally referred to ones in which a rigorous application of legal reasoning would work undue hardship on the losing side.[4] (Only later did it take on the meaning it usually has today, cases where the best answer is *hard* to discern because of the strong arguments on both sides.) A *hard case* in the older sense of the phrase has a correlative, though one that is less often discussed and has no name of its own. To keep the terms parallel, one might call it a *soft case* (the antithesis of a *hard case* in the newer sense being an *easy case*): one in which the result that the law appears to dictate seems too soft on one of the parties, so that the judges are tempted to bend the law to make it harsher. If they do, bad law (bad by the consensus of the other courts of the day or by some other yardstick) may be made in order to punish an unappealing individual.

Was *Riggs* a case of this kind?

This hypothesis, too, cannot be accused of inventing a previously unknown phenomenon for the purpose of explaining another. Almost everyone will admit that the circumstances of a particular case can and sometimes do warp the legal reasoning of the court that hears it away from what that court would hold were the matter stated in purely abstract terms. In his *Wiltberger* opinion, speaking of occasions when a judge had—improperly, in his view—read criminal penalties into a statute that its language did not authorize, Chief Justice Marshall suggested that they had involved "cases of considerable irritation, which it would be unsafe to consider as precedents forming a general rule for other cases."[5] Justice

Oliver Wendell Holmes similarly spoke in 1904 of so-called *great cases* as illustrating, like hard cases, how legal judgment can be thrown off course by "some accident of immediate overwhelming interest which appeals to the feelings and distorts the judgment. These immediate interests exercise a kind of hydraulic pressure which makes what previously was clear seem doubtful, and before which even well settled principles of law will bend."[6] The circumstances in *Riggs* could indeed have been causes of "considerable irritation," in Marshall's words, and of the "immediate overwhelming interest which appeals to the feelings," in Holmes's, to the Court of Appeals judges considering them, and could have produced the kind of doctrinal anomaly both warned against.

The legal scholar Frederick Schauer, in an article titled "Do Cases Make Bad Law?," has suggested that the problem of "case-driven distortion in judicial rulemaking" may be a pervasive one in a common-law legal system.[7] The development of rules only out of individual cases, Schauer observed, is often supposed to be one of the great strengths of such a system. It forces the judges to face the concrete realities of the situations their decision will henceforth regulate, and the stake the litigating parties have in the outcome helps ensure that the arguments on all sides will be fully and energetically presented. Yet, Schauer argued, it is a serious offsetting disadvantage that the specifics of the particular case in controversy are bound to weigh heavily, and perhaps too heavily, in the judges' minds as they seek a just and appropriate resolution to it. The result may be a decision that is ill-adapted to most cases of the same sort that it will nonetheless govern as a precedent. In the longer term, the result may also be an undesirable degree of change and instability in the law as new decisions distorted by new particulars at hand overturn older ones that were distorted in a different direction.

A decision closely contemporaneous with *Riggs* seems to have been very much swayed by the specifics of the case: the United States Supreme Court's ruling in *Mutual Life Insurance Company v. Hillmon*, handed down in 1892, and as famous in its own sphere as *Riggs* is in its.[8] In *Hillmon*, the court created, more or less out of nothing, a novel and enduring exception to an important rule of evidence in American courts, the ban on hearsay. What a witness heard another person assert—or, more generally, any statement made outside of court that is reported in court only at second hand—will ordinarily not be admitted as evidence of *what* it was that the other person asserted in a way that a witness's own statement to that effect will. The rationale is simple: such assertions are unreliable as evidence because their truthfulness cannot be subjected to the safeguards usually employed in a trial. The person who is their source is not placed under oath nor subject to cross-examination by the lawyers for the other side. (Statements of fact made out of court by a defendant and reported by another person, such as Elmer's to Willis Doud, were not and are not normally considered hearsay at all; the only party who could want to challenge them by cross-examination being the very person who had made them.) A number of recognized exceptions to the rule exist, one of them added to the list by the Supreme Court in *Hillmon*: the so-called state-of-mind exception. Evidence that would ordinarily be excluded as hearsay could be admitted as indicating the absent speaker's state of mind or intentions at the time of the statement. There are, as Marianne Wesson has shown, no compelling grounds—legal, psychological, or other—for such an exception, nor is it a corollary of or closely related to the other clusters of exceptions to the hearsay rule. It exists, and today forms part of the Federal Rules of Evidence, solely because the Supreme Court laid it down in deciding *Hillmon* in 1892.

Why did the court do so? In 1879, a resident of Wichita, Kansas, named John Hillmon took out three substantial insurance policies on his own life, the beneficiary being his wife, Sallie, whom he had recently married. Shortly afterwards he and a friend set out looking for land to buy for a sheep ranch in the southwestern part of the state. According to the friend, John H. Brown, Hillmon was fatally shot in an accident. Sallie claimed payment on the insurance policies, but the companies, suspecting fraud, refused to agree that the body produced was in fact Hillmon's. They maintained that it was the body of one Frederick Walters, a drifter who had disappeared from sight at about the same time, and that he had been killed and his corpse used to impersonate the still-living Hillmon, presumably gone into hiding to await the payoff from his swindle. A letter they produced as evidence from Walters to his fiancée, written from Wichita shortly before Hillmon's departure, strongly supported this version of events. In it, Walters mentioned that he had met a man named Hillmon and would be leaving shortly with him on a business venture. The trial judge, however, excluded the letter under the hearsay ban, Walters himself being unavailable for questioning: the ruling that the Supreme Court, to which the case was appealed, created its state-of-mind exception to override. It apparently did so in order to remove a legal obstacle frustrating what it considered the clear fact of the matter, that the claims were fraudulent. Wesson concluded that "the Court would not have invented the hearsay exception but for the pressure of a nearly irresistible desire to ensure that Hillmon did not succeed in his criminal schemes."[9] (As her research has also established, the court was almost certainly wrong about the insurance claims, appearances notwithstanding, for the body most likely was Hillmon's after all, and the Walters letter can be quite plausibly accounted for on other grounds.)

It would be difficult, then, against the hypothesis presented to explain *Riggs*, that such things simply do not happen. Experimental research among state and federal judges conducted in the early twenty-first century similarly indicates that their interpretations of disputed points of law are affected by their emotional responses to the situation and the litigants involved.[10] Nor is the suspicion that the result and the reasoning in *Riggs* owed much to the specifics of the case one that no observer at the time, closer than we are to the events involved, expressed. Shortly after the Court of Appeals announced its decision, an article on the case in the *New York Sun* frankly and matter-of-factly ascribed the judges' action to the light punishment that Elmer Palmer had incurred for his crime. "Their whole decision is based upon the supposition that had legislators supposed that a prospective legatee might estop a testator from changing his will by murder, *and then, though convicted of the murder, be set free to enjoy the estate*, laws would have been made to meet the emergency" (emphasis added).[11] Judge Earl's opinion, of course, stated no such qualification. But at least one otherwise well-informed contemporary believed that it could be read between the lines.

Likewise, one sentence of Gray's dissent—"The law has punished him for his crime, and we may not say that it was an insufficient punishment"—takes on a more pointed meaning in light of that supposition than it carries at first glance.[12] It suggests that what made Elmer's case unusual was that his punishment might well have seemed insufficient to the other judges; further, that they had in fact decided that it was insufficient and needed to be stiffened by a disinheritance that the law at the time, as generally recognized, did not impose; and that they had manufactured a rule that did not previously exist, though they pretended otherwise, solely for that purpose. Earl's reply, that the court was not taking anything away from Elmer, but merely applying the law as it stood and finding that the estate had never descended to him in the first place, is valid only if that was indeed how the law was generally understood. But the judges in the *Riggs* majority stood nearly alone in their day in so asserting.

Nor, finally, had the prospect of Elmer, having gone free, taking pleasure in his undeserved inheritance gone unmentioned in the argument of the case. As noted already, Russell and Sanford's brief for the appellants called the court's attention to what might come to pass if they upheld the decision of the General Term. The world, they observed, would witness the revolting spectacle of Elmer "clothing his possible mistress in gold," and in other ways enjoying the full possession and use of the estate.[13]

It cannot be said, therefore, that this explanation for the outcome is purely something projected from the present onto past actors to whom such a possibility would never have occurred. Having survived this initial objection, it warrants a serious and closer look.

Testing a Hypothesis: New York v. the Other States

That the majority in *Riggs* acted in this way is a counterfactual hypothesis. It implies that they would have ruled differently had Elmer, say, been sentenced to life in prison, or at least not gone free by the time of the decision. Like any historical counterfactual, it cannot be put to a direct empirical test. The human past cannot be run again in a controlled experiment with a single variable changed. We can know with some confidence only what happened under the circumstances that occurred and not what would have happened had they been different, and we can only seek as many indirect tests of the hypothesis as can be devised.

The hypothesis I have offered is supported, for example, if *Riggs* seems to be an uncharacteristic judgment for the particular state court that made it, and as noted already, it does. A second test, and a key one, has likewise in part been performed. If most American appeals court judges in legally similar situations during the same period decided them contrary to *Riggs*, then the hypothesis receives some support. Their actions offer a proxy for how the New York judges might have acted had Elmer's case been a more normal one. And in fact almost all of them did decide differently, even though the existence of *Riggs* by the time they did so as a precedent laid down by a highly respected state court pulled in the opposite direction.

These results, though, are only compelling if Elmer had indeed gotten off much more lightly than any of the would-be heirs convicted of murder in the cases decided elsewhere previously (*Owens*) or over the next quarter-century. As it turns out, he had. At the time the courts were considering their rights or those of their heirs or assignees, none of the other culprits was at liberty or within plausible sight of liberty, as he was, to enjoy direct possession of the inheritance in question.

In two of the cases (the sole one, in Missouri, decided in agreement with *Riggs*, and the Tennessee one that gave rise to *Box v. Lanier*), the claimant had departed the scene immediately: the murder had been a murder-suicide. In Nebraska, the murderer had been sentenced to death, as had the prospective heirs in Ohio, Pennsylvania, Kansas, and Illinois (though a quirk in the administration of law in Kansas made a death sentence in that state, such as Thornton Brant's, into, in effect, one of life in prison).[14] In the *Owens* case preceding *Riggs*, the wife who had conspired to kill her husband was serving a sentence of life in prison, as were the convicted murderers in Iowa, Oklahoma, and Minnesota (both 1908 and 1910).[15] In the Texas case (*Hill v. Noland*), murder by the dead man's widow and prospective heir-at-law was alleged in the lawsuit, but there had been no trial and no conviction. Charges (never, apparently, resolved) were still pending at the time of the appeals court decision, and a related case decided around the same time referred to the murder as the act of "persons unknown."[16] In the Dale suit in Indiana, as in the *Ellerson* case that would come up in New York, no one had been tried, let alone convicted. The inheriting murderers in the two lower-court cases in California, Frank Belew and Adolph Weber, were both executed, as was also J. Warren Jenkins in Wyoming; Ward Hedger, the convicted murderer in the Wisconsin case, was sentenced to life in prison, and so was Van Buren Baker in West Virginia.[17] There would have been no occasion for the courts in any of these cases to have to step in and stiffen the punishment by preventing the convicted offenders from enjoying in freedom the profits of their crimes, as Elmer Palmer was poised to do until the decision in *Riggs* blocked his way.

Thus to write off *Riggs* as merely a chance anomaly, even one embracing all five judges in the majority, would be to ignore a pattern in the cases that itself calls for explanation. The principal case in which a surviving murderer was denied inheritance from the victim was also, and by a considerable margin, the one in which the murderer had been most lightly punished: indeed, Elmer Palmer, and he alone, had actually been discharged by the time the state appeals court ruled on the case, and could have been said without hyperbole to have been on the verge of getting away with murder for profit. (The *New York Sun* in 1889, after recounting the details of the case, found it hard to understand "why the verdict was not made in the first degree, and why the Judge, who had the option in the matter, did not send Elmer to prison for life."[18]) That the coincidence between the two is a random occurrence is substantially less likely than that the *Riggs* anomaly, standing alone, was one.

Another difference between New York and the rest of the country is suggestive. It is the dissent in *Riggs* that contains the only clues in the printed appellate record to how light Elmer's punishment had been: "at the time of the commencement of this action," Gray wrote, "he was serving out his sentence in the state reformatory."[19] The qualifying clause, the reference to the particular institution with its indeterminate but generally modest terms of imprisonment, and the past imperfect tense of the verb would have hinted to anyone reading closely what had indeed occurred, that Elmer had been released by the time of the Court of Appeals decision. Judge Earl's opinion, by contrast, is entirely silent on the matter. Yet in all but two of the aforementioned cases decided in other states through 1914, the law report (and, most often, the majority opinion) mentioned the sentence for the homicide (which had been either death or life in prison) that had been handed down, and the two exceptions are easily accounted for. In Texas, there could be no mention because there had been no sentence; no one had been convicted of the murder. And the Iowa case had been a sufficiently sensational and familiar one throughout the state (as the Palmer murder had not been) that any mention of the penalty would have been unnecessary. Sarah Kuhn's conviction and life sentence had aroused much interest, and the question of pardoning her (a power, in cases of first-degree murder, that could be exercised by the governor only at the request of both houses of the legislature) had been a major electoral issue in the races for the state senate, and one settled against her by a vote of that body more than six months before the Supreme Court released its decision on her inheritance rights.[20] As a rule, then, the offender's sentence evidently seemed a natural and relevant datum for the opinion of the appeals court to mention, if only to emphasize that he or she had been severely punished. That Earl said nothing about Elmer's punishment supports the hypothesis that he had it in mind but preferred not to mention it and perhaps provoke speculation about why the decision had been made.

Testing a Hypothesis: New York's Retreat from *Riggs*

Another test is whether the judges of what I earlier called state A (and if possible, some of the same judges themselves) maintained their stance when faced with a second case presenting less extraordinary facts but the same legal question. Just such a second case arose in New York less than a decade after *Riggs*, and when it did, the Court of Appeals found its earlier reasoning unsatisfactory and shifted its response. Though committed beyond complete retreat, it made, in 1896, a fairly drastic repudiation of much of its earlier holding. A wealthy resident of Otsego County named Munroe Westcott had died in 1891, and his will left his estate under a set of conditions to his widow, Elizabeth, whom it also named as an executor. Munroe's sister, Catharine Ellerson, and several other relatives of his contested the will, asserting that he had been poisoned or in some other way murdered by Elizabeth and that, under the law as stated in *Riggs*, the will was therefore invalid and title to the estate should pass to them as Munroe's heirs at law. The appellate term of the New York Supreme Court agreed that such would be the case if the murder were to be established and accepted by the probate court as a matter of fact (there had so far been no criminal conviction or even proceedings to that effect), noting that *Riggs* had "involved precisely the issue presented here."[21]

It had indeed. And so in reversing the decision, as it did early the next year in *Ellerson v. Westcott*, the Court of Appeals, without acknowledging it, abandoned the commanding ground it had claimed earlier in *Riggs*. In particular, it tacitly denied that the maxims whose authority Earl had asserted overrode either the language of the statute where they conflicted or the provisions of a will in such a case, preventing the title to the property in question from passing legally to the murderer. Such had been the plain message of the majority opinion of 1889. The unanimous opinion in *Ellerson*, written by Chief Judge Charles Andrews, in effect overruled it. In *Riggs*, Andrews asserted, "the court did not decide that the will was void," nor did it in any way annul or add to the provisions of the statute. In *Ellerson*, no less than in the earlier case, he held, "the devise took effect on the death of the testator and transferred the legal right given her by the will."[22] Judge Earl, of course, had concluded his *Riggs* opinion by declaring that the provisions of Francis's will passing title to Elmer were void, never having made him the owner, and that the estate belonged legally to the plaintiffs.

The 1896 Court of Appeals had, in fact, come up with a new and, to its mind, much sounder and more secure foundation for the result in *Riggs* than the one that Judge Earl had articulated. It succeeded, to its own satisfaction at least, in reestablishing the result on that ground while pretending that the earlier decision had merely been misunderstood. The new ground it had chosen was the Anglo-American judicial domain of equity, which had developed in parallel with that of law proper.[23] Law's business was to determine the rights, entitlements, and obligations of the parties in a case according to the rules and precedents laid down by judges in their decisions and by legislators in statutes. Courts of equity, for their part, could supply corrective remedies where strict adherence to the law's rules and precedents would lead to a patently unjust or unfair outcome for one of the parties involved. They did not presume to alter the law, only to interpose to redress a particular unconscionable outcome that it had produced. Though they might over time develop rules of thumb for dealing with similar cases that could harden into law-like rules, their chief business was with the unique situation presented by each case. To a court of law, it would be a reproach that it had decided a contested matter in an ad hoc way. A court of equity existed to do just that when the occasion and circumstances called for it.

Such was the essential rationale for the joint existence of the two systems, though other differences between law and equity also developed. Traditional courts of equity dealt chiefly with cases involving property, though not presuming to determine property rights and titles, which belonged exclusively to law. Their distinctive concern with matters of conscience and individual responsibility made them the natural forum for disputes involving trusts and guardianships, situations where one person's powers over another person's vital interests might easily be abused if not carefully watched. Dispensing with the juries customary in legal cases, equity judges decided suits on their own and had wide latitude in the forms and substance of evidence that they would consider. They could take into account matters that a court of law would normally ignore: for example, whether parties asking for equitable relief had themselves behaved with scrupulous fairness. The remedies available to judges in equity were typically limited to injunctions: commands to parties in a case to perform or to refrain from performing certain actions, and enforceable, if they were ignored, by the penalties for contempt of court. Equity, to its defenders, represented the necessary complement of a domain of law based on rules. It allowed the demands of justice to be satisfied in those cases where the strict application of the rules would have frustrated them.

Though a deep distrust of judicial power and discretion made equity less important in the United States than it was in England, in its essential features it existed on both sides of the Atlantic. New York State, for the first seventy years after the revolution, maintained separate court systems for law and equity. The former was administered by a Supreme and lower courts. Equity pleas for relief were heard by the Court of Chancery under a chancellor, who outranked the chief justice of the Supreme Court as the head of the state's judiciary. When a new constitution ratified by the voters of New York in 1846 abolished the office of chancellor, the legislature then merged the two systems into one. Yet the union of law and equity into the domain of a single set of courts did not erase the distinction between them. Nor, though it tended to make them less visible, did it abolish the courts' equity powers.[24]

What Judge Andrews's opinion in *Ellerson* did was to apply to the case of a murdering heir an old equity remedy, the constructive trust, the word *constructive* in this term indicating a legal fiction of the *as-if* variety. Under this device, sometimes also called an involuntary or a remedial trust, when one had through one's wrongful actions (usually fraud) acquired legal title to a piece of property, the judge could redress the unconscionable result by declaring that the property was in reality a legal trust and the acquirer its trustee ex maleficio or ex delicto (as a consequence of wrongdoing), commanded by the court's decree to deliver its proceeds to whatever other person the court regarded as having the better moral right to them.[25] In effect, the income or other benefits from the property would pass to that person, though title, being a matter of law rather than equity, would remain the wrongdoer's. *Ellerson* announced that in New York State, a murdering heir would receive legal title to a legacy that met all of the law's conditions, but would be deprived of its use, being made by the courts a constructive trustee for the benefit of whomever the victim's property would most appropriately descend to.

Andrews himself had taken a major step years earlier in enlarging the scope of the constructive trust. Traditionally, courts had seen it only as appropriate when the parties had already been in some formal relationship of duties or obligations to one another. In 1877, he spoke for the Court of Appeals in the case of *Newton v. Porter* in making persons who had received stolen property and were aware of its tainted origins constructive trustees for the persons robbed when the normal legal course of action—recovery of the property or its equivalent from the thieves themselves—was useless because they had no assets in hand.[26] Thus the old requirement of a preexisting fiduciary relation for the creation of a constructive trust no longer held. Such a trust could be decreed to redress any situation in which property had been acquired in a lawful but quite unconscionable manner and effectively convey it to its rightful holder.

In adapting this broadened remedy to the murdering-heir situation in 1896, Andrews may also have drawn on a note that had five years earlier appeared anonymously in the *Harvard Law Review* and was later revealed as the work of James Barr Ames, then a professor in the Harvard Law School and shortly to become its dean.[27] In a fuller analysis he published in 1897, Ames rejected *Riggs* and its interference with the statutory transmission of title as an unwarranted and indefensible act of judicial legislation. Yet he found the alternative of letting someone in Elmer's position inherit equally unacceptable. It would leave "our law open to the reproach of permitting the flagrant injustice of an atrocious criminal enriching himself by his crime." To avoid the undesirable features of both of these options, he suggested a resort to equity through the device of a constructive trust. It would also forestall, he argued, a problem that the *Riggs* doctrine would produce in some cases, including the three that had immediately followed it in the supreme courts of other states. By confirming the murderer's legal title, it protected the rights of third parties who had in good faith acquired portions of the estate from the murderer.[28]

What *Ellerson* kept from *Riggs* was the end result and not the way in which it was achieved or justified. One of the most basic principles of equity held that its remedies were not available to anyone who had clear and adequate recourse through the law. For the court to resort to equity in a case so closely equivalent to *Riggs* was to acknowledge that the dissenters in the earlier case were correct and that the law in fact did grant Elmer title to his inheritance. *Ellerson* reformulated, as far as New York was concerned, a judicial assertion of the power to amend a clear and unambiguous legislative statute into something far more modest and restricted: merely a notice that the state's courts would use their equity powers in such unusual cases to prevent murdering heirs from enjoying the legally guaranteed fruit of their crimes at the expense of worthier claimants. It forestalled the same distasteful outcome as *Riggs* did and disposed of the Palmer estate in the same way. Yet confined so narrowly, it did not have, as judges of the period might have seen matters, the same potential to metastasize throughout the law as *Riggs*'s novel and radical assertion of the courts to apply traditional legal maxims to add to or invalidate statutes that conflicted with them. It did not involve statutory interpretation at all, as *Riggs* has generally been understood as doing. It won the support of Gray, the lone dissenter remaining on the Court from the earlier case, suggesting that he found the new method of arriving at the same result an unobjectionable one.[29]

Andrews's use of the constructive trust in *Ellerson* was by far the most satisfactory stopgap expedient that the courts of the day could employ when faced with challenges to claims by murdering heirs, at least for an initial case in a state that had not yet enacted a slayer statute. A Minnesota judge who endorsed his reasoning expressed surprise that it should not have been the course taken everywhere.[30] James Barr Ames thought that only the fusion in most states of law and equity courts, and the consequent eclipse of the latter's distinctive powers, had blinded the courts in *Riggs* and the two *Shellenberger* decisions to the availability of a solution so obviously superior to the ones they had adopted, and so much less objectionable in the precedent it might set.[31] The eminent legal scholar Roscoe Pound in 1905 offered the same explanation for the mishandling, as he saw it, of the murdering-heir cases by most American courts.[32]

Yet Ames's hopes for his brainchild rested largely unfulfilled. The constructive-trust approach was not widely taken up by courts that, unlike New York's, began with a clean slate rather than an existing decision that had somehow to be accommodated but that stood in need of a better rationale. When the Missouri Supreme Court, in 1908, went counter to the national trend, it affirmed Judge Earl's reasoning and presented its decision as one of statutory interpretation. It did not even deign to mention the *Ellerson* solution, by then the governing one in New York.

The constructive-trust approach was certainly open to criticism for its costliness and cumbersomeness, requiring as it might the filing and hearing of a separate plea in equity to accomplish what a statute, or even a judge-made rule like that in *Riggs*, would dictate more or less automatically. And because it achieved the result desired by all, of depriving the culprit of the inheritance he or she had killed to obtain, and offered a model that would apply to future cases of the same kind, it took some of the pressure off the legislature to enact a slayer statute that spelled out all of the principal rules. New York remained one of the few states never to enact such a statute. The predictability and consistency of its law would suffer as a result, and would suffer even more from the subterfuge employed in *Ellerson* to reconcile it with the earlier case. A key point on which they differed and which a well-drawn statute would have spoken, whether legal title passed to the murdering heir or not, was left unresolved and became a chronic source of inconsistency in New York decisions thereafter. An expert on inheritance law writing in 1931 urged, though in vain, that the passage of an explicit slayer statute by the legislature would "clarify the confusion of thought found in the eight New York decisions dealing with this problem."[33] A decade and a half later, a professor at the New York University School of Law found matters still worse, a 1939 decision having muddled the doctrine laid down in earlier cases so badly as to create "a state of confusion and contradiction which is difficult to describe."[34] Similar complaints about mutually irreconcilable decisions and calls for a clarifying New York statute, thus far, unavailing, have continued to appear in legal periodicals into the twenty-first century.[35]

Although it had little influence on the law elsewhere, the route taken in *Ellerson* is significant for what it says about *Riggs*. The spokesman for the court in the later case was Chief Judge Andrews, who had been a member of the majority in 1889. Thus not only the 1896 court, without a dissenting voice, but also the only judges who sat in both cases, Andrews and Gray, disclaimed the most revolutionary assertion made in Earl's opinion, and the one to which *Riggs* owed most of its later celebrity: that of the court's power to deny Elmer title to the Palmer estate by inferring an exception into the statute. That the later court had found itself unable or unwilling to assert this power, and that the result in *Riggs* required such tinkering as to amount to an abandonment of its original basis, bolsters the suspicion that it had not been a considered statement of legal principle. *Riggs*, in this light, looks like something that Earl patched together, largely out of the materials handed to the judges in the brief for the appellants, to justify the result that he and four of his colleagues wished to reach in the particular situation that confronted them. That situation, on the hypothesis advanced here, was Elmer Palmer's claim on an estate he had committed murder to obtain and been so lightly punished for doing.

That the initial solution should have been a makeshift one is not surprising. The New York Court of Appeals, throughout the last decades of the nineteenth century, labored under a heavy burden of cases that kept it chronically behind with its work.[36] Its judges could spare relatively little time for considered reflection on the best way to resolve a difficult case raising novel issues. It would be no wonder if the person assigned to write for the court in *Riggs* had grasped as if at a life preserver at the generous array of arguments and materials that Russell and Sanford had thrown in his direction, as offering respectable cover for the result, and without too much effort to make them cohere. Yet had it fallen to Andrews and not Earl to write the opinion of the court in 1889, the result might have been a decision in equity and not in law: the *Ellerson* constructive-trust doctrine announced some years before it actually was. In that event, *Riggs v. Palmer*, as a run-of-the-mill instance of a court using its equity powers to redress a lawful but unjust outcome, would have faded long ago into obscurity.

Ellerson is significant for another reason. It shows how the options open to the courts in states still lacking a slayer statute were not in fact limited to the stark choice between letting a murderer inherit and usurping the powers of the legislature. The equity powers that the courts of New York and the other states retained allowed them to escape both horns of their apparent dilemma, by making the murderer a constructive trustee for the worthier heirs of the victim. An enacted slayer provision, in the long run, made a more satisfactory solution, but even in its absence the judges were not obliged to connive at rewarding a crime if they balked at amending a statute. That the constructive-trust expedient should have been so little used attests powerfully indeed to what Ames, Pound, and others deplored as the eclipse of much of the equity tradition in America by the beginning of the twentieth century—and what others similarly deplored at the beginning of the twenty-first.[37]

Why the Divided Court of Appeals?

That the decision in *Riggs* was, without being avowed as such, an ad hoc and an ad hominem one—that the majority of the Court of Appeals crafted its general argument as an expedient to deny a specific individual, Elmer Palmer, his inheritance—seems a possible explanation of the result. It is arguably a better explanation than any other, making sense as it does of the outcome, of its general failure to win acceptance elsewhere in cases where the facts were less unusual, and of its retraction in 1896 by the Court of Appeals itself. But we are still left with the question of why the court divided on *Riggs* as it did and why two judges, and the particular two who did, dissented.

One conceivable answer is partisan affiliation. The candidates for a seat on the Court of Appeals were nominated by the opposing political parties and chosen in the regular state elections (vacancies were filled by interim gubernatorial appointments). Yet partisanship was muted by the length of their terms (fourteen years), by the considerable overlap between Democrats and Republicans in this period on many fundamental issues, and by an unwritten but uniformly obeyed rule that a judge who had performed acceptably for a full term would be renominated by both parties (though an open seat usually produced a vigorous contest).[38] Most of the court's decisions, like most of those of American appeals courts in the past and today, were unanimous. Most of the rest did not follow partisan divisions. Some that did so arose, not surprisingly, in cases involving contested elections and legislative apportionments.[39] Others concerned racial discrimination: the Republican judges voting to uphold, and the Democrats (with one partial exception) to overturn, a statute requiring that places of public entertainment impartially admit white and black customers, while in another, a majority composed entirely of Democrats held against the two dissenters, both Republicans, that there was no constitutional ban on the maintenance in New York of racially separate public schools.[40] The Republican judges in this era also tended somewhat more strongly than the Democratic ones to uphold state regulations on business and property. In any event, the disagreement in *Riggs* cut squarely across party lines. The majority consisted of three Democrats (Chief Judge William C. Ruger, Earl, and Judge Rufus W. Peckham Jr.) and two Republicans (Andrews and Judge Francis M. Finch), the minority of one Democrat (Gray) and one Republican (Danforth).[41] Similarly, at the lower level, Elmer's right to inherit had been upheld by a Democratic referee, Sawyer, and by an appellate court made up of one Republican (Landon), who wrote the opinion in the case; one Democrat (William L. Learned); and one apparently apolitical jurist who had successively been appointed to judgeships by governors of both parties (Augustus Bockes).[42]

Some other candidate answers hold up equally poorly to scrutiny. Both dissenters were more than ordinarily insulated from the voters, conceivably a factor in a stance, that of seeming to reward an unworthy heir, that might have proved an unpopular one. Danforth, reaching the age of seventy, took mandatory retirement at the end of 1889, just a few months after the decision. Gray, elected to a full term in the fall of 1888, was not up for reelection until 1902. Yet two members of the majority, Ruger and Andrews, were also due to retire before they would have had to run again (though Andrews did stand, and successfully, as the nominee of both parties, for the position of Chief Judge in 1892 when it fell vacant after Ruger's death). Nor, should some kind of generational explanation for the divide be posited, does it correlate with age, the two dissenters being respectively the youngest and the oldest members of the court at the time.[43]

Brian Leiter has looked to other opinions by Earl and Gray (both Democrats, it will be recalled) for clues to clashing worldviews that could help account for their divergence in the Palmer case.[44] For the disagreement in *Riggs* might still have originated in some other ideological divide cross-cutting the partisan platforms of that era. But the mouthpiece for the court in any case it decided was not necessarily the most outspoken advocate of the position taken, if the practice of assigning opinions in advance of the arguments and decision on the Court of Appeals of which we have accounts from 1901 and 1929 was already being used in 1889, raising some questions about any attempt to attribute the outcome in *Riggs* to differences between Earl and Gray alone.[45] A full answer must be able to account for the stances taken in *Riggs* by all seven of the judges, Certainly, in so overworked a court, whomever had been assigned to write the opinion might indeed have put more of his individual stamp on it than the rest, and whoever took the time to write a dissent must have felt quite strongly about the issues that it raised. But what most calls for explanation in *Riggs* is the decision itself and not the reasoning by which the majority opinion justified it.

In any event, the answers that Leiter based on a mere pair of opinions by Gray and Earl and contemporaneous with *Riggs* are unpersuasive. In one case handed down in the same year (*Haynes v. Sherman*), Leiter suggested, Judge Earl had insisted on the duty of the courts to respect a testator's stated wishes as far as possible, and in another (*Bockes v. Wemple*), Judge Gray had spoken of the need to interpret statutes according to their authors' underlying intentions. As the two decisions appeared to reverse the positions the two judges had taken in *Riggs*, he concluded that their disagreement in that case could not have rested on a profound commitment by either of them to any overarching legal principle. Instead, each must have been arguing in an opportunistic way for the result he personally favored. In *Bockes*, Gray "seems to have wholly forgotten the literalism of his *Riggs* dissent" and to have issued "a resounding endorsement of intentionalism" as a legitimate correction to the plain meaning of a statute.[46]

Earl's opinion in *Haynes* offers little support for this argument. Writing for a unanimous court, he indeed noted that a testator's intentions would always be honored if possible. He added, however—and it was the central point of his opinion—that in the case at hand, those intentions ran contrary to a statutory prohibition and thus were invalid.[47] What the example most tellingly illustrates is Earl's (and his colleagues') usual deference to the authority of the relevant statutes, a deference puzzlingly absent from his and the majority's stance in the Palmer will case.

And what Gray said in *Bockes v. Wemple* does not at all contradict his reasoning in his *Riggs* dissent, as an account of the principal point in question will make clear. The plaintiff was a justice of the New York

Supreme Court who had been retired from the bench on reaching the age limit of seventy. An 1870 law set a justice's annual salary at $6,000, with an additional five dollars per day for expenses when away from home hearing cases. In 1872, the legislature abolished the provision for expenses, substituting, in lieu of it, an additional annual payment of $1,200. An 1880 amendment to the New York Constitution guaranteed that a Supreme Court justice whose service was ended by the age limit would continue to receive the "compensation" he had been receiving on the bench for the remaining years of the term to which he had been elected. Bockes, since his retirement, had been paid only $6,000 per annum, and he sued the state comptroller to claim the additional $1,200, which had been refused as not part of what the word "compensation" had been intended to cover. Gray held that "where language is explicit, we should not allow ourselves to lose sight of its plain meaning, and to wander in the wastes of conjecture." Only when language was unclear was it necessary or appropriate to speculate on the intentions underlying it. For him and for all but the one dissenting judge in the case, the meaning of the key word, "compensation," was plain and unequivocal, covering as it did all that a Justice was paid (in this instance, $7,200) while holding the office. "I think," he concluded, "that the People meant the full force of the words chosen to express their will. Had they intended to limit the receipt of compensation to salary as originally fixed, they could well have said so."[48] Far from conflicting with Gray's dissent in *Riggs*, his opinion in *Bockes* expresses the same view of a judge's obligation to follow the plain language of a statute. As seen in the reaction to *Riggs* of the courts of other states, it was the prevailing view in American jurisprudence at the time. The *Riggs* dissenters, Gray and Danforth, were insisting on what a legal consensus at the time regarded as the correct answer. Earl and his colleagues in the majority appear to have been drawn from that path by some element of the case that overrode their professional judgment.

Leiter also found signs in another opinion contemporary with *Riggs*, a dissent in *People v. Budd* (1889), that Gray espoused a laissez-faire ideology arguably congruent with his vote in the Palmer will suit. Thus, he wrote, "it should hardly be surprising that he objected to the effort of the majority in *Riggs* to undo a testator's liberty to dispose of his property as he had intended. Judge Gray's opportunistic literalism in *Riggs* in all likelihood has more to do with his ideological opposition to state interference with property rights than with a considered view of statutory interpretation."[49] In *Budd*, the owner of a grain elevator in the city of

Buffalo had been convicted of charging rates in excess of the maximum ones set for that business by a state law. The case closely paralleled that of *Munn v. Illinois* (1876), in which a majority of the United States Supreme Court had rejected the claim that a similar state regulation exceeded the constitutional powers of the legislature. Speaking for the Court of Appeals in *Budd*, Judge Andrews largely adopted the reasoning advanced in *Munn*: that governments possessed a police power to address threats to the public welfare, and that the regulation of businesses that possessed, beyond their purely private character, a distinctively public interest as well, lay within the scope of that power.[50]

Gray's dissent in *Budd* argued for a narrower view of the government's regulatory authority.[51] It does indeed express the worldview of what would come, after a famous case of the early twentieth century, to be called Lochnerism, an insistence on private property rights and liberty of contract. But it is not clear that Gray was much more of a Lochnerite than Judge Earl himself, spokesman in 1885 for a unanimous court (which Gray had yet to join) in *In re Jacobs*, a decision that some historians have seen as more of a landmark of laissez-faire jurisprudence than *Lochner v. New York* itself.[52] And Gray was at least somewhat less of a Lochnerite than was one of his *Riggs*-era Court of Appeals colleagues, Rufus W. Peckham Jr. Like Gray, Peckham dissented in *Budd* and in the companion case of *People v. Walsh*, and in his opinion in the latter, appended to the former, he stated grounds similar to Gray's doing so. The regulation of grain elevator rates, he wrote, was "vicious in its nature, communistic in its tendency, and . . . an illegal effort to interfere with the lawful privilege of the individual to obtain such compensation as he can for the use of his own property. . . ."[53] Faced in 1895 with a challenge to a state requirement that master or employing plumbers obtain a certificate of competence from a state board, Gray, writing for the court, upheld the law as a (barely) legitimate exercise of the police power to protect the public health.[54] In a sharply worded dissent, Peckham called the majority's reasoning "very absurd."[55] And in 1904, Gray concurred, though narrowly and grudgingly, in upholding the same state law limiting the hours of work in bakeries that Peckham (translated in the interim to Washington) struck down in the following year for a closely divided US Supreme Court in *Lochner v. New York*, as a violation of a constitutionally guaranteed liberty of contract.[56] So if we are to understand that Gray reacted to the Palmer will case as he did because of his views of political economy, we should expect to find that Peckham reacted in the same way. But the expectation is not borne out, for Peckham sided with Earl and the majority in *Riggs* and not with the dissenters. For his part, Judge Danforth, who concurred in Gray's *Riggs* dissent, voted with the majority to sustain the elevator-rate limits in *Budd* and *Walsh*. His doing so would be inexplicable if *Riggs* were really a disguised debate over the proper role of government in the marketplace.

Leiter also inferred from another opinion written around the same time in a divorce case that Judge Earl had a pronounced streak of moral rigorism that drove his refusal to allow Elmer Palmer to inherit from his victim. But this speculation as applied to the decision (and not merely the reasons stated for it) in *Riggs* is again problematic, focusing as it does on the characteristics of a single judge, as conjectured from a single opinion of his, to account for a result agreed upon by four of his colleagues as well. Leiter did not attempt to demonstrate, as the argument requires, that Earl's outlook differed significantly even from Gray's in this regard or that it was congruent with that of the judges who joined him.[57] Finally, he proposed, building on Kim Lane Scheppele's work, that *Riggs* was Earl's way of getting around the result in *Avery v. Everett*, in which the court—with Earl alone in dissent—had held that persons sentenced to life in prison following a conviction for second-degree murder were not subjected to the distribution of their property through consignment to the state of "civil death."[58] But he did not try to explain why the four judges who joined Earl in the majority in *Riggs* would have wanted to help him circumvent a decision that all of them, plus Danforth (Gray did not sit in *Avery*), had agreed with, and which one of them (Andrews) had stated in the opinion of the court. It seems most implausible that they did.

The literary and legal scholar Stanley Fish attempted in 1978 to account for the division in the Court of Appeals in terms of his theory of interpretation.[59] What gives some generality and stability to the reading of a text—here, New York's statute of wills—Fish maintained, is not some control exerted by the words of the text itself, but rather the assumptions shared by a community of its readers. Earl and Gray, he proposed (like Leiter, he did not mention the other five judges) differed in their response to the case because they belonged to different interpretive communities, the former supposing the maxim "no one should profit from his own wrong" to be part of the implied content of the statute, and the latter not. But as an explanation of the divide, it is empty and circular because Fish offered no evidence that they did subscribe to such conflicting assumptions independent of what the opinions in this one case say.

In one sense, the fact that Gray and Danforth dissented does not require explanation. As we have seen, they were merely upholding the settled and accepted doctrines of American law at the time. All the same, a question does arise: why, if the reason suggested here for the anomalous holding in *Riggs* is correct, did the two of them not also find that reason a compelling one? What made them less susceptible than their colleagues to the distorting pressures of the facts in the Palmer case? It may be significant that Gray's law practice before he joined the Court of Appeals had included service as "referee in a number of large will cases," a background that could have particularly disinclined him to violate the accepted assumptions and procedures regarding inheritance or to tamper with the unhindered freedom, not so much of individuals in general, but specifically of testators by setting a dangerous precedent for judges to approve or disapprove of the bequests they had made.[60] It was a professional specialization that none of his Court of Appeals colleagues appears to have shared.

For his part, Danforth had been particularly outspoken on an issue central to the divide in *Riggs*. An earlier opinion of his, in *Bonnell v. Griswold* (1880), formed the basis for a second, lower-court holding cited both in the brief for the respondent and in Gray's dissent.[61] In it, Danforth had emphatically condemned attempts by judges to add to the punishment for an offense by inferring provisions not plainly spelled out in a law: "I cannot imply a term into a statute for the purpose of extending or imposing a penalty. If the Legislature has not used words sufficiently explicit to include all the cases which fall within the mischief intended to be prevented, the court is not competent to enlarge them."[62] A judge who had expressed himself so strongly on that point in an earlier case might well have found the majority's decision in *Riggs* impossible to accept. (Judge Earl dissented in *Bonnell* but did not submit his views in an opinion.)

The clearest pattern aligning with the vote in *Riggs* lies in the backgrounds of the judges. Gray was the only member of the court in 1889 from New York City, and he belonged by birth and upbringing to wealthy metropolitan society. His fellow dissenter, Danforth (born, moreover, in Boston, and the only judge not native to the Empire State), was from Rochester, the largest of the upstate cities then represented on the court. Four of the five justices in the majority came from smaller cities (two from Syracuse, one from Albany, and one from Ithaca).[63] The pattern is not perfect, for Albany, where Peckham was from, had been larger than

Rochester until the 1870s, but it is nearly so. Moreover, all of the judges in the majority except Peckham had been born and spent their early years not in cities, even small ones, but in small towns or on farms.[64] Robert Earl, the least urban of the five in his background, had been a lifelong resident of the Mohawk Valley town and village of Herkimer, save for his college years and his time on the bench in Albany.[65]

What the pattern means is less clear. It is at least consistent with one possibility, though a rather speculative one. If there is any basis to the stereotypes of large-city urbanity and impersonality and of rural moralism and particularism, then the split court in *Riggs* becomes more understandable. The backgrounds of the majority and dissenting judges approximately mirror within New York State the socio-geographical divide that Karsten correlated nationally with the split between the jurisprudences of *heart* and *head*. In his examples of the former, he emphasized judicial sympathy with the parties. But judicial antipathy, of the sort that Elmer's story might well have inspired, is no less a matter of what Karsten called heart as opposed to head. The lenient treatment that Elmer received from a rural judge and jury at his murder trial is consistent with the pattern. By the impersonal law of *head*, his crime clearly fitted the definition of first-degree murder, but the jury, swayed by his youth, character, and circumstances, went so far as to try to downgrade it, ignoring the plain letter of the law, to manslaughter, apparently repelled by the prospect of his undergoing the punishments attached to a murder conviction. Judge Potter, from a similar background, chose not to impose the usual punishment for murder in the second degree. At the same time, had a strictly impersonal interpretation and application of the law prevailed, it would have guaranteed Elmer, or his heirs, his legacy under Francis's will, while rural *heart* would have revolted at so unjust an outcome and devised, as the majority in *Riggs* did, a novel legal argument to forestall it.

And while Peckham came from the most urban background of any of the judges in the majority, it is perhaps not irrelevant that he impressed a close observer as a man of unusually forceful dislikes and as intolerant of beliefs and behaviors of which he disapproved. Justice Holmes, who sat with Peckham for some years on the United States Supreme Court, wrote of his onetime colleague: "I used to say that his major premise was God damn it, meaning thereby that emotional predilections somewhat governed him on social themes."[66] A student of Peckham's career on the United States Supreme Court has commented on the "inflexibility, passionate prejudices, and decidedly subjective approach to the law" evident in his opinions when his deepest feelings were engaged, something apparent in the vehement, self-assured, and even bullying tone of much of his judicial prose. The same scholar has also seen signs in his opinions in criminal cases of a "prosecutor's mentality," little concerned about procedural irregularities that might have infringed on the protections guaranteed to defendants by the constitution or the statutes.[67] It is difficult to imagine him dealing patiently and dispassionately with Elmer Palmer's claim on his grandfather's estate, no matter what the accepted legal principles of the day might have said about it. But this too is speculative, as an explanation will tend to become the more it emphasizes the characteristics of a single individual rather than the response of a group.

Chapter 5

A Case Transformed

Beginning in 1921, *Riggs* underwent a remarkable metamorphosis. It migrated from the junkyard to the museum; from a widely disparaged decision, it became a leading case taken by many as a paradigm of how judges reason and ought to reason. Though it has been cited a respectable number of times in judicial opinions in support of one point or another, it has found its principal niche not in law in practice, but rather in higher-order discussions *about* law: what it is and how it operates. Within this ongoing conversation, it happened to acquire some notably respected and influential defenders whose writings pulled it from obscurity and made it a familiar case throughout the American legal community. But they did not popularize it gratuitously or by mere chance. The case possessed some qualities that made it an exceptionally useful resource for certain jurisprudential projects of the time. Its advocates alone could not have rehabilitated *Riggs* if the law as a whole had not been moving in a direction that eventually made the decision seem as self-evidently correct in legal terms as it had once seemed plainly wrong.

Cardozo

The earliest commentator of the first rank to have an unequivocally good word to say about *Riggs* carried such weight that he is probably more responsible than anyone else for the prestige and currency that the decision acquired in the twentieth century. Benjamin Nathan Cardozo (1870–1938) joined the New York Court of Appeals by gubernatorial designation in 1914, winning appointment to a regular seat on the court in 1917, election to that seat in November, and election to the chief judgeship in 1926, and departing only in 1932 when he, though a Democrat, was appointed by a Republican President, Herbert Hoover, to succeed the retired Oliver Wendell Holmes on the United States Supreme Court. In his first few years on the Court of Appeals, Cardozo established a reputation as a judge of outstanding intelligence, judicial craftsmanship, and literary style. These qualities won him an invitation from the Yale Law School to deliver, in 1921, the annual Storrs Lectures, which were published in the same year to wide acclaim under the title *The Nature of the Judicial Process*.[1]

In these lectures, Cardozo sought to correct the popular picture of judges as invariably and mechanically applying preexisting law to the cases that came before them. On the contrary, he maintained, judges deciding cases always had choices to make. Even when clear precedents existed, they chose whether to follow them or not. Inevitably, they created law, if only, in the vast majority of cases, where a clearly correct legal answer was apparent, by recreating it. Scholars who would become known as *Legal Realists* were beginning to make similar arguments against what they decried as formalism. Cardozo's statement of a moderate realism gave it considerable currency and respectability. But more emphatically than these critics would do, Cardozo denied that judging need be arbitrary or idiosyncratic. Even in cases left wide open by previous decisions, he maintained, ways existed to identify, if not right and wrong answers, at least clearly better and worse ones. He devoted most of *The Nature* to expounding the methods that judges could employ to reach the best answers to seemingly indeterminate questions. In the first of his lectures, devoted to "The Method of Philosophy," he drew on, among other cases, *Riggs v. Palmer* to illustrate and bolster his argument.[2]

Discussing *Riggs* in a single long paragraph spread over four pages of the published book, Cardozo presented it as a striking instance of a lawsuit that seemed at first glance as if it could have been decided either way with equal validity. Yet, Cardozo maintained, one of the possible answers was indeed better than the other. For him, the case exemplified the importance of two steps in resolving such a case, both of them illustrating the uses of philosophical methods for law. The first step consisted of discerning and articulating the fundamental principles that were in conflict. The second step lay in weighing those principles to determine which were the greater ones and which were the lesser. As he described the situation in *Riggs*: "There was the principle of the binding force of a will disposing of the estate of a testator in conformity with law. That principle, pushed to the limit of its logic, seemed to uphold the title of the murderer," and it was joined, moreover, by a second accepted principle pointing in the same direction, "that civil courts may not add to the pains and penalties of crime." "But over against these there was another principle of greater generality," he continued, "its roots deeply fastened in universal sentiments of justice, the principle that no man should profit from his own iniquity or take advantage of his own wrong. The logic of this principle prevailed over the logic of the others." Why had it prevailed? Because, Cardozo answered, "of the conviction in the judicial mind that the one selected led to justice . . . in the end, the principle that was thought to be most fundamental, to represent the larger and deeper issues, put its competitors to flight," and he thought, rightly so.[3]

Cardozo's account of *Riggs* has serious flaws, but ones so deftly concealed that they take some effort to tease out and state. He carefully papered over the fact that the original decision in *Riggs*, which he nowhere distinguished from its substantial retraction by the Court of Appeals in *Ellerson*, was an assertion of the judges' power to amend a statute, and not, as he implied, the enunciation of a doctrine in the common law. As he observed later in *The Nature*, and quite correctly so far as the practice of most courts went: "The fissures in the common law are wider than the fissures in a statute, at least in the form of statute common in England and the United States," and judges likewise enjoyed "greater freedom of choice in the construction of constitutions than of ordinary statutes," the former being worded in much more general terms and thus requiring more judicial interpretation to decide upon the scope of their application.[4] By setting his discussion of *Riggs* in the context of his first lecture, he allowed readers who did not know better to believe, incorrectly, that it was a common-law decision and not one involving statutory interpretation at all. For early in the same lecture, he had asked where a judge finds the sources for a decision and replied: "There are times when the source is obvious. The rule that fits the case may be supplied by the constitution or by statute. If that is so, the judge looks no further," though even with statutes, he continued, gaps, ambiguities, and apparent injustices could require judicial interpretation.[5] But from that point on, he avowedly confined himself to discussing how judges reasoned in the common law, and all of the cases except *Riggs* that he discussed in detail in the lecture lay in the distinctively common-law fields of torts and contracts. By saying nothing to the contrary, he gave the impression that *Riggs* belonged to those fields as well, and that the judicial law-making that it involved was of the same relatively uncontroversial type.

Moreover, by conflating the two Court of Appeals decisions, and treating *Ellerson* as if it had been a mere application or restatement of *Riggs*, Cardozo hid from view the degree to which the later decision had repudiated the earlier one. He spoke as if the device the court in *Ellerson* had used to extricate itself, that of a constructive trust, had in fact been a part of *Riggs* and as if the two decisions had rested on the same doctrinal foundations. Making effective use of the passive voice, he wrote: "Consistency was preserved, logic received its tribute, by holding that the legal title passed, but that it was subjected to a constructive trust."[6] He thereby escaped having to say precisely *who* had so held (the court in *Ellerson*) and who had *not* (the court in *Riggs*, which had explicitly denied that the legal title passed to Elmer), or to acknowledge that *Riggs* had in any way lacked the "consistency" that the constructive-trust elaboration in 1896 had "preserved" or the "logic" that it had honored. The result was to save from blemish the image both of the Court of Appeals, of which Cardozo was a loyal and devoted member, and of its 1889 decision as well.

Passing over in silence the existence of a dissenting opinion in the Court of Appeals, he likewise ignored the refusal of most of the other state courts to assent to *Riggs*. On his account of the matter, it could only have resulted from their inferiority in weighing philosophical principles. He did not make that corollary explicit, and it would have been an awkward one to have to defend. He thereby dodged, instead of acknowledging and addressing, the additional legal principles that came into play beyond the ones he presented and the reasons other courts had given for deciding cases similar to *Riggs* differently: above all, their doubts about the authority of the courts to amend a clearly expressed legislative statute. He reduced the apparent question involved to something it was not, a simple clash between moral maxims in which the deeper and more compelling of them prevailed.

Nor, finally, did his interpretation of the decision fully answer to the use he was trying to make of it. He began by offering *Riggs* as an example of how the "method of philosophy" could be used to resolve seemingly indeterminate cases. By identifying the plaintiffs' arguments as supported by the deeper and more compelling moral principle, the judges had correctly denied Elmer his inheritance. But Cardozo wound up his discussion of the case by suddenly grounding the decision in a different rationale. "The murderer lost the legacy for which the murder was committed because the social interest served by refusing to permit the criminal to profit by his crime is greater than that served by the preservation and enforcement of legal rights of ownership." Justice and "social interest," as critics of utilitarian philosophy are fond of pointing out, may not be the same thing. "My illustration, indeed," Cardozo acknowledged at this point, "has brought me ahead of my story," for this added rationale for the decision belonged, not to his "method of philosophy," but rather with that of sociology, the subject of the third of his lectures.[7] Cases that did not involve the use of both methods would have exemplified each of them much better than one that did.

Why, then, did he choose a case so problematic in so many ways to discuss at all? Though the actual history of *Riggs* would have complicated his task a great deal, the issues that his amputated account of it presented made it an excellent choice to illustrate the point he wanted to make and defend: the legitimacy and indeed necessity of the exercise of choice by judges. For it sugarcoated a message that at least some readers, both lay and legal, would have found unpalatable if it had been argued aggressively in the abstract or by using an example with a less pat and pleasing outcome. Most readers would have sympathized so strongly with the end result that the Court of Appeals reached in 1889 that they would have been little inclined to quibble with the way it was achieved.

Riggs had another attraction for Cardozo as well. *Ellerson*—the case he was really describing in his discussion of *Riggs*—had made an expansive use of the Court of Appeals' equity powers in proposing a constructive trust as a response to a murdering heir. Cardozo was his judicial generation's most eloquent advocate of equity's methods and remedies in general, and of the constructive trust in particular, as means of rendering substantial justice.[8] In an opinion two years before his Storrs Lectures, he had written: "A constructive trust is the formula through which the conscience of equity finds expression. When property has been acquired in such circumstances that the holder of the legal title may not in good conscience retain the beneficial interest, equity converts him into a trustee," adding citations to several cases to bear out his point. "A court of equity," he added, "in decreeing a constructive trust is bound by no unyielding formula."[9] He did much to extend the use of the device in American law to situations where nothing like a trust or a fiduciary relation had previously existed between the parties. In doing so, he continued the work of Judge Andrews, the author both of the *Ellerson* opinion and, to similar effect, of *Newton v. Porter*. (Cardozo, according to his biographer, regarded Andrews as the greatest judge ever to sit on the New York Court of Appeals.[10])

Cardozo's treatment of *Riggs* bears some of the marks of his characteristic procedure in deciding cases as a judge. It also exhibits the damage that such methods can do to historical understanding. Other judges and lawyers admired his opinions for the thoroughness with which they reviewed the existing precedents and seemed to bring them all into harmony with the decision he announced, making it appear to be their logical and necessary outcome.[11] Less often, but often enough to be noteworthy, his reasoning provoked and has continued to provoke unease among some readers who have sensed an element of illusion in the way he wove all of the elements into a seemingly seamless fabric of argument. Critics have taxed him with disingenuousness, even deviousness, in his handling of both facts and precedent, noting a frequent selectivity and even misstatement of the former and cavalier interpretation of the latter, both undertaken with the goal of making the outcome at which he aimed and the rule he sought to establish appear more inevitable and unquestionable than they really were.[12] The goal may have been a professional virtue. A judge must reach a decision, and one that will persuade, while advertising its novelty and unsettling the law as little as possible. In rewriting *Riggs* in *Ellerson* while pretending not to, Andrews had done the same. Bad legal history may be good jurisprudence—and vice versa. Cardozo's discussion of *Riggs* is impressive to one who knows of the case and its background only the facts that he provides. It is inadequate and evasive to one who knows more. The decision he described was a very pretty one, but he should not have called it *Riggs*.

The weaknesses in Cardozo's argument were so well concealed, and his praise of the decision so eloquent and so apparently sensible, that *Riggs*'s fame spread as *The Nature*, an instant classic in the American legal literature, gained additional reflected luster from the rest of its author's distinguished career. (He had only been on the Court of Appeals for seven years in 1921 and had yet to write many of the opinions for which he is best known.) To be introduced to the case through his account of it, as most readers probably were, made it more difficult to see it in any other way. It is probably not by chance that in the dozen or so years following 1921, the balance in state court opinions concerning murdering heirs shifted somewhat. *Riggs*, though remaining the doctrine of a minority of states, was accepted as authoritative by seven more that had not previously passed judgment on the matter: Massachusetts (1923), Washington

(1926), Wisconsin (1927), Michigan (1930), South Carolina (1930), South Dakota (1932), and Maryland (1933).[13] During the same years, only one state, Nevada, followed the earlier consensus in rejecting *Riggs* in 1927.[14]

And if Cardozo indeed had something to do with this trend, the fact that although actually arguing for the constructive-trust approach taken in *Ellerson*, he endorsed *Riggs* by name may have some significance. Only two new courts adopted the constructive-trust approach of the later New York case: those of North Carolina, in 1927, and New Jersey, one of the few states that still had a separate court of equity, in 1933.[15] (Both of these states, as well as all of those adopting *Riggs* during the 1920s and 1930s, later enacted slayer statutes rather than leave the matter to judge-made case law.) In New York itself, conflating *Riggs* and *Ellerson* as if they were equivalent, as Cardozo did, only perpetuated the confusion over whether the former was good law or not. It bore particularly sour fruit in a New York decision in 1939 that utterly confounded the issue between them: whether the formal legal title passed to the murdering heir or not.[16] The basic inconsistency on this point of the two leading cases has continued to plague the state's judge-made slayer rule. It suggests, by contrast, the virtues of the slayer-statute alternative, one that New York has yet to adopt, and of the explicit equity solution of a constructive trust not employed in *Riggs* as an expedient in the interim.

Hart and Sacks

The Harvard Law School professors Henry M. Hart Jr. (1904–1969) and Albert M. Sacks (1920–1991), each of whom would serve as dean of the school, undoubtedly knew *The Nature of the Judicial Process* well. It was probably Cardozo's book that called *Riggs* to their attention as a useful vehicle for introducing students to the challenges of legal reasoning. Hart and Sacks in 1946 put together a mimeographed volume of readings, commentary, and questions to serve as a textbook for a course they offered under the title "The Legal Process: Basic Problems in the Making and Application of Law." They continued to revise the text through 1958, guiding students at the nation's most prestigious law schools ("The Legal Process" was widely adopted elsewhere) toward a point of view that has been dubbed the *Legal Process* approach.[17] The harsh realities of legal compulsion, Hart and Sacks maintained, had to be legitimized by grounding them in general and generally accepted principles that formed an internally consistent whole. Asking how this harmony of doctrine could best be achieved, they proposed a larger role than earlier American legal scholars had found acceptable for judicial initiative and creativity in making the law more coherent, whenever judges were the ones best positioned to act—which, to their mind, would not be infrequently. Judges had, after all, a better understanding of the law as a system than a large and heterogeneous body of legislators could possess. They could also act far more swiftly and decisively. When the opportunity arose for them to improve the law's integrity, rationality, and unity by their rulings, even if they seemed to be disregarding the language of a statute, it was not only their right but their duty to do so.

Seeing matters in this way, Hart and Sacks naturally viewed *Riggs* more favorably than the decision's contemporaries had done, and indeed in their hands the case became "one of the classic heuristic tools of process jurisprudence."[18] They centered one of the two introductory chapters of *The Legal Process* on the questions raised by the phenomenon of the murdering heir.[19] They made Judge Earl's opinion central to their discussion, as addressing what they called "the differences between enacted and decisional law": law, that is, made by legislatures versus law made by judges. That they fundamentally preferred the latter to the former much more strongly than they anywhere said outright is the clear impression left by their book, and by their chapter on the murdering heir in particular. What earlier writers had thought to be a question of how power was to be allocated and restrained, they saw instead as one of how tasks were to be most efficiently divided up. Confident that judges would do some things that needed doing better than the other branches of government would do them, they found in *Riggs* a model for students to ponder and absorb.

The way they went about it, though different from Cardozo's, similarly subordinated historical accuracy to programmatic justification. Throughout *The Legal Process*, they proceeded in the manner customary to American law-school teaching, that of posing questions for discussion rather than decreeing conclusions. But they took full advantage of the scope that the method allows for enforcing a professor's own views while pretending not to. One can carefully select the background materials provided for discussion. One can ask certain questions that will move the discussion in the preferred direction and refrain from asking others, equally cogent, that might deflect it. And one can phrase the questions tendentiously enough to make it clear what answer the professor (and future grader of one's performance) wants to hear.[20]

In their chapter on murdering heirs, Hart and Sacks contrasted the approach adopted in *Riggs* (printing Earl's majority opinion, but not Gray's dissent) with the history of the problem in Ohio. They documented the consistent refusal of the Ohio courts to allow a person convicted of homicide of any degree to collect a life insurance claim on the victim, as well as the state's courts' rejection of *Riggs* in 1892 in *Deem v. Millikin* (which they also printed). They also provided the text of the Ohio slayer statute, which went into effect on the first day of 1932 and denied inheritance to any person "finally adjudged guilty, either as principal or accessory, of murder in the first or second degree," of any part of "the real or personal estate of the person killed," whether under the will of the victim or the laws of descent and distribution.[21] It followed that a conviction of manslaughter would, just as before, fail to prevent inheritance by the person convicted. They made it clear, not by saying so but by the questions they posed for "discussion," that the courts ought to apply the ban to manslaughter as well, in defiance of the law's wording and on their own authority.

They dramatized what Ohio law would mean in practice through an invented and rather contrived history unrolling in the years just before the passage of the state's slayer statute.[22] "Ronnie Reckless" had led a dissolute life, abandoned (without divorcing) his wife, and killed his well-to-do father, Richard Reckless, when the latter reproached him for his conduct and announced his plans to leave his money to a fund for research into juvenile delinquency. At the ensuing trial for first-degree murder, "[h]is counsel played upon the sympathy of the jury by dwelling upon the death of Ronnie's mother in childbirth and his lonely and unhappy childhood. The jury, instead of bringing in a verdict of murder in the first or second degree, as the evidence would have warranted, brought in a verdict of guilty only of manslaughter in the first degree."[23] (The parallel with the initial verdict in Elmer Palmer's trial was presumably mere coincidence. There is no indication that Hart and Sacks knew more of his case than was spelled out in the appellate opinions.) The probate court granted Ronnie his father's estate directly and the proceeds of an insurance policy on his father's life, naming him as beneficiary, indirectly: under Ohio law, it was denied him as an insurance payment, but as his father's estate was named as the next beneficiary in line, it came to him by that route.

Hart and Sacks weighted the details of the story, to an almost comical degree, to nudge students toward the conclusion that they were supposed to arrive at. The specific culprit under discussion was an individual who, rather than being correctly convicted of murder, or of manslaughter, had in reality committed murder and had unworthily escaped conviction for it. There was no good reason for that twist in the tale other than to incline a reader towards an outcome, however dubious legally, that would see Ronnie punished properly after all. Hart and Sacks also had Richard, before his death, handwrite and sign an addition to his will providing a substantial legacy to his mother, the elderly Ruth Reckless, which the probate court nullified on a technicality, giving Ronnie the money.[24] Irrelevant to the legal question of the rights of a murdering heir, this passage likewise functioned only to stack the emotional deck further against Ohio law as it stood.

The contrast Hart and Sacks drew between the law in Ohio and in (supposedly still) *Riggs*-governed New York was unequivocally in the latter's favor, and much assisted by some judicious editing of their materials. They quoted Cardozo on the 1889 decision with evident approval.[25] They ignored his actual reliance on *Ellerson*, however; ignored the later case's withdrawal from much of the ground taken earlier; and carefully excluded Cardozo's references to the equity remedy of a constructive trust as the proper response to the case. They cited James Barr Ames in support of the maxim that wrongdoers should not benefit from their misdeeds, but they concealed from the reader Ames's emphatic rejection of *Riggs* in the same article.[26] They quoted Roscoe Pound's criticisms of *Riggs*, only to undercut his position with a set of leading questions hostile to his argument.[27]

Characterizing the two options open to a court and to the textbook's reader to choose between in such a case—that is, barring inheritance for manslaughter as well as for murder by judicial fiat, or leaving the matter to be resolved by statute—they labeled the one the New York majority had chosen "a much more tough-minded approach."[28] The phrasing was hardly calculated to make the typical law student of the 1950s speak up in favor of the alternative. And anyone preferring the law of Ohio, they implied, was not merely a sissy, but was irrationally inconsistent, or at least deplorably tolerant of inconsistency in the law. The Ohio slayer statute, by clear implication, permitted inheritance when the crime was manslaughter. That the statute's authors might have had good reasons for making the distinction they had made, Hart and Sacks would not allow. It made no sense to them that murder and manslaughter—or intentional versus unintentional killing—should be treated differently in this connection. That the statute as worded did treat them differently marred the rationality and integrity of the law. Disagreeing with it as they did, they presumed it could only have reflected sloppy thinking and drafting by the legislature, which had left a loophole for miscreants like Ronnie Reckless to wriggle through by speaking of murder when it should have said unlawful homicide.[29] The mistake should be corrected, but not by the legislature itself, which had bungled the job once already and which was a cumbersome and time-consuming machine to try to put in motion.[30]

Judge Earl in *Riggs* had furnished two main rationales for the Court of Appeals' decision: that it implemented the actual, though unexpressed, intention of the legislators, and that it best cohered with the long-established principles of the law. Hart and Sacks made clear their indifference to the first argument and their approval of the second. The Ohio courts, when a case arose under the slayer statute, were, apparently, to decree on their own authority that the word *murder* in the statute also meant manslaughter. Again, Hart and Sacks said so, but again not in the declarative mood, but, at least nominally, in the interrogative. "Does not a legal system require some means for rationalizing the fabric of its law as a whole? Is a legislature a better institution for doing this job than a court?"[31] By now, the students had presumably gotten the message and understood that the expected answer to the last question was "no." But just to be on the safe side, Hart and Sacks drew their attention to some of the reasons one might have for giving that answer. For good measure, they threw in another set of heavily loaded questions, solemnly asking readers to decide for themselves whether the "wooden technique" of statutory legislation was better or worse than "the flexible method of growth" in the law through judicial decisions.[32] And in one of the most peculiar passages in *The Legal Process*, they disparaged the notion that legislative problems should be handed to the legislature to resolve as "the flagellant theory of statutory interpretation . . . that it is the court's duty to discipline the legislature by taking it literally whenever it forgets to deal with special cases or otherwise fails to speak clearly. The notion is that if the legislature is firmly and unvaryingly punished in this way for permitting uncertainty to creep into its enactments, pretty soon it will start writing laws which are clear and certain, and the courts and the people will then be spared the pain of having to think for themselves about what the laws mean."[33]

As well as pondering the questions that they did ask, one might note the questions that Hart and Sacks did not. They did not ask students to reflect on how the fact that most American courts, Ohio's included, had sided with the *Riggs* dissenters squared with the theory that the courts will produce the right and rational answer that a legislature will not. Nor did they invite students to consider, among other slayer statutes excluding manslaughter from their terms, that of Pennsylvania, which, though passed by the legislature, had been drafted for it by an expert legal commission that was responsible for whatever faults it displayed. *The Legal Process* said nothing about the possible disadvantages of establishing the law piecemeal as the questions to be answered came up one by one before the judges in particular cases, as compared with a statute setting out its main provisions at once. Nor did it say anything about what was to happen and whose judgment was to prevail if the legislature genuinely disagreed with the judges about where the boundaries in cases of this kind should be set, or if the judges disagreed with each other.

Elsewhere in *The Legal Process*, Hart and Sacks signaled, though again chiefly by innuendo, their disdain for many of the concerns that had led state courts in the late nineteenth and early twentieth centuries to reject the *Riggs* doctrine. They offered a skeptical treatment of the rule of lenity, or, as they put it, "the traditional canon in favor of the strict construction of penal statutes." Asking their students to consider "what are the foundations in reason and policy of this canon, and what part should it play in an enlightened and properly functioning legal system," they implied that the correct answer was: not much. Such, at any rate, was the message conveyed by the specific questions for discussion they offered, all of them loaded against the rule.[34] Similarly, they presented some annotated materials on what they called "The Problem of Common Law Crimes," or actions declared to be criminal by judicial rather than legislative action, one of the bêtes noires of eighteenth- and nineteenth-century American legal thought and public opinion, but whose rarity and unpopularity they passed over lightly and that seemed to their mind not to represent real problems at all.[35] They deftly juxtaposed such crimes to the traditional maxim *nullum crimen sine lege*, or "no crime without a law," rather than to its close corollary *nulla poena sine lege*, "no punishment without a law." The former was less likely than the latter to raise an awkward question in students' minds and start them thinking critically. Most people would be more comfortable with the idea of judges declaring a certain course of action to be, or not to be, criminal than they would with the idea, however necessarily related, of a judge decreeing what punishment should be inflicted for it. Employing two of their favorite pedagogical devices, the loaded question and the slanted antithesis, Hart and Sacks ended their discussion by asking students to consider: "Which constitutes the greater danger to liberty—gradual accretions by judicial recognition to the list of customary crimes, or the unthinking proliferation by modern legislatures of novel regulatory crimes?"[36] The broader concern that lawmaking by legislatures had a legitimacy in many people's minds that its amendment by judges lacked seems to have struck them as puerile. Their response to it was a contemptuous silence.

Comparing their discussion to Cardozo's helps measure the changes that had occurred in mainstream American legal thought in the few decades between his time and theirs. Cardozo had extolled a decision he called *Riggs* that was actually *Ellerson* and that had shorn *Riggs* of its most controversial and problematic pronouncements. Hart and Sacks revived *Riggs* in its full original breadth, ignoring its repudiation by the Court of Appeals in the later case. The earlier decision was more in line with their program for judicial action, as an attractive example of the kind of legal action they liked and wanted to teach others to like as well.

Dworkin

The third of the twentieth-century commentators to whom *Riggs* owes much of its fame was Ronald Dworkin (1931–2013), the most prominent American legal theorist of his time. He first drew on the case in a series of publications beginning with "The Model of Rules," an article published in 1967 and worked into a book, *Taking Rights Seriously*, that appeared a decade later.[37] In these early writings, Dworkin used *Riggs* to challenge a view he thought exemplified in the work of the Oxford professor of jurisprudence H. L. A. Hart, whose book *The Concept of Law* (1961) characterized law as consisting essentially of two kinds of rules.[38] Primary rules forbid or prescribe certain kinds of actions and state the consequences of their infraction. Secondary rules dictate how primary rules are altered or how the very existence of a valid and binding rule is recognized. Hart's rules, of either sort, had what Dworkin saw as an "all-or-nothing" character.[39] When questions arose, one needed only to apply the rules, which normally indicated a clear answer. But cases would arise—"hard cases," in the modern sense of the term—to which the set of existing rules did not provide such an answer. In such cases, which Hart called open ones, law was lacking, and the courts had the freedom to decide them as they considered appropriate, though thereby creating a precedent that might itself become a rule for future cases.

Rather than challenging either the notion of law as the application of clear rules or the existence of open areas created by their absence,

Dworkin disputed both simultaneously. Law, he argued, involved more than the first notion allowed, and the additional resources it possessed for deciding cases made situations to which it could give no right answer highly unlikely to arise. For its resources included, in addition to rules, principles, or maxims stating "a requirement of justice of fairness or some other dimension of morality." Legal principles lacked the inexorable, either/or character of rules. "Even those which look most like rules do not set out legal consequences that follow automatically when the conditions provided are met."[40] Principles also lacked the clearly recognizable credentials that rules possessed, their enunciation in a specific constitutional clause or statute or leading case. They had authority nonetheless, deriving it from what Dworkin called "a sense of appropriateness developed in the profession and the public over time."[41] It was an authority that, for a judge conscious of the need to make the law a coherent (though always evolving) system, could on occasion override both clear rules and other, competing, but less compelling and authoritative principles. If law were understood in Hart's terms as a system merely of rules, it was indeed more than likely that the rules at hand at any one time might not clearly cover a case that arose. Understood as a system of both rules and principles, Dworkin maintained, it almost always furnished a right answer.

In *Taking Rights Seriously*, he posited the existence of a judge he called *Hercules*, one whose intellect could comprehend the law in its entirety as a consistent whole. Hercules—the apotheosis, it could be said, of the Legal Process thinker—would develop the panoramic vision of the law that made the best sense of it and grasp what it required in a particular case. (To do so, Dworkin observed, he would have to recognize some past decisions, and even some statutes, as mistaken because conflicting with the law's coherence and integrity.[42]) Thus right answers existed, though in ordinary practice there might often be doubt as to what they were, and the legitimacy and the moral claims of the law, particularly its obligation to treat similar cases similarly, were vindicated.

One of the cases on which Dworkin relied most heavily to support his case against Hart was *Riggs v. Palmer*. There was no doubt about the answer that the rules seemed to dictate. If they alone determined the outcome, then the dissenters were correct. What separated the two opinions was the majority's willingness to employ the full resources of the law and consider some of its principles, embodied in broad legal maxims, as also relevant. The maxim they had most relied upon, and had found to outweigh the rules, held that no one should be permitted to profit by his own wrong. Though a part of the law, Dworkin observed, this maxim did not operate as a rule. In many situations, persons were indeed allowed to hold onto the profits of their wrongful actions. The doctrine of adverse possession, for example, turned trespassing that had gone on long enough without being objected to into a legally recognized right of access.[43] The maxim against profiting from one's wrongs was, rather, what Dworkin called a principle. There were principles on the minority's side as well; he mentioned those of legislative supremacy and adherence to precedent. Like Cardozo's, his argument allowed for the possible existence of conflicting principles. Like Cardozo, he thought that such conflicts did not mean that no better and worse answers existed, for in a given case, the principles would be of unequal weight and applicability. He differed from Cardozo in regarding principles not as external tools to which judges could legitimately resort for guidance in difficult cases, but as themselves parts of the law. That the decision in *Riggs* had been made as it was, Dworkin argued, showed that courts did, in fact, accept the *legal* authority of principles as well as rules, and of some principles as carrying more weight in a particular case than others, supporting his account of law over Hart's.

In a later book, *Law's Empire* (1986), Dworkin again leaned heavily on *Riggs*, which this time he referred to as "Elmer's Case."[44] He put it to use in a new way complementing his earlier analysis, employing the majority and minority opinions this time to underpin an analysis of the character of disagreement between judges. Such disagreement, Dworkin proposed, can be understood in one of two ways. It may represent a genuine debate over what the law really is, and he emphasized that that was how both Earl and Gray seemed to understand what they were doing.[45] Or the show of legal disagreement may merely be covering up essentially political contests over what the law should be made to be: that is, "when lawyers and judges seem to be disagreeing about the law they are really keeping their fingers crossed."[46] They make arguments about what it requires but do not really believe them. Dworkin rejected this second view. He insisted that the opinions in *Riggs* and in judicial disagreements more generally should be taken "at face value" and indeed that "we have no justification for taking them in any other way." If judges who disagree were merely engaged in a power struggle and were not sincerely disagreeing about the right legal answer, it would be futile for them to have maintained for so long what would have been merely a public "pretense" and "charade" of disinterestedness.[47] Thus Gray was not trying to impose an extralegal result under the cover of legal reasoning. He acknowledged that a system of law under which Elmer did not inherit would be superior to the one he thought existed and under which Elmer did inherit.[48] There was, Dworkin emphasized, a respectable school of thought in 1889 that underwrote Gray's dissent even though Earl's opinion today read as the more compelling one. Earl's views had triumphed, on Dworkin's account, because arguments within the law about what it requires have improved it and improved our understanding of it.[49]

Dworkin's either/or framework, though, omits the possibility that in a particular disputed case, one side may be arguing for the right answer as it understands the law, while the other argues opportunistically in favor of the outcome it prefers, and that it was Earl for the majority who was doing the latter. The facts that a legal archaeology of the case turns up about *Riggs* point to just that interpretation. They suggest that the majority's arguments covered up a determination to impose its favored outcome, having reached it in spite of what all of the judges would normally have understood the law to require, over the protest of the dissenters. Dworkin's image of judges pretending to reason impartially and objectively while "keeping their fingers crossed" describes to a tee what the majority appears to have been doing in *Riggs*, presenting a legal argument merely for show. If so, then much of what has been said and supposed about the jurisprudential debate between Earl and Gray misses the point of what it was about. It reads deeper issues into the opinions than the ones that were actually in play: the accepted norms and principles of judicial decision at the time versus their temporary suspension for the purpose of preventing a result that the majority in a particular case found intolerable.

Many of Dworkin's critics have suspected that he developed his theories not to understand the law objectively, but with a definite practical end in view: to furnish a principled rationale for a set of decisions by the Warren and Burger Courts of which he strongly approved and that their detractors regarded as abuses of judicial authority lacking valid legal grounding. If that is indeed what he was doing, it is not hard to see why he found *Riggs* so attractive. As an exercise of such authority, it came from a highly respected state court in an era that the critics themselves would have been likely to regard as far sounder in its understanding of the proper judicial role. Moreover, having been treated by writers of the stature of Cardozo and Hart and Sacks as a member of the canon of classic decisions, ones almost beyond question or challenge, it had in effect become such a decision by 1967. What Dworkin said about it in "The

Model of Rules," that it was "chosen haphazardly," and that "almost any case in a law school casebook would provide examples that would serve as well," may be doubted.[50] The extreme rarity of what *Riggs* offered, a canonical decision using legal maxims to override statutes and to achieve an appealing result, would have left him with few other choices.

Dworkin's Hercules would reach his conclusions through an exhaustive survey of legal precedent to unify it into a coherent whole. Dworkin himself tended to use a different method, dwelling at length on a few cases as crucially telling ones. For that method to work, the cases so emphasized must be capable of bearing all of the weight placed on them. *Riggs*, it should be clear by now, is not. Dworkin supported his view of the law, and not merely the law of his own day, by the fact that the New York Court of Appeals decided the case in the way that it did. The recurrent implied ground of his arguments is that if *Riggs* is correct, such-and-such must also be so, with *Riggs*'s correctness itself taken as a given. *Riggs* may indeed support his arguments, but what supports *Riggs*? Almost all of the other state courts of the period rejected it, and the New York court gutted it of its principal claims only a few years later. Dworkin could have defended it only by appealing to the correctness of his view of the law, thus making the argument circular, for *Riggs* was supposed to furnish evidence for his view of the law. A decision so unusual in the era when it was handed down, so isolated and generally repudiated, makes a poor foundation for any argument about what judges as a rule actually do or should do.

To say so is not to say that it is anything but correct by today's law, but that is because the law happens to have evolved in a way that makes it now seem correct. Rapids on a river that in one period of history are a problem—a barrier to navigation, say—may in another time become a valuable resource (for power generation, or for recreation or scenic tourism), merely because the society environing them is different. That the law changes, and with it the usefulness of particular decisions embedded in the landscape of the appellate reports, Dworkin fully understood, while ascribing it (which is more debatable) to the law's own internal and autonomous processes of self-improvement. He wrote in *Law's Empire* that "questions considered easy during one period become hard before they again become easy questions—with the opposite answers."[51] *Riggs* illustrates the point, though only with a twist. It is an easy case today, and it was an easy case in 1889. But it was one that the Court of Appeals, for very specific reasons of its own, decided *against* the then-prevalent understanding of what made it easy and what the law plainly called for.

Criticizing Dworkin's account of judicial disagreement, Brian Leiter supposed that both sides in *Riggs* were arguing with their fingers crossed, hiding their support for the outcomes that each preferred behind a screen of legal reasoning.[52] On his account, Earl was driven by an outraged moralism visible in another opinion of his and incensed at the idea that Elmer Palmer might profit from his crime, Gray by a dislike, apparent in his *Budd* dissent, of state restraints on economic liberty that made him uncomfortable with judicial interference with the provisions of a will.[53] It is odd that both Leiter and Dworkin, using *Riggs* to inquire into the reasons for judicial disagreement, should have done little or nothing to find out more about the actual case that the disagreements were about. For Leiter no less than for Dworkin, *Riggs* represented a paradigmatic instance of judging, one that shows in miniature how it is done. But like Dworkin, he made far too much of what turns out on closer inspection to be an extremely eccentric and atypical case, one that might have tempted any court to step well out of the usual bounds. *Riggs* is such an oddity and an outlier, even within the small corpus of early murdering-heir cases, that it cannot tell us much about how judges work.

The "core claim" of American Legal Realism, Leiter has also argued, is essentially that judges are not constrained by rules, but decide cases in accordance with their sense of fairness and aptness given the specifics of the case: the deserts of the parties or the consequences for public policy, even if they conflict with the existing legal rules.[54] Taken in isolation, *Riggs* supports the claim, as does the 1908 Missouri case. But the other murdering-heir cases of its era contradict it, and they are considerably more numerous. No judge anywhere thought that the murderers merited their inheritances, but most felt constrained by what they thought that the law as it stood at the time required. There are no good grounds for singling out *Riggs* for attention while ignoring the decisions that contradicted it.

There is still another problem with Dworkin's use of *Riggs*. He presented it as supporting his view of the role of principles, as he defined them, as integral elements of the law. On this view, it will be recalled, they function differently from rules, lacking the latter's all-or-nothing character, and calling for expert judgment as to when they do and do not come into play and override what the rules seem to call for. "A principle like 'No man shall profit from his own wrong,'" Dworkin wrote, "states a reason that argues in one direction, but does not necessitate a particular decision."[55] But that is not how Judge Earl presented the master maxim he invoked in his opinion. Echoing Russell's and Sanford's brief, he treated it as a rule, indeed a super-rule, seeing "all laws" as "controlled in their operation and effect by general fundamental maxims of the common law" of this sort, ones that had not been enacted into statutes themselves, but had not been and indeed could not be overridden by statutes.[56] Dworkin's picture of the law may or may not be correct. But it is not a picture exemplified by the majority opinion in *Riggs*. And Earl's assertion of the overriding power of principles as *he* understood them has few if any counterparts in the law of his time: a fact consistent with it having been custom-made to fit one particular case and not meant seriously beyond it.

Recent Commentators

There has been plenty of discussion of *Riggs* in more recent scholarship. What is surprising is how little debate there has been. Some past decisions belong to what has been called an *anticanon* of leading cases, the Supreme Court's *Dred Scott* ruling of 1857 and *Plessy v. Ferguson* of 1896 foremost among them: ones now generally regarded as supremely and disastrously mistaken.[57] They live on as powerful examples of what courts should not do and of ways in which they can go wrong. Advocates of conflicting schools of jurisprudential thought have long tried to show that *Dred* or *Plessy* exemplifies the errors of the approaches they most dislike and that the court would have avoided its grievous error by following the one that they favor.[58] *Riggs* comes close to being these cases' mirror image. In 2004, a retired judge of the New York Court of Appeals looked back on *Riggs* as one of the landmark achievements of that tribunal's history and as too obviously correct to need any lengthy defense: "Should the Court of Appeals have permitted the grandson named in the will of the grandfather to inherit, even though he murdered the grandfather to obtain the inheritance? Almost all reasonable persons today would, I believe, answer 'no.' "[59] Few contemporary writers have a bad word to say about the decision. Nearly all commentators want to claim it for their own or feel obliged to show its consistency with their own preferred jurisprudential stance. It has been read, in fact, as exemplifying the virtues of an array of legal philosophies usually taken to be incompatible with one another. To some extent, it may by now be accepted because it seemingly has to be, as some people are famous for being famous. Cardozo and, to a lesser extent, Hart and Sacks had to argue for its correctness. Writers from Dworkin onward could and even had to accept it as a jurisprudential given, as almost a fact of nature, the way physical anthropologists long had to try to incorporate the doctored fossils of Piltdown Man in their reconstructions of the past. *Riggs*, having now become, by citation and repetition, a leading case, and the cases contrary to it having faded from view, has become an apparent datum that theories must be able to justify.

In a book dedicated to Dworkin and echoing his call to make the law a philosophically coherent whole, Jeremy Waldron has argued at length that the courts of one country ought to be receptive to precedents from the legal systems of others.[60] For Waldron, *Riggs* represents an admirable early model of such receptivity in a country that has often failed to display it. The majority opinion apparently accepted the authority in an American case of non-American or English legal wisdom. Judge Earl "cited foreign materials, from the Civil Code of Lower Canada, the Code Napoléon, civil law in general, and the principles of Roman law." "Jurists have not treated *Riggs v. Palmer* as an instance of reliance on foreign law," Waldron observed, "though it is." He concluded: "the majority in *Riggs v. Palmer* did not say simply that we can learn something from the French or from the Canadians. They had a sense that there was a body of jurisprudence constituted jointly by a consistency among decisions in the world that could be held out as a resource."[61] Like Dworkin, Waldron offered the case as a key foundation for his argument, and like Dworkin he took as given its authority as a model and a precedent.

In one sense, what he said about *Riggs* is entirely correct. The majority opinion cited the foreign sources in question and is unusual in its time (or in ours) in doing so. Precisely why it cited them is another question. Waldron himself noted that many who object in the present day to the practice of foreign citations in American decisions assert it to be nothing more than an attempt to buttress a desired result when sufficient domestic precedent is lacking. Judges who rely on such materials come under the suspicion of "simply imposing their own subjective preferences—and calling in support the views of 'like-minded foreigners' to make that imposition look legally respectable."[62] That appears to have been just what Judge Earl in *Riggs* was doing. The principal non-United States sources he referred to were mentioned in Russell's brief and (disparagingly) in Justice Landon's opinion in *Preston v. Palmer*. He did not have to go to any great trouble to find them, and his citations do not necessarily indicate any deep interest in, acquaintance with, or even curiosity about them beyond their usefulness for the task at hand, that of helping to justify a result for which there was not much else, legally speaking, to be said.[63] Nor was Earl, on the face of things, the member of the Court of Appeals likeliest to have used such materials in any more than a superficial and opportunistic way. The most cosmopolitan by far of the seven judges in 1889 was Gray, who as a boy had gone to school in Geneva and who had studied civil law at the University of Berlin in between his undergraduate education and his entrance to Harvard Law School.[64] In his *Riggs* dissent, Gray simply dismissed the authority in a New York State case of the materials Waldron discussed, just as Justice Landon had done.

Approving citations of *Riggs* have by no means been confined to those who in some way or other agree with Dworkin. Writers who would have courts, in making their decisions, routinely consult not only positive law (the written enactments of identifiable human legislators), but also natural law (the supposed commands of a code of right and wrong intuitively known to or knowable through reason to all human beings), have approved strongly of Judge Earl's opinion. For one of them, this 1889 case speaks to us from "an era when the law of nature served as a valid source of law," and the dissent is a harbinger of a then-rising tide of amoral legal positivism that would—deplorably—all but sweep away the acknowledgment of the authority of such deep-seated and universal imperatives.[65] Another eminent defender of a natural-law jurisprudence has similarly treated *Riggs* as a decision of profound wisdom and authority.[66]

Pragmatists who, for their part, would have judges liberate themselves from a sense of duty to follow the supposed demands of natural law—or, for that matter, of precedent, or statutory text, or legislative intent—whenever they would obstruct the most sensible and just decision also tend to approve of *Riggs*. Richard Posner, legal pragmatism's leading American champion and a federal appeals-court judge himself, endorsed it a number of times as plainly correct even though granting that it involved the judicial amendment of a statute.[67] The majority's solution, he argued, better carried out what must have been the intentions of both the legislature in the law it passed and the testator in the will he left. The dissent, for Posner, illustrated the silliness of insisting on the letter of the law even when doing so means an obviously unjust outcome. To uphold Elmer's right to inherit from his grandfather "would have been a goofy interpretation."[68] In a dissenting opinion in 1989, Posner cited *Riggs* as authority for courts to depart from a literal reading of statutory language, and he noted pointedly that, having been handed down when it was, it could not be dismissed as "the work of newfangled judicial activists."[69] Ronald Dworkin was a fervent admirer of what others called the judicial activism of the Warren Court and of the outcomes it achieved, and by whatever name one calls it, certainly the majority's opinion in *Riggs* furnishes a model for such judging. Yet most of the proponents of natural law in American academia have not, to say the least, been admirers of the Warren Court, and Posner-type pragmatists, for their part, have little common ground, politically or intellectually, with either. And yet all regard *Riggs* as a model.

So, though in a somewhat different way, do proponents of legal realism, which is a theory less of how judges ought to reason than of how in fact they do.[70] It emphasizes the pervasive presence and importance in legal decision-making of what are conventionally considered non-legal considerations, and the pervasive indeterminacy of the supposedly controlling legal ones, to deny that judges do, or perhaps even can, exclude the former from their thinking. Interpreting the divided Court of Appeals in *Riggs* as essentially debating the proper role of the courts in the economy, Brian Leiter assimilated it to legal realism as readily as other readers have tied it to their favored approaches.[71] In doing so, he incurred the same objection they are vulnerable to. Realism claims to tell us how judges often or usually behave, not of how they behave in freakishly exceptional cases. The effectiveness of Leiter's use of *Riggs* depends on the presumption shared by most of these writers, that it is in all key respects a paradigm case of judicial behavior, and thus one against which we can usefully test theories of such behavior. A close look at the case's history does much to undermine this presumption.

One might suppose that legal positivists, for whom law is whatever the formal commands of the accredited sources dictate, would express some doubts about *Riggs*. There could hardly be stronger testimony to the decision's exalted status than for an article published in 2018 in defense of legal positivism to assert its entire correctness. On strictly legal grounds, Dennis M. Patterson wrote, an outcome other than the one stated by Earl for the majority "was all but impossible." Its interpretation of what the law of the time required is simply "more persuasive than that offered by the dissenting opinion," bringing the case more successfully into harmony with the entire body of legal authorities and expectations. How do we know that it was more persuasive? Because "Judge Gray was alone in dissent. His decision attracted no one, while the majority got the votes."[72] As well as being inaccurate (Judge Danforth, of course, concurred with Gray's dissent) and circular (we know that Earl was persuasive because the majority agreed with him, and their agreement with him is explained by the persuasiveness of his opinion), the last claim is contradicted by two awkward facts from history. The decision failed dismally to persuade the other state courts of the time, for whom it was agreeing with *Riggs* that proved "all but impossible," and it was essentially retracted only a few years later by the court that had made it: ample evidence, one would think, of its lack of persuasiveness in its own day. Yet it is not easy to read *Riggs* in the twenty-first century with anything but twenty-first-century eyes and see it instead as it would have struck a contemporary.

The most prominent self-described formalist and textualist in modern American jurisprudence did voice his disapproval of the approach taken in *Riggs*. In a book he coauthored with Bryan A. Garner, US Supreme Court Associate Justice Antonin Scalia made the murdering-heir problem a vehicle for defending judges who "apply an unwise law as written"; they thereby remain true to their assigned role in the system of government and encourage the legislature to perform its own task and revise the law. Scalia and Garner pointed to the spread of slayer statutes across the United States in the wake of such decisions as illustrating the feasibility of the approach. "The statute books will become more complete, and improvised judge-made exceptions that cannot be found in the text of enacted laws will be less common."[73] Yet when Scalia criticized the use of the absurdity rationale for judicial intervention, he used *Holy Trinity* as his principal target rather than *Riggs*.[74]

Presenting only two choices, moreover, Scalia and Garner oddly made their own task, to persuade readers that the murderer in a case like *Riggs* must inherit, more difficult because less appealing. They ignored the third route open to judges, the equity solution of a constructive trust. Yet it is not difficult to understand why. A celebrant of the virtues of what he called "a law of rules,"[75] Scalia had little to say in his non-judicial writings about equity, though it is as much and as venerable a part of the Anglo-American court system as law is and its natural counterweight to remedy the defects of excessively rigid formulae.[76] The bias carried over into his work as a Supreme Court justice. In 1999, against vigorous dissent, he marshaled a bare majority of the bench behind the proposition that the equity remedies available to federal judges are only those that were clearly enunciated and used at the time of the adoption of the Constitution in 1789, and in that opinion he likened equity unaffectionately to a nuclear weapon.[77] Prizing rules for the predictability they offer and the constraints they place on judicial action, Scalia was reluctant to acknowledge even the existence of the parallel system created to remedy the defects and failures of justice resulting from law too rigidly applied. Though rejecting *Riggs*, he tacitly accepted the *Riggs* majority's assumption that the courts had no way other than reinterpreting the statute to keep a murdering heir from inheriting. He had little else in common with Ronald Dworkin, but the realm of equity was alien territory to both, in Dworkin's case (as indeed with Hart and Sacks as well) as a threat to the principled coherence, unity, and integrity he saw as the law's highest achievement.

Another defender of legal formalism, Frederick Schauer, has been the chief *Riggs*-skeptic of recent times. Though also inattentive to the equity solution advanced in *Ellerson*, he has usefully pointed out the eccentric and unrepresentative character of the 1889 decision within the American law of inheritance in its own time, challenging attempts to use it as a model of what judges actually do. He has likewise noticed and emphasized the implied repudiation of *Riggs* by the choice of almost all of the American states to rely on statutes rather than case law to deal with murdering heirs, both in its own time and more recently, similarly under-cutting attempts to use it as a paradigm case of judging at its best.[78] Yet his success in using historical materials, albeit only of the kind customary in conventional legal research, to clarify *Riggs* creates a new puzzle. On his account of the matter, it makes little sense that five judges of the New York Court of Appeals could have agreed on a decision for which so little could apparently have been said. A fuller use of history offers an answer to that question, too, illustrating thereby its value, and sometimes its indispensability, in making sense of legal decisions.

The Death of a Case?

Many biographies have been written of people who are still alive, and many of them are excellent pieces of work. Around even the best of them, however, hovers a sense of incompleteness. If there is a single demand that biography as a literary form imposes on its practitioners, it is that they trace the entire arc of the human life being studied: "all biography . . . moves inexorably towards death."[79]

Similarly, a case biography may be written about a decision that remains very much alive in legal argument. Its validity may be contested, its authority may be challenged, and its meaning may continue to evolve. It may even be so discredited and even abhorred as to become a universal example of what judges ought not to do. So long as a case retains its vitality, in one of these ways or in some other, its biographies will carry a provisional and incomplete air.

But what was once a leading case may die. It may have been so thoroughly assimilated into legal doctrine and practice that specific reference to it is no longer necessary and is no longer made, or because some better exemplar of the doctrine it stated has taken its place. It may pass away because the legal point it made, or indeed the whole domain of legal doctrine to which it belonged, has gone into desuetude. It may also disappear permanently from use because of the recognition, however belated, that it never really established what it was thought to establish. For that reason, upon the facts presented in this book, I venture to think that *Riggs* has now died. Its main use has been to demonstrate the long-standing acceptance of certain assertions about law and judging. It can no longer credibly be taken to demonstrate anything of the sort. And though those assertions remain alive and well, they now have bases entirely independent of *Riggs* and its supposed lessons.

But though a biography is only formally complete if it reports the death of its subject, that report need not, and very often does not, occupy its final page or chapter. The life's course ended, it is quite common for the last chapter to review its patterns or to propound its lessons. That is what the next chapter does with *Riggs*.

Chapter 6

Riggs, Case Biography, and Legal Archaeology

A recent review identifies two related sources of malaise prevalent among scholars in legal history. One is the fear that their separate studies, taken together, add up to very little other than a recurring emphasis on the contingencies and specificities of particular times and places. The other is a sense of being ignored and considered irrelevant by practitioners of law, who appear uninterested in and uninfluenced by what legal historians have found.[1] Does a detailed study of *Riggs v. Palmer* merely add one more limited and idiosyncratic case study to the mass of such studies we had already? Or can something of wider interest and value be generalized from them all?

There will never be any difficulty in showing that the appellate-court report of a case excludes some facts about it, or in turning up a wealth of such facts through outside research. But to do these things is not to demonstrate that their absence from the law report matters. Case biography and legal archaeology, both involving the historical study of a past case or set of cases through sources beyond the appellate opinions, are not valuable or worthwhile in themselves, but rather to the extent that they can help answer certain important questions, using historical source material, better than other available approaches can.

Not all of the uses of the two methods that one study illustrates will be significant in another. Conversely, a single study may illustrate more than one. *Riggs* displays several that echo ones arrived at in other studies: the value of historical research in accounting for a certain outcome by correcting or supplementing the knowledge of the facts of a case as derived solely from the law report; how variables external to the universe of accepted legal argument may have influenced a decision that for one reason or another seems a surprising or puzzling one for the court rendering it to have given; and the ways in which what is accepted legal doctrine can change with developments in the wider social environment. Collectively they make it possible to identify certain recurrent and stereotyped ways in which ahistorical legal inquiry and practice can—most people would agree—go wrong.

The Facts of a Case

Legal scholarship normally relies on the appellate-court opinion for the facts of the case it discusses. But as Richard Posner wrote in 1990: "The appellate court will usually state the facts as favorably to its conclusions as the record allows, and often more favorably."[2] Selective and purposefully so, the opinion frames matters by highlighting some things and withholding others, and it may contain outright distortions or inventions. It presents the result it announces as following from the facts of the case it states, yet the relation may run the other way; it may be the result in view that dictates which facts are presented (and which are not). Summing up his own and others' research in legal archaeology, Paul Lombardo noted how "continued near-exclusive reliance on a court's version of the 'facts'" in conventional scholarship disregards how "the official factual account contained in an appellate opinion may have only the most tenuous relationship to the events that actually led the parties to court."[3] Karl Llewellyn earlier observed along the same lines that in reading such an opinion, "we have had removed from our sight a very considerable number of hard facts, which may, for all we know, have much affected the actual outcome of the case." As he observed,

> even an appellate court officially concerned with rules alone has been known to strain itself and to strain the rules that it laid down in order to produce what seemed a just result in the case at hand . . . [S]o far as facts or factors not shown in the report were at work in the court, the opinion gives us a misleading picture of what happened, and, therefore a misleading basis for prophecy of what will happen in the future. . . . For we may expect that in future cases, as in the case at hand, *one* of

the possibilities will be that rules will be twisted out of their apparent shape in order to produce what seems a just result.[4]

Because their accuracy and completeness are always open to question, simply confirming through the use of external sources that the facts of a significant case were as the opinion states them is not a waste of effort. A thorough legal archaeology of the contracts case of *Ploof v. Putnam*, decided by the Vermont Supreme Court in 1909, for example, clarified the social origins and background of the dispute but largely confirmed the court's statement of the legally relevant situation.[5] Facts not mentioned in the appellate-court opinion in another contracts case from the same period, *Alaska Packers' Association v. Domenico*, on the other hand, offer considerable support for other interpretations than the one that the court chose, as Debora Threedy has shown.[6]

There is no guarantee that legal archaeology will transform what we know about any case it investigates or even that it will often or usually do so. But what research might show cannot be known until it is done. External sources themselves, of course, do not provide the full and unmediated truth about a case that cannot be found in a judicial opinion. They also must be weighed and interpreted. But in A. W. Brian Simpson's words, "to try to supplement law reports with other material in the hope that this will at least bring us closer to historical reality" is a more sensible course of action than to confine ourselves dogmatically to the one source alone and trust it to tell us all that we need to know about what happened.[7]

One side benefit that could be claimed for the method has struck some critics as no benefit at all: that the real-life details of a case under study will bring it alive for law students, especially beginning ones, who are apt to be confused and repelled by a relentlessly abstract discussion, based wholly on the law reports, in which the parties and their actions and motives remain shadowy at best. The critics fear that the injection of human interest, in the form of details that are irrelevant to the legal doctrine laid down in the case, will obstruct and delay rather than help a student's education in the law. For it panders, counterproductively, to the very habits of mind that lawyers need to overcome and slows the acquisition of the reasoning skills that they need to develop.[8] The objection may underrate the value of vivid and concrete detail in arousing a student's initial interest if people in fact are as they are. It is certainly vulnerable to a deeper criticism. Emphasizing the close reading of published appellate opinions—the standard case method of legal instruction introduced by C.

C. Langdell at Harvard after the Civil War—obstructs the development of other skills and deprives the student of an essential challenge. In the case method, the relevant facts of the case have already been chosen by the decision's author, as have the legal categories they best fit. The student is not asked to select the relevant facts from the raw material of the case and discard the rest, or to formulate the most appropriate conceptual framework for them. The writer of the opinion has done both jobs; its readers, barred from looking outside the opinion, can only discuss the materials as handed to them. They are not taught the craft of thinking legally in the best way, by having to do the work themselves. Or so it seemed, at any rate, to as much of an insider as Jerome Frank (1889–1957), legal scholar turned federal appeals court judge, who in 1947 bemoaned the hegemony of the Langdellian method. "What would we say," he asked, "of a medical school where the students were taught surgery solely from the printed page? . . . Who would learn golf from a golf instructor, contenting himself with sitting in the locker-room analyzing newspaper accounts of important golf-matches that had been played by someone else several years before?"[9]

But let us take the case method as given. In law school, students are required to make sense of the cases they are assigned. In legal practice, a case, to be usable, must be understandable. Supplementing the law report with other sources is sometimes not only worthwhile but also imperative. For appellate-court opinions can be impossible to understand even on their own stated terms, and for reasons that no amount of the remedy that is usually proposed or resorted to—closer and closer reading of their text—can cure. By using ambiguous language, omitting facts essential to their line of reasoning, or making assumptions or carrying them over from the case record without stating them explicitly, they often invite and sometimes demand speculation of a reader obliged to make them make sense. Such a reader must, consciously or otherwise, introduce material not stated in the opinion to fill its gaps. The gaps can be filled in one of two ways: by the reader's imagination, or through research. If it is objected that the historical sources that legal archaeology exploits lie outside the official legal record, the only possible reply is that the same is true for what imagination provides instead, and it lies outside the historical record as well. Legal archaeology is far less likely to introduce errors than conjecture is.

A core tenet of the approach, that frequently "one needs to look outside the opinion in order to read it," is true at a variety of levels, and not least at the simplest and most literal ones.[10] Sometimes the entire basic situation as the opinion states it is a puzzling one. The Supreme Court's opinion in the classic absurdity case of *United States v. Kirby* asks the reader to believe that the offense of arresting a postal carrier wanted for murder, and thereby violating a federal law against obstructing the delivery of the mails, was what had actually landed the defendant in the dock. David Achtenberg's legal archaeology of the case provides a vastly more credible account of its origins.[11] Legal archaeology can as usefully confirm as challenge the accuracy of doubtful-sounding facts in an opinion that might tempt a reader into erroneous conjecture. The plaintiff in the English contracts case of *Leaf v. International Galleries* (1950) had bought a painting supposedly by John Constable (1776–1837) in 1945 for £85. Such a low price for a work by so renowned an artist has led later readers of the case to assume that Leaf should have known that its authenticity, a central issue in the litigation, was highly speculative. But research on art-price history and its vagaries by Angela Fernandez in turn undermines that easy assumption and the conclusions about the case that have been drawn from it.[12]

Kirksey v. Kirksey, decided by the Alabama Supreme Court in 1845, has been a staple of contracts instruction in American law schools. Isaac Kirksey, a well-to-do plantation owner, offered his brother's widow, Angelico, and her children a place to live. Angelico accepted the offer, and the family left the farm where they had been living and relocated, only for Isaac, two years later, to order them to move out. Angelico sued for damages. Analyses of the case turn on whether Isaac's promise had been a gratuitous one that he was not obliged to keep, or whether it was a bargain for which he had received some benefit in return ("consideration," in legal terms) that made the agreement an enforceable contract. The short appellate opinion leaves it unclear why Isaac acted as he did. Readers have filled the lacuna with a variety of assumptions: that Isaac wanted a sexual liaison with his sister-in-law, or that he wanted the cheap labor of Angelico's children to cultivate his land, or that on closer acquaintance he found Angelico too disagreeable a neighbor to put up with. William R. Casto and Val D. Ricks in 2006 published a thorough legal archaeology of the case that demolished all of these hypotheses and set out an entirely new and convincing explanation. The key to Isaac's behavior, they established, lay in the changing laws governing the preemption rights of squatters on federal land and in his hopes to use them, with his sister-in-law as a claimant, to enlarge his holdings. In Casto's and Ricks's words, "no one who has ever taught the case has had any real understanding of what actually happened."[13] The history of *Kirksey* offers a clear and negative test of the ability of close reading plus imaginative conjecture to make sense of an elliptically stated case from the past, and an illustration of legal archaeology's capacity for doing much better.

When conjecture is preferred over research, as it usually is in traditional legal scholarship, Judith Maute described what may happen as a result and often does. A "folklore" develops around a leading case. It consists of "imagined facts," ones that were supposed into existence to flesh out gaps or resolve inconsistencies or implausibilities in the appellate opinions, or that simply appear to follow commonsensically from things that the opinions do state. They may eventually come to be treated as actually part of the official record, their imaginary character forgotten.[14] *Riggs* offers several examples of the phenomenon.

Some writers have described Francis Palmer as a wealthy man, one whose assets would have made Elmer rich had he succeeded in acquiring them.[15] Judge Earl's opinion indeed referred at one point to Francis's "considerable" property."[16] But *considerable* is a vague term, and the trial record and briefs in the case, as well as the opinion in *Preston v. Palmer*, specify the approximate sum in question. No doubt his grandfather's farm and other possessions represented wealth in Elmer's eyes. Their total value, however, fell between five and six thousand dollars: a comfortable sum at the time, but even then falling well short of what most people would have used the words *wealth* or *riches* to describe.[17]

Many commentators on the case have ascribed Elmer's crime to a fear that Francis would change his will in favor of his new wife.[18] In doing so, they have read into the text of the decision something that is not there and that is not borne out by any other sources. Judge Earl wrote of Elmer: "He knew of the provisions made in his favor in the will, and that he might prevent his grandfather from revoking such provisions, which he had manifested some intention to do, and to obtain the speedy enjoyment and immediate possession of his property, he willfully murdered him by poisoning him."[19] Earl's opinion mentioned Francis's remarriage at an earlier point.[20] It is easy to suppose a connection between these two statements, and many readers have inferred one. But the opinion does not make one, and neither does the record of the trial. Nowhere did Earl say anything about a planned or even contemplated change of will in favor of Eliza Palmer. The testimony to which he was referring ascribed Francis's only explicit threats of disinheritance to his irritation with Elmer's behavior, and particularly with his "extravagant" spending and his romantic attachments, not to any plans to benefit his new wife. At the trial, neither the prosecution nor the judge mentioned the possibility of a new will transferring the estate to Eliza. District Attorney Lang summed up Elmer's motives for the crime as he saw them: "Elmer expected his grandfather's estate except a few small legacies, and he wanted it at once. . . . Elmer was exceedingly desirous of marrying. Mr. Palmer was sternly opposed to it. . . . Also Palmer did not like the way he was squandering his own property and he threatened to disinherit Elmer, if he did not change his course."[21] Judge Potter recited the same set of alleged motives, and no others, in his charge to the jury.[22] The action that Cecelia Preston and Lorette Riggs initiated in 1883 offered identical reasons for the crime and again made no hint that the prospect of a new will made for Eliza's benefit had played any role:

> Elmer was captious and disposed to do about as he pleased, regardless of the wishes and directions of said Francis B. Palmer, staying out late at night, spending money for useless articles, and waiting on or courting girls with whom said Francis B. Palmer did not desire him to associate; that said Francis B. Palmer often remonstrated with said Elmer for his conduct and often threatened him that unless he behaved himself better and did as he wished he would make a new will and not leave him his property; that he would not give him any of his property; that this state of unpleasantness continued between them until the 25th day of April 1882; that said Elmer E. Palmer was greatly desirous to come into the possession and ownership of the property of said Francis B. Palmer and was fearful and apprehensive that said Francis B. Palmer would make a new will and not leave him much or any of his property. . . .[23]

Russell and Sanford in their briefs for the plaintiffs would hardly have failed, if they could have done so, to mention a point that would have shown Elmer in a particularly unattractive light, as having committed murder to enrich himself at the expense of a stepmother whom Francis intended to make his heir. The record contains no evidence of any such plans. Francis's criticisms of his grandson's behavior were most vehement when it came to Elmer's successive courtships. If Elmer worried about being disinherited at all, so far as we know it was chiefly on this basis. It is far clearer that he felt intolerably constrained and eager to obtain his legacy right away than that he feared losing it. Judge Earl himself erred, and has been followed by many others, in attributing equal weight to two factors, impatience to inherit and fear of disinheritance, when the testimony overwhelmingly pointed to the former. It is, of course, possible that thoughts of the latter were also on his mind, as so many commentators on the case have assumed. But there is no evidence that they were.

Both of these errors illustrate the dangers that may await anyone who reads an opinion, in Carl Becker's phrase, "without fear and without research."[24] Neither of them seriously distorts an understanding of *Riggs*. Another imagined fact equally lacking any basis in the record has been much more harmful. Commentators who have erred in their assumptions about the sentence Elmer received have invariably supposed it to have been more severe than it was: "Although we do not know Elmer's sentence, we can guess that it was imprisonment for life"; "he [Elmer] was duly sentenced to a long prison term"; "he was convicted of second degree murder and sent to prison, probably for life"; "Elmer [at the time of the Court of Appeals decision] is already in jail for his crime"; he "was serving his sentence in the state penitentiary at the time the case was decided"; "his prospects for life in prison."[25] These undocumented embroideries on the record show a commendably accurate awareness of what the normal punishment for Elmer's crime in that era was. But they assume incorrectly that Elmer received such a punishment. He was sentenced, in fact, not to prison, but to the reformatory, and he had gone free by the time the challenge to his inheritance was finally decided. The effect of these misstatements has been the same as produced by Judge Earl's reticence on the same point in the majority opinion: to obscure, if the preceding analysis is correct, the factor that most likely motivated the court. What did happen to him is stated, albeit incompletely and obliquely, in the dissent (in Gray's observation that when the suit was launched, Elmer was serving a term in the reformatory), but in a way hardly any later analyst of the case has noticed. If the decision was indeed influenced by what had (or, more precisely, what had not) happened to Elmer, it is far better and more accurately understood when the facts of his case are added.

With the full facts of the case invisible in the Court of Appeals opinions, equally invisible is the unique situation to which the decision seems to have been a response. Modern discussions of *Riggs* have typically treated it as an exemplary or paradigmatic case of judging, as a decision that any theory of law or legal reasoning is obliged to show itself consistent with. But one might as reasonably try to develop a general theory of the sovereign state on the basis of Monaco or the Vatican City: something that indeed exists and belongs to the category in question but differs profoundly from most of its other members. In its time, *Riggs* was regarded as a good example of how cases should not be decided. It accepted a set of arguments rejected by almost every other court that heard them or that heard a parallel to them in the same years, including the New York Court of Appeals itself only a few years later. The decision's unusualness emerges clearly from a recovery of the details amid which it arose, and what also emerges is a more likely explanation for the outcome than any that can be unearthed merely from a close reading of the opinions. The Court of Appeals in *Riggs* was faced with an extraordinarily provoking claim. A convicted murderer had been released in his early twenties and stood ready to take lawful possession of the property he had committed his crime a relatively short time earlier to obtain. The judges doubtless wanted to rule against Elmer, but if they were to do so, their decision, to command respect, had to be couched in accepted legal terms. Having greater freedom than the courts below to lay down new law, though still obliged to present it as old law, they found the best means readily at hand for doing so in citing the maxims and principles that the plaintiffs' brief provided as overriding the literal meaning of the wills statute, in a way neither they nor other American courts of the time normally did. *Riggs* was a quite idiosyncratic case that produced a quite idiosyncratic ruling, though for reasons invisible in the majority opinion. Legal archaeology asks (without prejudging the matter in either direction) whether the key facts of the case that came before the court were "the facts of the case" as the court stated them. The assumption that they were is a convenient one, but convenience is a poor guarantee of reliability, as *Riggs* and other cases illustrate.

Explaining a Decision: Extralegal Factors

If the outcome in *Riggs* did owe much to factors hidden from view in Earl's opinion, it would not be unique in that respect. Legal cases too numerous to list are generally recognized to have been influenced or even wholly determined by *extralegal* considerations, ones other than those that a court is supposed to take into account in deciding a case: racial, class, sexual, cultural, and ideological leanings or preconceptions, political pressures or expediency, the supposed imperatives of military or economic or medical emergency, simple contingencies involving the individuals who happen to have been involved. Frequently, the fact of their having been so influenced was a matter of common remark at the time they were decided and has remained so ever since. In other instances, though, some such external factors have seemed to be present without being readily identifiable. All that can be sensed is that the court's decision was a surprising one for it to have reached and that its stated reasoning falls well short of satisfactorily explaining the outcome. Legal archaeology has more than once shown its usefulness in making sense of such puzzles in a way one might instead liken to legal astronomy: looking for the undiscovered planet whose gravitational pull would account for irregularities in the orbit of a known one.

One set of possible disturbing factors lies in the ways in which a dispute is litigated by the nominal parties to it. American courts have always recognized that the decision of a case, with all that it may mean as a precedent for similar cases in the future, requires the best possible statement of the arguments pro and con. As one corollary, they have been appropriately distrustful of what are called *collusive* or *feigned* cases, in which the seemingly antagonistic parties are actually working together in order to control the presentation of facts and arguments and secure a ruling to their benefit.[26] The courts have been less attentive, though, to a much more common phenomenon, familiar to lawyers yet rarely mentioned in judicial opinions, that in practice can have similar consequences: the frequent disparity in resources between the two sides in litigation, which may lead to one side being presented much more effectively than the other. A classic of legal archaeology, Judith Maute's study of the 1962 contracts case of *Peevyhouse v. Garland Coal & Mining Co.*, emphasized how much both the result and the rule that emerged owed to this factor.[27] Such disparities occur quite often and can matter quite a lot. Legal-archaeological research exploring the effect they have on shaping individual cases and, through them, legal doctrines makes a valuable contribution.

To be sure, neither side in the litigation in *Riggs v. Palmer* was vastly richer or poorer than the other. All the same, one side was significantly overmatched by the other. The chance interest that Leslie W. Russell took in the possibilities presented by the case had much to do with its final outcome. He brought a wealth of ingenious arguments and usable citations to the appellants' brief that the Court of Appeals could plunder to rationalize a decision in their favor. Simply by arguing their case, too, he conferred legitimacy on a legally outlandish claim, giving it the prestige and support of a former state attorney general and a familiar and trusted advocate before the court. An appeal researched, drafted, and argued by C. E. Sanford alone would most likely not have given rise to the *Riggs* that we know.[28]

Legal archaeology may also uncover hidden and extralegal motives that a court had for resolving a case in the way it did. Consider a decision extraordinarily far-reaching in its consequences: *Johnson v. M'Intosh*, decided by the United States Supreme Court in 1823 in an opinion by Chief Justice Marshall, the single most important case in American Indian law and indeed in American property law in general. Marshall's opinion laid down two rules of enormous future consequence: first, that a civilized power, by the right of discovery, acquired title over the lands inhabited by the "savage" indigenous peoples they encountered, though the latter (the American Indian nations, in the case of the United States) retained the right of use and occupancy over their territories; and that only the sovereign state, not private individuals, could acquire lands by purchase or cession from their Indian occupants. *Johnson* has baffled later readers for two reasons. One is that Marshall's opinion, especially in enunciating the first of these rules, went far beyond what it needed to do to decide the suit at hand. Why? A second is that Marshall less than a decade later found his decision in *Johnson* a serious embarrassment when faced with another case that took its reasoning to its logical and, to him, unacceptable conclusions. Why, then, had he made it in the first place?

In a study published in 2005, the law professor and historian Lindsay Robertson raised both of these questions and proposed answers to them.[29] The chief actors in *Johnson*, who quietly organized and financed both sides of the lawsuit, were the shareholders in a land company. They went to court in an attempt to legalize a vast and dubious purchase the company had made in the early 1770s, just prior to the American Revolution, from two Indian nations in parts of present-day Indiana and Illinois. They had against them the fact that a British government proclamation issued in 1763 had outlawed such purchases by private parties, a ban that the subsequent policy of the United States had continued. The flimsy legal foundations of the purchase and the evidently contrived and collusive character of the action used to bring it into court made the claim an impossible one for Marshall to accept. Denying it, as invalid under the British law of its time, would ordinarily have been simple enough. But Marshall and the court, as Robertson established, happened in the early 1820s to be at the center of two other and much more contentious sets of issues.

They had gravely offended the legislature and courts of the then-powerful state of Virginia by a series of decisions, particularly *Cohens v. Virginia* (1821), that had affirmed the superiority of the federal judiciary over questions that many regarded as lying outside its domain. And they faced the prospect of having to decide a heated controversy between Virginia and Kentucky over the latter's attempts to deny the validity of land grants the former had made when Kentucky was still a part of Virginia (it separated in 1792). The two states were, at the same time, very much at odds over a related but narrower issue they were trying but failing to resolve by negotiation. Before the separation, Virginia had issued warrants allowing its Revolutionary War militia veterans to claim state-owned lands in a part of the Kentucky district that was, until they relinquished it in a federal treaty in 1818, occupied by the Chickasaw Indians. Virginia asserted, and Kentucky denied, that the veterans possessed an enforceable property right in the lands to which they had received warrants now that it had become available for white settlement.

Not only did Marshall have personal connections and sympathies that would have inclined him to favor the Virginia militia claimants, Robertson established, but the furious resentment that *Cohens* had aroused in a powerful state also jeopardized his court's still shaky authority within the American political system. He had strong reasons to want to avoid antagonizing Virginia further and indeed to pacify it if at all possible. Going well beyond the issues central to the case, Marshall used most of his opinion in *Johnson* to set out a theory of the relations of European conquerors with the indigenous peoples of the countries they had conquered: the discovery doctrine, in short. The doctrine was unnecessary to decide the case at hand, which could have been much more narrowly and simply resolved by finding the purchases illegal under British law in the 1770s. But it furnished a basis for settling the Virginia-Kentucky controversy in favor of the claimants from the former, were the court ever asked to do so. It affirmed—ignoring much evidence to the contrary, which could the more easily be ignored because it had not arisen in the argument of the *Johnson* case—that Virginia had possessed a sovereign title over the Chickasaw lands even while they were still under Indian occupation, and thus could make grants of future title to them to individuals. None of these influences on the decision in *Johnson* are stated in or can be readily inferred from the text of the opinion in the case. Spotting them requires a knowledge of the historical context in which the court was operating at that moment: in Robertson's words, of "just what was on the minds of the participants in the case at the time it was crafted, pleaded, argued, and decided."[30]

As Robertson observed, Marshall had every reason to suppose that the doctrine he was asserting would not affect any future cases or find any wider application.[31] The federal government had long since taken over the management of Indian land title, usually according it a tacit recognition by negotiating terms of purchase. The states had long since stopped making grants of the kind in question. But in the late 1820s and early 1830s, the decision rose from the grave. The State of Georgia, eventually with the support of President Andrew Jackson, sought to establish control over the large ancestral territory of the Cherokee Nation lying within its borders after the tribe refused to discuss selling it. Georgia's governor and legislature asserted title to all of the Cherokee lands not held in individual ownership, defined their occupants in essence as tenants whose leases were now being canceled, and declared that the state's laws henceforth applied in the Indian territory. A Jacksonian majority in Congress cooperated by passing a bill affirming Georgia's stance and setting aside federal lands in the western territories to be given Indian nations in exchange for their eastern homelands. Proponents of the new policy of compelled Indian removal invoked *Johnson* in support of its legality. Writing for the Supreme Court in *Worcester v. Georgia* (1832), a challenge to the state's claim of jurisdiction within Cherokee territory, Marshall repudiated the reasoning he had earlier laid down, denying now that discovery transferred title to the land to the civilized discoverers. But he failed to uproot a doctrine that too conveniently served the interests of expansionist whites not to establish itself firmly in American law, and Jackson's and his successors' numerous appointees to the Supreme Court over the next several years tipped the judicial balance ever more strongly in its favor.[32]

If Robertson's explanation of *Johnson* and the one I have suggested of *Riggs* are correct, then a couple of parallels between the two cases become both noticeable and understandable. One is a fact otherwise hard to account for: that the court that handed down each decision attempted, within a decade, to scale it back quite significantly: *Johnson* in *Worcester* and *Riggs* in *Ellerson*. Such is what one would expect of a decision that had been made, not on the basis of established legal principles, but rather for reasons of expediency in dealing with a specific situation, only for its broader implications to become troublesome once made apparent. The other and related likeness is the remarkably high level of generality at which each opinion is pitched. Marshall grounded *Johnson* in a capsule history of the modern world and in a grand theory of the legal relations of advanced with "savage" peoples. Earl, writing for the majority in *Riggs*, swathed the court's judgment in sweeping maxims purporting to govern the law in its entirety and to express the accumulated wisdom of civilized human society. Professional conjurors use gestures, suggestions, and glances to direct the audience's attention away from what they are doing. The opinions in *Johnson* and *Riggs* carry the reader aloft into a realm of abstract first principles. That they do so would not be surprising if some very down-to-earth specifics were what had most mattered to the outcome. The Anglo-American legal system enshrines objectivity and impersonality high among its ostensible norms. It requires that the decision of a case be uninfluenced by the persons of the parties or the consequences to them or to others. In such a system, the more a decision is motivated by such forbidden factors, the more it is likely to be justified by lofty generalizations, accompanied as little as possible by details and specifics that might give the game away. The majority opinion in *Riggs* fits the profile remarkably well. It is largely a matter of chance that the same qualities—mistaken for the actual reasons for the decision—would give it a much later celebrity among readers taking its philosophical pretensions at face value. But it is just as credulous to accept the rationale for a decision on the say-so of the judge as it is to accept the facts as the opinion states them. Each claim calls for testing when it can be had.

Legal-archaeological research has shed light on a number of similarly puzzling decisions. An example is Marianne Wesson's study of the origin of the "present intention" exception to the hearsay ban in *Mutual Life Insurance Company v. Hillmon*, discussed earlier. Another is the legal historian Sally Greene's investigation of a landmark decision in the antebellum American law of slavery, North Carolina Chief Justice Thomas Ruffin's opinion in *State v. Mann* (1830). Ruffin overturned the conviction of John Mann, a socially and economically marginal figure in Chowan County white society. Exasperated by the recalcitrance and attempted escape of a female slave, Lydia, whom he was renting from her owner, Mann shot and wounded her. A jury found him guilty of assault and battery for having exceeded the rights of chastisement that, as a mere slave hirer, he possessed. As Greene documented, the verdict reflected the law as then understood both locally in Chowan County and across the South generally. Ruffin disregarded that understanding in asserting that the absolute dominion of the master, by lease no less than by ownership, was a necessary element in the existence of slavery as a social institution. In so ruling, he portrayed himself as merely and perhaps regretfully following the dictates of the law as it already stood, disingenuously presenting change as continuity. His reasons, as best they can be identified, were those being advanced in the late 1820s and 1830s by like-minded upper-class conservatives in Ruffin's native Virginia. Alarmed at new signs of the fragility of the Southern social order, they sought ways to solidify it, among them the rejection of traditional restraints on the power of white in general over slaves.[33]

Additional examples come from the landmark 1860s English common-law tort case of *Rylands v. Fletcher*, which involved an action for damages caused by the failure of the defendant's reservoir and the resulting flood. Rejected by the lower courts, the claim was upheld as valid on appeal. At the time, Anglo-American law was moving toward a rule of making defendants liable for harm caused by their activities only when they had been negligent or had failed to take reasonable precautions. The result in *Rylands* surprisingly staked out a novel claim, which has proved an enduring and fruitful one, for the much tougher standard of strict liability, holding a person liable regardless of fault or negligence, in a rather nebulous and flexible class of instances that one opinion in the case defined as those involving dangerous materials and another as any unnatural use that owners make of their land. Later commentators strove without great success to make doctrinal sense of the decision in the light of the law as understood at the time. In the mid-1980s, A. W. Brian Simpson pointed out that it had been handed down shortly after the worst dam failure disaster in English history, the great Sheffield flood of 1864, which cost 240 lives. And in the text of the principal opinion, which otherwise studiously avoided any reference to the recent calamity, he found, among other signs of its influence, "a slip of the pen" indicating that the Sheffield flood was in fact on the author's mind. Speaking of the importance of reservoir failures, it mentioned the victims drowned in such disasters, though no one had been drowned by the failure of the reservoir in *Rylands*.[34] A later study by another scholar found that the acceptance by American appeals courts of the strict liability standard advocated in *Rylands* was related, more closely than to any other likely cause, to the occurrence of serious dam-failure disasters in the United States and especially to the worst of them ever, the devastating Johnstown, Pennsylvania flood of 1889.[35]

For a historian or for a student of law as a social institution, such studies of cases can illustrate the relations between legal doctrine and the wider environment in which it develops. For neither kind of scholar are they particularly problematic in principle. For lawyers and judges, though, they raise a more difficult set of questions. *State v. Mann* is no longer authority for any legal proposition, but what of the others, which still are? If Marshall was placing politics above law, if the Court of Appeals ruled as it did because Elmer Palmer seemed to it not to have been punished severely enough and the Supreme Court in *Hillmon* because it thought (erroneously) that it smelled a rat, if *Rylands* and its acceptance in the United States largely responded to recent events rather than to recognized legal doctrine, does that undermine each decision's authority as precedent for future cases? On Robertson's account, indeed, *Johnson* is doubly tainted at its source. Not only may Marshall have decided it for improperly extralegal reasons, to defuse a dangerous quarrel between the Supreme Court and the state of Virginia, but the previously unexamined papers of the land company also show that the suit itself was an improperly collusive one. Centering the case on an artificially crafted situation rather than a genuine dispute between two parties, it narrowly restricted the points argued and the interests represented before the court in order to increase the shareholders' chances of winning a decision in their favor. Robertson's findings, if accepted, would certainly lessen the weight that later courts might give *Johnson* as precedent and might even seem to require its abandonment.

But history is a field notoriously short on consensus. Robertson's book reads very convincingly, and it earned generally favorable reviews by legal historians. Yet at least one close student of the same case has questioned the importance it ascribed to the Virginia-Kentucky dispute in explaining Marshall's actions.[36] When scholars disagree, it might be asked, whose authority does a court accept? Does it have to play historian itself and assess their arguments and evidence? The interpretation of *Riggs v. Palmer* suggested here, that it was an ad hoc decision made for reasons generally regarded as illegitimate in the law, is far from being demonstrably or unquestionably correct. Should that interpretation deprive the decision of its authority? In more general terms, would using historical research help to screen out bad precedents and make better doctrine? Or would it merely increase the area for disagreement instead of narrowing it, and invite advocates on both sides to practice tendentious *law-office history*, as it is often called, something quite different from serious and impartial investigation?

The objections are not empty nor trivial. And yet they would apply to much else that courts do consider, and when considering those matters it is assumed, reasonably enough, that evidence in dispute can be weighed and argued over and better and worse conclusions distinguished from each other. "The skills necessary to be a good historian—critical thinking, analogical reasoning, proper evidentiary weighting—are skills that lawyers and judges use every day. . . . If lawyers cannot do history merely because we are not historians, then I wonder whether we can really do this thing called 'law' at all."[37] The problem is not lawyers' inability but their unwillingness to conduct historical research and learn from its results.

Moreover, appellate opinions themselves teem with statements of asserted or assumed truths—not only historical, but also political, sociological, and economic—that have not been established by a process of rigorous legal demonstration either. One legal scholar has aptly called them "doctrinal facts," "empirical arguments enlisted in the service of some doctrine, but with little or no supporting authority." Assertions regarding the original intent or understanding of those who framed and approved the Constitution, he continued, are the most prominent and the most frequent, but they are far from alone. "Federalism is repeatedly championed on the basis of empirical claims such as 'the value of the states as laboratories of experimentation,' or 'states operate as a check to national power in order to preserve individual liberty,' or 'states more effectively implement local interests.' "[38] None of these sweeping assertions can be described as empirically established, and yet they are staple ingredients of judicial decisions that invoke them as such. The narrower and more modest claims made by Robertson and Wesson concern singular events rather than whole classes of them and stand on considerably firmer foundations.

It might be objected that the findings of historical research are and should be inadmissible because they did not undergo the procedural tests used to identify legally valid evidence that the material that made it into the official record passed. But the materials of legislative history—reports, hearings, debates, and the like—that courts now freely and routinely use to interpret statutes have not passed such tests either. And this objection does not touch a good deal of what legal archaeology unearths. Legal scholarship and argument normally focus on the appellate opinions in a leading case, neglecting to consult the trial record and the briefs submitted by the opposing parties. Consulting these materials for whatever light they can shed on the case should not be controversial. To show that the decision misstated the facts as presented at the trial in no way transgresses standard boundaries of legal argument. Elmer Palmer's sentence to the reformatory rather than to a term of life in state prison is an impeccably documented fact even from a strictly legalistic point of view.

Appellate courts, though, function chiefly as judges of law rather than of fact, and it is in that realm that the findings of legal archaeology pose the most awkward questions. Charles Barzun observed in 2013 that "despite the fact that efforts to historicize court precedents fill volumes of law reviews, neither courts nor legal scholars have devoted any serious attention to asking whether, and if so when, a past court's actual motivation might properly bear on the precedential status of its decision." One basis for answering "no," he continued, was that "such an argument hardly seems to be a *legal* argument at all," for as matters are usually understood, the decision ought to stand or fall on the justification that the majority opinion provides for it.[39] And yet, he pointed out, not only have advocates in cases before the Supreme Court offered such arguments, but justices themselves have also advanced them in their opinions.[40] The majority in *Mitchell v. Helms* (2000), a case involving the extent of permissible government aid to religious schools, rejected a standard stated in earlier decisions as having its roots in "a period . . . that the Court should regret" and "a shameful pedigree that we do not hesitate to disavow": specifically, anti-Catholic bias widespread in the nineteenth- and twentieth-century United States and infecting the earlier court.[41] In *Seminole Tribe of Florida v. Florida* (1996), a dissenting opinion signed by three justices invoked several works of legal history to suggest that *Hans v. Louisiana*—an 1890 decision denying the right of citizens of a state to sue that state in federal court without its consent—had been a doctrinal aberration inconsistent with the text and the earlier history of the Eleventh Amendment to the Constitution and prompted by political rather than legal factors.[42] And although the majority opinion in that case, which depended heavily on *Hans* as a precedent, objected strongly to such a use of history as improperly introducing extralegal considerations, all but one of the justices in the *Seminole Tribe* majority agreed with the opinion in *Mitchell* four years later that used history in an essentially similar way.[43]

Reviewing the possible reasons for resisting an attempt to "impeach" (or, more mildly, to "impugn") a past decision's authority as precedent, Barzun nonetheless concluded that it should not in principle be considered illegitimate. Much of the unease that such attempts elicit, he noted, may reflect a fear that if successful they would erode the prestige of the law and through it the rule of law itself. "Even if lawyers and judges might recognize that previous decisions are less authoritative for having been based on 'extralegal' considerations, to state as much explicitly would be to undermine the Court's legitimacy in the eyes of the public."[44] Acknowledging the force of the objection, he countered that the court's prestige might on the whole be enhanced by a willingness to acknowledge and to redress past violations of its own norms of judging.[45] Paul Lombardo's investigation of *Buck v. Bell*, in which the United States Supreme Court in 1927 upheld a Virginia statute for the compelled sterilization of the "feeble-minded," furnishes good legal grounds to justify discarding a highly dubious precedent that has never been clearly repudiated. Among other things, his archival research showed, it was a demonstrably though clandestinely collusive case argued energetically by the one side and lackadaisically by the other to win a favorable verdict for the statute.[46] Repudiating its decision would do the court's moral authority nothing but good.

Open-minded historical research, moreover, is not always destructive. It can help to dispel as well as create doubts about a decision's validity with respect to the law of its time. That the Chicago anarchists convicted of murder in the Haymarket bombings of 1886 were condemned for their political views and not on the evidence in the trial, and that the Illinois and United States supreme courts upheld the convictions on the same illegitimate grounds rather than on sound legal ones, has been generally accepted for many decades. It has recently been challenged by a historian who for the first time has examined the entire courtroom record and the wider background of the event rather than rely, as previous writers had done, on a heavily and tendentiously abbreviated trial transcript published soon after the verdict by its critics.[47]

There is no question of rejecting the traditional internal analysis of legal scholarship in order to replace it with an assumed priority of external factors. Both approaches merit attention for whatever light they can shed on a case. The former will often, and even usually, be the more rewarding. Neither need inquiry in external historical sources be undertaken for all or even many important decisions, only those cases where there is some need for further light or some cause for suspicion. Precisely what flags *Riggs* as problematic and strongly invites legal-archaeological inquiry is that its reasoning and its result run so contrary to internally accepted doctrine in the era it was decided. That discrepancy calls for explanation, and the discovery that the circumstances of the case were indeed such as might have tempted judges to bend or even ignore the law sounds an alarm. It should, at least, prompt another and closer look at what the judges in *Riggs* did, and it suggests that a later court that relies too heavily on such a decision, one that stands out for its oddity, may be building on insecure ground. American judges of the greatest eminence have offered similar warnings: Marshall when he cautioned against relying on rules derived from "cases of considerable irritation," Holmes against precedents affected by "some accident of immediate overwhelming interest."[48] Similarly, those who are using such a decision, as many have used *Riggs*, for less official purposes, to understand the nature of law and the character of legal decision, should be careful about the conclusions they draw from it. Nor, indeed, should they rely too heavily on any single past decision without some help from legal archaeology: by consulting research on the case, or, if none exists, doing it themselves to ensure that it conceals no buried skeletons.

The broader objection, felt even if not articulated, seems to be that the rule of law would be threatened if the presence of such extralegal factors in some decisions were acknowledged. But what threatens the rule of law is their presence and not the honest recognition that they are sometimes present. Apparently, what legal archaeology really menaces is the determination to see no evil, the comforting but untenable faith that all legal decisions are made on objective legal grounds. As an ideal, it is a worthy one, and it is sometimes transgressed in practice. How often, how significantly, and how objectionably it is transgressed, legal archaeology is essential to clarify. If violations of the ideal are indeed undesirable, the best way to prevent them is surely not to close one's eyes or look the other way when they occur.

Becoming Right or Wrong

If one question about a past case is how the decision squared with the accepted legal doctrines of the time, another is whether and how those doctrines have themselves changed under the influence of extralegal factors. Here again, legal scholarship as traditionally practiced and limited is in some ways a barrier rather than a help to understanding.

A pioneering work of both legal archaeology and case biography addressed this question, among others: Richard Danzig's study, published in 1975, of the leading English contract case of *Hadley v. Baxendale* (1854).[49] That case involved a claim for damages by the owners of a Gloucester flour mill against Pickford and Co., a transportation concern. An engine shaft having broken, the mill lay idle while the damaged part was being shipped to a firm in Greenwich that was to fashion an identical replacement. Because Pickford ended up sending the shaft by canal and not, more rapidly, by rail, the substitute did not arrive until five days later than it had assured the Hadleys that it would, resulting in lost profits for the mill, which its owners claimed as damages from Pickford's proprietor, Joseph Baxendale. Though the jury awarded damages, on appeal the verdict was overturned on a decision limiting liability to losses either "arising naturally" from a breach of contract or that both parties understood would be likely to arise from it. The doctrine, which had very few antecedents in English law, rapidly became authority for a new rule that became a staple of contract law, and of contracts courses in law schools as well.

But the way such a case is taught, Danzig continued, illustrates a serious limitation of the case-centered method in legal scholarship. As he wrote, "cases are normally treated like doctrinal fruits on a conceptual tree"; they are analyzed and differentiated from each other according to the content and the seeming cogency of their reasoning, "but all are quite erroneously treated as though they blossomed at the same time, and for the same harvest." In fact, he continued, cases "arise in different settings," and if one ignores the circumstances of their origin, one cannot "comprehend the processes of doctrinal innovation, growth, and decay." [50] A leading case, he emphasized, becomes a leading case. It is made and not born one, and it may become one for reasons that the law reports themselves—emphasizing its philosophical cogency and harmony with the supposed existing bedrock principles and doctrines of the law—will often fall far short of explaining.

On Danzig's analysis, *Hadley* and its rapid acceptance as authoritative reflected the legal needs of an industrializing economy. The decision adapted previously existing law as it did to limit and control the scope of damages that actors might have feared in the course of their normal operations, and thereby offered business greater security and assurance to proceed and to expand. At the same time, Danzig proposed, the rule has features distinctly of its earlier time that may now make it less suitable to these purposes, because of changes in the economy and in its institutional framework. It was laid down when businesses had less access to the range of tools for limiting liability, such as incorporation or contractual disclaimers, that they now have and that make the rule less essential for their protection. It also appeared before the onset of both highly fragmented and subcontracted and high-volume business operations made its stipulation of a clear understanding between the parties an increasingly unrealistic one. Danzig observed further that the rule suited the needs of the mid-nineteenth-century English judicial system, when an explosive growth in the number of possible cases threatened to overwhelm the courts' ability to hear and review them. It diminished the volume of litigation and appeals by making the outcomes much more predictable. It appealed, as well, to judges by withdrawing what they might have considered a dangerously wide discretion for juries to award damages as they saw fit.

Danzig offered his study as what he called "a counterpoise to the tendency to regard some rules of law as 'fixed stars' in our legal system."[51] *Hadley* was a novelty when announced, quickly became a leading case, and over time has seen its status and its usefulness gradually diminish. *Riggs* offers a contrasting trajectory through the legal skies, but one similarly inconsistent with the *fixed stars* model of leading cases, though the term perfectly captures the way it is usually regarded. It existed on the books for a long time before it became the leading case and legal landmark that it is today. Because nothing in the text of the decision has changed, the reasons for its changing status can lie only in changes in the eyes through which it is read. At one level, the history of its reception by lawyers and legal scholars is, like *Hadley*'s, that of evolution in legal doctrine. It is also, more fundamentally, the history of some broader extra-doctrinal reasons for that evolution that must be sought outside the texts of appellate opinions.

On anyone familiar with the American jurisprudential climate of the late nineteenth century, *Riggs* should have had the effect of tomato sauce in a film set in ancient Rome or a wristwatch in a Western. But their usual ahistorical modes of argument leave lawyers with a weak sense of anachronism, of what does not ring true for an earlier period. *Riggs* was an anomaly at the time it was handed down, as witness its chilly reception by other courts of the era and its rapid abandonment by New York in *Ellerson*. Subsequent American law happened to develop in certain directions that made what was jurisprudentially preposterous in 1889 the common sense of later generations. Seeing things according to their own assumptions, readers of *Riggs* from Hart and Sacks onward have noticed nothing odd about it. The principles that had prevailed earlier and had discouraged the courts of other states from following New York have lost much of the power and authority that they then possessed.

Foremost among them is the plain-meaning rule in statutory interpretation. Its demise was announced starkly in the 1940 decision of the
United States Supreme Court in *American Trucking Associations, Inc. v.
United States.*[52] The majority opinion let it be known that henceforth, even
when a statute's language was unambiguous and led to no absurd results,
the court would not exclude other sources that might help it in understanding how it ought best and most reasonably to be interpreted. Such
sources might include its legislative history, or what was said and written
about it on its course to passage; the overall policy evidently aimed at by
the act; and the provisions of other and related statutes. The court laid
down its new policy only by the narrow margin of five to four, but the
way it divided made it clear what was to be expected henceforth. The five
justices in the majority were the five newest members of the Court, none
of whom had served on it for as long as three years; the four dissenters
were the four senior justices. The change in the court's personnel, itself the
result of wider changes in national politics, signaled a shift toward more
creative statutory interpretation in the future. And indeed, subsequent
decades saw the clear-meaning rule dwindle into the assertion that what
earlier generations would have regarded as the commanding force of an
unambiguous text was merely one of the factors that judges interpreting
a statute ought always to take into account. More recently, advocates of
an approach most often called *textualism* have campaigned for the rule's
revival. They have achieved no more than scattered and partial successes.
The consensus in the rule's favor that did so much to make *Riggs* unacceptable in the late nineteenth and early twentieth centuries no longer
exists, because perceptions of the proper scope of judicial interpretation
are not what they were. A reader formed by contemporary assumptions
does not react to the case as most judges did at that time.

The taboo on overt *judicial legislation* cited by so many of the earlier
judges repudiating *Riggs* has met the same fate. Indeed, the conscious del-
egation of, in effect, lawmaking power by the legislature to administrative
agencies and to the courts has proceeded so far that the principle that
Marshall stated authoritatively in *Wiltberger* carries today far less weight.
Much the same holds true of another canon he made central to that
decision. In a book on the history of statutory interpretation in American law, William D. Popkin wrote: "The importance of the rule of lenity
canon has clearly declined during the twentieth century," and though still
often cited, it rarely controls a decision.[53] Popkin suggested two reasons

for the rule's decline. The widespread use of penal sanctions such as fines to regulate economic activity may have diminished the stigma that once attached to them and that the rule sought to spare respectable citizens from incurring. And vocal public concern about crime has made a canon of interpretation that seems to weigh the scales of justice in favor of the accused, rather than in favor of protecting society, an unpopular one. The latter concern has eroded another obstacle that many courts saw to accepting the doctrine in *Riggs*. Forfeitures, by an ingenious use of legal fictions adapted to the goal of fighting crime, have become quite commonplace in American law, without being struck down as violations of the language in the federal and most state constitutions that once appeared an insuperable bar to them.[54]

Several other developments that might have worked against *Riggs* have, for one reason or another, not done so. To take one example, subsequent decisions have not notably expanded the scope of the absurdity rationale for judicial intervention—but neither have most modern readers seen it as the principal ground for Judge Earl's opinion. To take another, it was long accepted without serious question that courts were effectively free to make new law applying ex post facto by their rulings, as legislatures are not. In 1964, however, in the case of *Bouie v. City of Columbia*, the United States Supreme Court held that a judicial interpretation of a statute as making certain conduct criminal violated the Constitution's guarantee of due process of law if the interpretation was one that the defendants could not reasonably have expected: if it constituted, in Justice William Brennan's words, "an unforeseeable and retroactive judicial expansion of narrow and precise statutory language."[55] Whether the same applies to an interpretation that, instead of making particular actions criminal, increased the punishment for them, in ways likewise not previously announced or implied, the court did not say. Several federal circuit courts of appeals in subsequent cases have held that it does.[56] Their reasoning could be taken to invalidate the way the New York Court of Appeals treated narrow and precise statutory language in *Riggs*. And yet it has not been so taken, for most readers have accepted the 1889 decision as Earl framed it, as regulating the process of inheritance, rather than as inflicting an added punishment, the way most late nineteenth- and early twentieth-century judges saw it.

The decision and the reasoning in *Bouie* itself, moreover, may have owed much to the specifics of the case, and the rule it announced is one that the Supreme Court has applied only narrowly and infrequently in subsequent cases. Several black civil rights protestors had seated them-selves at a drugstore lunch counter that was generally understood to be for whites only, but that no signs explicitly announced as such. They were arrested for remaining at the counter after the management had twice asked them to leave, and the South Carolina courts held them guilty of criminal trespass. The state's highest court sustained the verdict by ruling, with no apparent support in its previous line of decisions, that the statute, which defined criminal trespass as the act of entering upon someone else's property after having been given notice not to do so, included also the act of entering without such notice and then refusing to leave when asked. The United States Supreme Court approached the matter with con-siderable sympathy for the petitioners, which may have led it to bend established law in the area back in their favor. The court's reasoning was persuasive on its own terms, and yet broke with its tradition of restraint in dealing with the interpretation of the law by state courts, a step it quite possibly would not have taken in a less charged case and has often declined to take subsequently.

Finally, and at the most general level, the expansive use of judicial powers to reach desirable outcomes, in the way exemplified by the Court of Appeals, and defended by Hart and Sacks, is today so well accepted, among the general public as much as within the field of law, as to make *Riggs* look like a run-of-the-mill decision and the dissent to seem the odd-ity. The American legal historian Lawrence Friedman noted the growth during the twentieth century of a "general expectation of justice," the belief that where a wrong occurs in society a legal remedy must also exist.[57] Courts met the heightened demand for remedial decisions by willingly increasing the supply, thereby increasing their own powers. Judicial activ-ism was first deplored over the course of the twentieth century by the left and then by the right. By the beginning of the twenty-first century, it had become their common property.[58] And if one had to choose a single formula to state what *Riggs* stands for, it would be an active role for judges in making and altering law.

No case has been more influential in American legal thought since the mid-twentieth century than the Supreme Court's *Brown v. Board of Education* decision of 1954 striking down racially separate systems of pub-lic schools. Hardly anyone questions the decision's rightness. The prestige in the profession and the public alike that *Brown* has now achieved bestows a like prestige on any decision whose patent justice similarly seems to make the ability of the courts to justify it on established doctrinal grounds a matter of lesser concern. It has never been clear just how constitutional law as understood by the mainstream of the profession in 1954 supported the result that the court reached. But that, instead of discrediting the result, has done much to discredit the demand that patently just results be so supported. "In this respect," as one legal scholar commented in 2001, "*Brown* represented a sea change in attitudes about the proper role of the judiciary."[59] Though it has been seriously questioned how pathbreaking and how important was the court's leadership in school desegregation and civil rights more generally, what has mattered has been the belief that it was both. The immediate result of *Riggs*, Elmer Palmer's disinheritance, though far less socially consequential, is no less obviously just. So it now seems far from posing any kind of puzzle, as it did to commentators before 1921, or from requiring explanation from any circumstances outside of the mere facts of the case stated in the majority opinion. What now seem to call for explanation are Judge Gray's dissent and, when they are noticed, the preponderance of other state court opinions rejecting *Riggs*. To ascribe them to an archaic and simplistic formalism today is the obvious answer. But that answer drastically oversimplifies a more complex history, and it imposes on the past the assumptions of the present as if they were valid for all times. *Riggs* looks today like a fixed star that should always have looked like one, but it has not, in much the same way that the name Elmer, which in the 1860s suggested glamor, dash, and bravery, holds far different connotations now, though its spelling and pronunciation have not changed one bit since then.

Appellate-court opinions can thus escape from their creators' control, for the words they used under one set of circumstances can take on new meaning and importance under another. If we accept Robertson's interpretation of *Johnson v. M'Intosh*, that leading case, one that has had an immense subsequent influence, became a leading case entirely against the intentions of its author, Chief Justice Marshall. "I believe that the Court viewed *Johnson* as a relatively insignificant decision when rendered," Robertson wrote, "and that the case achieved landmark status as a result of political circumstances unrelated to its origin."[60] For its part, when *Riggs* became a leading case in discussions of the nature of law itself, it was for qualities that were not at all admired at the time it was made, and ones that, if my interpretation is correct, had little to do with the actual reasons motivating the judges. The New York Court of Appeals asserted what it did in 1889 in order to meet an immediate emergency. It issued, to adopt a famous figure of speech used by a Supreme Court justice in 1944 to express his dismay at the decisions his colleagues were producing, "a restricted railroad ticket, good for this day and train only."[61] Its later status as a model decision, and one to be taken at face value, would have astonished its contemporaries and probably even its authors.

"Legal theories," in the words of a modern scholar, "gain authority by explaining why good cases are good and bad cases are bad."[62] Their goodness or badness stem from how well their results live up to a present-day consensus about what is just and acceptable. *Brown* in the early twenty-first century is the ultimate *good* or canonical case, one that a theory, if it is to gain acceptance, cannot hold to have been incorrectly decided. Conversely, a case enters the *anticanon* of universally reprobated decisions—*Dred Scott*, *Plessy*, and the like[63]—less because the reasoning of the court that handed it down is demonstrably faulty by some timeless standard than because its result comes to seem so wrong as to impeach the train of arguments by which it was supported.

To maintain the fiction of a fixed set of permanent and fundamental legal principles, a popular modern expedient is to describe an anticanonical case as having been "wrong the day it was decided."[64] It can thus be repudiated as a governing precedent without the authority of precedent itself being put in question. But it is quite rare for any case to be decided against the law as understood at the time, even if one does not define law itself as what the courts at any one time apply. It makes far more sense to say that cases can become wrong because the law does change. The formula "wrong the day it was decided" is another expression of the mythology of fixed stars in the legal sky, ones that mark out the abidingly correct way for judges to plot their course toward the right outcome.

Such a mythology is useful, as the constitutional scholar J. M. Balkin has observed, for two reasons. It allows courts to maintain the fiction that they are following legitimate precedent when in fact they are overruling earlier decisions, and it allows the public to feel it is honoring and keeping faith with the true traditions of the past instead of rejecting them. Yet it is more consistent with the record of the past, Balkin continued, "that the correctness of legal reasoning can and does change with changing times." Arguments that were at one time, as he put it, "off-the-wall"—that is, "inconsistent with the key assumptions of the legal culture"—can become so orthodox that to disagree with them is as futile and as irresponsible as it once was to advance them.[65]

If the formula "wrong the day it was decided" is ever validly applicable, it is to a narrow and unusual set of cases: those that in their own time went against the prevailing rules and standards as laid down and followed by almost all of the other courts. *Riggs*, in this sense, genuinely was wrong the day it was decided. Yet it is not wrong today. If a legal archaeology of its origins tends to impugn its credibility as a precedent, a case biography locates the reasons it gained its present authority. Wider developments have made it right, and not merely right in itself, but a standard against which to measure the rightness of other decisions. Those who treat it as authoritatively supporting certain views of how the law works or should work are in fact using those views to identify it as a case deserving to be treated as authoritative: as witness the many contrary decisions from the same era, equally on the books, that could be cited instead. It is particular beliefs that give it its standing and not its standing that justifies those beliefs. Yet legal writing characteristically employs a timeless present tense, speaking of arguments that "are" valid or not, even when referring to ones enunciated long ago, obscuring the way in which their validity can and does change.

Conclusion

This discussion does not pretend to exhaust the contributions that historical inquiry can make to legal inquiry. It examines only those that are exemplified by a legal archaeology and case biography of *Riggs*. These, taken together, exemplify a claim made by the twentieth-century English philosopher-historian R. G. Collingwood. In his *Autobiography*, published in 1939, Collingwood proposed that:

> . . . you cannot find out what a man means by simply studying his spoken or written statements, even though he has spoken or written with perfect command of language and perfectly truthful intention. In order to find out his meaning you must also know what the question was (a question in his own mind, and presumed by him to be in yours) to which the thing he has said or written was meant as an answer. . . . If you cannot tell what a proposition means unless you know what question it was meant to answer, you will mistake its meaning if you make a mistake about that question.[66]

The standard method of legal analysis closely resembles the one that Collingwood warned against. Its user expects to achieve an accurate understanding of past decisions by studying their written text. The method often, even usually works well. If it did not, it would long since have been dropped. But there are cases where it does not work well. Here, legal archaeology and case biography may provide a different and better understanding, by correcting errors about what question or questions the court, or the litigants, were actually posing and answering.

Those who have taken the majority opinion in *Riggs* at face value have treated it as an attempt to answer the question: Does the law implicitly prohibit murderers from inheriting from their victims? Or, more generally, Does the law incorporate the principle that people shall not profit from their wrongs? The majority appears instead to have been addressing a different question, and one with no clear implications for any other cases, that question being: In what way could Elmer Palmer, having been so lightly punished and so quickly released, be denied his inheritance in a way that did not too blatantly conflict with accepted legal doctrine?

Similarly, the American Supreme Court in deciding *Hillmon* was evidently thinking less about the abstract principles of hearsay evidence and its admissibility than about foiling what it took to be an attempt to defraud. In deciding *Johnson v. M'Intosh*, it had its eye on other kinds of issues entirely from the ones the case ostensibly addressed or those it would eventually be applied to. The English judges in *Rylands v. Fletcher* were not merely, or perhaps even mostly, trying to state a general rule about liability for accidents; the matter foremost in their minds was deciding how to treat a particular hazard, that of floods from broken reservoirs, that had lately caused much damage and loss of life—as it was for those American judges who faced the same challenge in the shadow of the Johnstown disaster in 1889. As Lombardo's research into *Buck v. Bell* makes clear, the arguments offered by the plaintiff's lawyer were not inept attempts to answer the question: What is the best legal case I can make against the Virginia sterilization statute? They were, rather, a skillful response to a different and concealed question: How do I appear to fulfill my professional duty to my client while minimizing her chances of winning? *Kirksey v. Kirksey* and *United States v. Kirby* have long been misunderstood because they do not state, and their readers did not correctly divine, the actual questions at issue between the parties. Danzig's analysis of *Hadley* makes it clearer to what pressing contemporary challenges the court's answer given in 1854 was thought to respond, why the response was so widely thought to be a good one, and why it may not be so now. The reasons why the answer given in *Riggs* was legally wrong at the time are not easy to see today.

Judicial decisions always address, at least nominally, both general and specific questions. A good decision is one that satisfies the demands of both and keeps them in harmony. Similarly, "ideas have two aspects. They are abstract and universal, and it is in virtue of this character that they allow communication to bridge such gulfs as person to person, epoch to epoch and culture to culture. But the thinking of any idea is also a specific occurrence which has a spatio-temporal location and a social context."[67] The writer of these words suggested that the latter aspect is what interests historians and the former what interests philosophers—and also, he might have added, lawyers and legal scholars. The general question and its answer, and the justification given for that answer, abstracted from the specifics of time and place, are their usual concern. Their normal assumptions include "treating cases decided in different eras as if all had been decided yesterday."[68]

There is nothing illegitimate or invalid in such a focus. But it makes it all the harder for those accustomed to it to recognize those instances where the pressures of the here-and-now so predominated that their role cannot realistically be ignored. When Frederick Schauer asked whether cases make bad law, he called attention to the way that the specific question may overwhelm the general one in the judges' minds. How much of a problem—how large and how frequent—are the distortions that result is a question that legal archaeology and case biography can contribute much toward answering. *Riggs* appears at least to offer another and previously unrecognized example of the phenomenon. And historical research can equally well cast light on the converse process, little apparent in *Riggs* but salient in some other cases. Inadequate justice may be done to the particular litigants by judges eager for one reason or another to lay down a general rule for reasons they find compelling at a particular point in time.[69] Such a failure is even less likely than the other kind to be apparent from the opinions themselves, and even more is it likely to require external research to be identified.

Epilogue

Second Lives

Once decided by the New York Court of Appeals, *Riggs* took on a life of its own, which this book has attempted to trace up to the present. Strictly speaking, what happened in their own later lives to the actors in the case is irrelevant to that story. But curiosity on that point is natural and legitimate, and to leave it unaddressed would leave the reader unsatisfied.

First, the lawyers. Lewis C. Lang, who prosecuted the murder charge against Elmer, remained district attorney of St. Lawrence County through the end of 1887. In that year, the county Republican convention defeated him for renomination for a third three-year term, less from any dissatisfaction with the job he had done than on the principle, widely accepted at the time, of rotating public offices among the different aspirants and the different parts of the county claiming their turn.[1] In the fall of 1891, he was elected as a Republican to the State Assembly, in which he had served two terms already in the 1870s. During his year in office, he worked energetically but unsuccessfully for a constitutional amendment ending the payment of their salaries to judges retired by the age limit for the rest of their elected terms, the provision Gray had interpreted in *Bockes v. Wemple* (it would be scrapped by a state constitutional convention in 1894).[2] Any further legislative career Lang might have had was cut short when a new and highly partisan state apportionment in 1892 deprived St. Lawrence County of two of its three assembly seats. Returning to private life and law practice, he died soon after, in December 1893, at the age of fifty-one.[3]

Elmer's chief defense counsel, Pardon C. Williams, enjoyed a longer and more distinguished career. Winning election in the fall of 1883 on the Republican ticket to the New York State Supreme Court, he served as a trial and appellate judge for almost thirty years, retiring in 1912 and dying in 1925 at the age of eighty-two. A highly regarded jurist, Williams sat in a number of famous cases both upstate and downstate. In 1894, a Democratic governor (a fellow native of Jefferson County) chose him to preside in a politically sensitive murder trial growing out of the election-day shooting of a Republican poll watcher in the city of Troy.[4] A verdict that Williams directed in a suit for damages in 1888 had the distinction of being reversed in a United States Supreme Court decision (*Lawton v. Steele*, 1894) that has remained a leading case in defining the scope of the government's police power, though his reasoning won the approval of three dissenters, including the chief justice and the senior associate justice.[5]

Carlton E. Sanford, who launched the legal challenge to Elmer's inheritance, largely gave up the practice of law in his later years to devote himself to business (including the presidency of a Potsdam bank he founded), civic affairs, and writing.[6] He published a history of the town of Hopkinton's early years that made no mention of the Palmer family, and an almost equally unrevealing volume of reminiscences; it lauded Leslie W. Russell for winning the appeal that established the *Riggs* doctrine as the law of New York, but said nothing about the case's local origins.[7] Russell himself maintained a dual residence and law practice in St. Lawrence County and New York City. In 1890, he was elected to Congress from the district in which the former lay, but he resigned a year into his term to accept a seat on the state Supreme Court, serving on it for a little more than a decade. He left the court to resume his legal practice shortly before his death in 1903.[8] In 1898, Russell delivered an address to the New York State Bar Association reviewing *Riggs v. Palmer* and asserting, rather fancifully, that the failure of the Court of Appeals to rule as it did would have been tantamount to legalizing murder, something he must have believed the other states that by then had rejected *Riggs* had done.[9]

Judge Potter was reelected to another fourteen-year term on the Supreme Court in 1885, not without some controversy regarding the eight years of compensation that, under the ruling in *Bockes*, he could look forward to collecting from the state after he reached the age of mandatory retirement.[10] He spent his last several years on the bench serving on a temporary second division of the Court of Appeals created to help it deal with its acute backlog of work.[11] Potter's Victorian Gothic residence in Whitehall, on the southeastern fringes of the Adirondacks, was placed in the 1970s on the National Register of Historic Places and in recent years has been open as a house museum.[12] Dying at his home in Canton in February, 1888, William H. Sawyer lived to see the conclusions of his referee's report upheld by the New York Supreme Court but not to see them repudiated by the Court of Appeals.[13] Judson S. Landon, who wrote the opinion sustaining Sawyer's findings in *Preston v. Palmer*, continued to serve on the Supreme Court until he reached the statutory retirement age of seventy in 1903. Like Potter, he spent the last few years of his judicial tenure seconded to the Court of Appeals, as one of three Supreme Court justices appointed by Governor Theodore Roosevelt under a new provision of the state's constitution to help work through yet another accumulation of undecided cases.[14]

The only member of the *Riggs* court still sitting by the time of Landon's special appointment was John Clinton Gray, who had written the dissent agreeing with his *Preston* opinion. Rufus W. Peckham Jr. had moved to Washington at the end of 1895 to take up the Supreme Court appointment tendered him by his old Albany friend President Grover Cleveland. Serving on that bench until his death in 1909, he vigorously upheld the doctrines he had expressed in *Budd* and *Walsh*.[15] Francis M. Finch, nearing the age limit, retired voluntarily to Ithaca at the end of his Court of Appeals term in 1895.[16] Robert Earl served briefly as chief judge by interim appointment following the death of William C. Ruger. Retiring in 1894 on reaching the age limit, he devoted the rest of his life (he died in 1902) to civic affairs and research on the history of his native Herkimer County.[17] Charles Andrews, the author of the *Ellerson* decision, was nominated for chief judge by both parties and elected in the fall of 1892, serving until he, too, reached the age of seventy, in 1897, and then enjoying two decades of retirement as Syracuse's leading citizen.[18] (His son William S. Andrews would also serve on the Court of Appeals and be best remembered for a dissent from Cardozo's single most celebrated opinion, in the torts case of *Palsgraf v. Long Island Railroad Co.*, 1928.[19]) George F. Danforth, his service on the court ended by the age limit a few months after *Riggs*, pursued a further decade of successful law practice in Rochester. Active to the end, at the age of eighty he collapsed and died shortly after completing an argument for a motion he was making before the trial term of the New York Supreme Court.[20] His fellow dissenter, Gray, reelected by a whisker after an unusual partisan contest in 1902, retired from the Court of Appeals on reaching the age limit at the end of 1913 and died in 1915.[21] Barely more than a month thus separated the departure from the Court of *Riggs*'s earliest critic from the arrival, initially by gubernatorial appointment, of Benjamin Cardozo, who did more than anyone to enhance the reputation of the decision that Gray had so eloquently deplored.

Among the actors in Hopkinton and Stockholm, Martin Doud spent his last years living in the households of his grown children, dying in his late eighties in 1906.[22] Myrtie Doud, the perhaps reluctant object of Elmer Palmer's infatuation, married a Stockholm farm laborer named Frank Simmons. The marriage apparently produced no surviving children, and Myrtie died in 1929 at the age of sixty-eight.[23] Willis Doud, who had briefly shared Elmer's position as lead suspect in the Palmer murder and then testified effectively against him, worked as a farmer and mill hand. Outliving anyone else involved in the trial, he died in 1963 at the age of ninety-six, himself survived by his wife of sixty-eight years and their one son.[24] Lorette Riggs's husband Philo gradually retired from farming, first taking a job as a postal deliveryman and then operating a store that he purchased in the Stockholm hamlet of Winthrop, to which the couple moved. Lorette died in 1909; Philo later remarried and lived until 1920.[25] The families of Francis's two daughters, the Vermont and New York branches of the family, might normally have drifted apart. They formed a new connection in 1896, however, when Cecelia Preston's elder surviving daughter, Etta May, married Lorette and Philo's son Leslie, her first cousin, and moved to New York's North Country. Cecelia's son Arthur lived with them for a time before also marrying and settling in St. Lawrence County.[26] I have not been able to trace what happened to Eliza Palmer in later years. But by the end of the century, her eldest son, Hendrick Bresee, and his family owned and occupied the Palmer house and farm in Hopkinton. The fact suggests that some amicable arrangement had been made among the parties involved to transfer title to Eliza and her heirs.[27]

Moving to Canada when he did, Elmer swam against a particularly strong net tide of migration flowing in the opposite direction in the 1880s, drawn by the opportunities that a more dynamic American economy afforded.[28] As mentioned already, he married shortly after his arrival, and he became a naturalized citizen sometime in 1889. The official record of his marriage correctly states his full name, his date and place of birth, and the names of his parents. By the time the Court of Appeals decided *Riggs*, he was a father. He worked in his early years in Canada as both the iron molder the Elmira Reformatory had trained him to be and the farm laborer he had been in Hopkinton. In time, he secured modestly more remunerative employment and eventually a small house of his own in London. His paper trail through Canadian documentary sources suggests an exemplary family man. The 1891 and 1901 censuses both found him living with his wife, Mary (née Gray), who was nine years his senior, their children (three sons and a daughter by 1901), and Mary's widowed mother, who apparently made her home with them until her death in 1908. By 1921, the children had all left, but Elmer and Mary were providing a home for three grandsons of theirs, aged eleven, nine, and five, whose mother, their only daughter, Ida, had died in 1916.[29] The irony was probably not lost on Elmer—though he most likely would not have shared it with anyone else—that around the time he reached the age when Francis died, he too was living with a sixteen-year-old grandson, though unlike Francis, he apparently suffered no ill effects from doing so (the grandson, it is true, was not his expectant heir). When Elmer died on July 11, 1934, aged sixty-nine, it was from complications following a prostate operation and after several weeks in the hospital. His remains rest under a granite tombstone in Woodland Cemetery in London, Ontario, inscribed "Beloved Husband of Mary Palmer." Mary, who outlived him by nine years, is buried with him. So are their eldest son, Edgar, Edgar's wife, Ona, Elmer and Mary's daughter, Ida Maude Palmer [Wood], and their youngest son, Percy Douglas Palmer, who died in his late teens in a drowning accident in August 1914.[30] There are questions that cannot be answered from the information that has survived: just how much of his past Elmer shared with his Canadian family, for example, or whether he stayed in contact with his Nichols relatives, or whether he ever knew of the fame that his case acquired in his own lifetime, particularly following Cardozo's discussion of it in 1921.

Elmer and Mary's second son, Russell Ethelbert Palmer (1892–1973), added some modest renown to the Palmer name, and in a more creditable way than his father had. Earning an MD from the University of Toronto, he reversed Elmer's trajectory by emigrating to the United States in the early 1920s. He soon after became the resident physician on Beaver Island in Lake Michigan. He tended for three decades to the year-round medical needs of the island's five-hundred-odd residents, aided by his wife, Suzanne (née Brisbois), a trained nurse. Newspapers acclaimed him as a hero. In later years, he and Suzanne, who died in 1961, enjoyed a well-earned retirement from the rigors of the island winters, first to a medical practice on the Michigan mainland and then to the sunshine of Florida.[31]

Russell and Suzanne had no children, but Elmer had and apparently still has direct descendants through Edgar and Ida, presumably unaware of the events that planted their family tree in new soil.

The impression of Elmer one gets from the events of 1882 is distinctly at odds with that produced by what we know of his later life. The talented novelist Harold Frederic served his literary apprenticeship as a young journalist in the small cities and countryside of upstate New York around the time of the Palmer murder trial. A knowledgeable character in Frederic's first book (published in 1887), a county district attorney, observed that the typical rural murderer "plans the thing in cold blood, and goes at it systematically, with nerves like steel. And so long as he isn't found out, he never dreams of remorse. He has no more moral perspective than a woodchuck. But when detection does come, it knocks him all in a heap. He blubbers, and tries to lay it on somebody else, and altogether acts like a cur. . . ."[32] The words make an uncomfortably accurate description of Elmer Palmer's behavior in 1882. They offer little that is recognizable as his later self, so far as it can be reconstructed. Whether the credit belongs to Zebulon Brockway and the Elmira Reformatory, or to the salutary shock of his brush with the law, or merely to the process of aging and maturation, he had apparently changed a good deal since 1882—just as the case that made him famous has changed a good deal since 1889, and has had as surprising a later life as its central actor did.

Notes

Introduction

1. In addition to works cited later, articles devoted primarily to the decision include Anthony D'Amato, "Elmer's Rule: A Jurisprudential Dialogue," *Iowa Law Review* 60, no. 5 (June 1975): 1129–46; Linda J. Maki and Alan M. Kaplan, "Elmer's Case Revisited: The Problem of the Murdering Heir," *Ohio State Law Journal* 41, no. 4 (1980): 905–71; Rodger Beehler, "Legal Positivism, Social Rules, and *Riggs v. Palmer*," *Law and Philosophy* 9, no. 3 (August 1990): 285–93; and Damiano Canale and Giovanni Tuzek, "Legislative Intentions and Counterfactuals: Or, What We Can Still Learn from Dworkin's Critique of Legal Positivism," *Ratio Juris* 36, no. 1 (March 2023): 26–47.

2. Philip Milton, review of David Lyons, *Ethics and the Rule of Law*, *The Modern Law Review* 49, no. 2 (March 1986): 279.

3. Henry E. Smith, "Fusion of Law and Confusion of Equity," in Dennis Klimchuk, Irit Samet, and Henry E. Smith, eds., *Philosophical Foundations of the Law of Equity* (Oxford: Oxford University Press, 2020), 227.

4. Curtis Nyquist, "Single-Case Research and the History of American Legal Thought," *New England Law Review* 45, no. 3 (Spring 2011): 592 (characterizing the rationale for the prevailing approach, not endorsing it).

5. John V. Orth, *The Judicial Power of the United States: The Eleventh Amendment in American History* (New York: Oxford University Press, 1987), 158.

6. Debora L. Threedy, "Legal Archaeology: Excavating Cases, Reconstructing Context," *Tulane Law Review* 86, no. 4 (March 2006): 1202.

7. A. W. Brian Simpson, *Leading Cases in the Common Law* (Oxford: Clarendon Press, 1995), 11, 12.

8. Caroline Jones and Jonathan Montgomery, "Competing Narratives in a Case Biography: A Tale of Two Citadels," *Journal of Law and Society* 47, no. 3 (September 2020): 416. They cited recent studies of sacred religious books framed as their biographies and similarly premised on the idea "that the printed text is neither the beginning nor the end of the life in question" (414).

9. Each of the nine legal archaeologies in Simpson's *Leading Cases in the Common Law*, for example, covered the background and origins of the legal dispute that reached the court more thoroughly than it did the subsequent histories of the doctrine that emerged. Many of the chapters in two series of edited volumes, the Foundation Press's American "Law Stories" and Hart Publishing's "Landmark Cases" in the UK, combine legal archaeology and case biography in varying proportions, as do many of the monographs in the University Press of Kansas's "Landmark Law Cases and American Society" series. Model studies blending the two emphases include Anthony Jon Waters, "The Property in the Promise: A Study of the Third Party Property Rule," *Harvard Law Review* 98, no. 6 (April 1985): 1109–210; Matthew Chapman, *The Snail and the Ginger Beer: The Singular Case of Donoghue v. Stevenson* (London: Wildy, Simmonds & Hill, 2010); and Joseph D. Kearney and Thomas W. Merrill, *Lakefront: Public Trust and Private Rights in Chicago* (Ithaca, NY: Cornell University Press, 2021).

10. Simpson, *Leading Cases*, vii.

11. *New York Trust Co. v. Eisner*, 256 U.S. 345, 349 (1921) (Holmes, J.).

Chapter 1

1. Émile Durkheim, *Le suicide: étude de sociologie* (Paris: Félix Alcan, 1897), 403.

2. Roger Lane, "Crime and Criminal Statistics in Nineteenth-Century Massachusetts," *Journal of Social History* 2, no. 2 (Winter 1968): 156–63; Roger Lane, *Violent Death in the City: Suicide, Accident, and Murder in Nineteenth-Century Philadelphia* (Cambridge, MA: Harvard University Press 1980); Eric H. Monkkonen, *Murder in New York City* (Berkeley: University of California Press, 2001).

3. Waldo L. Cook, "Murders in Massachusetts," *Publications of the American Statistical Association* 3, no. 23 (September 1893): 357–78. See also "Murders in the Small Towns," *Springfield [MA] Daily Republican*, February 20, 1893, 4.

4. James W. Darlington, "Peopling the Post-Revolutionary New York Frontier," *New York History* 74, no. 4 (October 1993): 359.

5. Manuscript schedules, United States Census of 1850, Town of Lincoln, Addison County, Vermont.

6. Manuscript schedules, United States Census of 1860, Town of Hopkinton, St. Lawrence County, New York; manuscript schedules, United States Census of Agriculture of 1860, Town of Hopkinton, St. Lawrence County, New York; *New Topographical Atlas of St. Lawrence County, New York, from Actual Surveys by S. N. and D. G. Beers and Assistants* (Philadelphia: Stone & Stewart, 1865), 41.

7. Lewis D. Stilwell, *Migration from Vermont* (Montpelier, VT: Vermont Historical Society, 1948).

8. Manuscript schedules, United States Censuses of Agriculture, 1860 and 1870, Town of Hopkinton, St. Lawrence County, New York.

9. "Byron Palmer (abt. 1842–1874)," "Cecelia G (Palmer) Preston 1843–1886," and "Loretta A (Palmer) Riggs 1848–1909," at https://wikitree (pages maintained by Wallace Philips, a direct descendant of the Palmer family; visited August 11, 2021).

10. Elmer's birth date and cause of Byron's death: Entry # 1249, Elmira Reformatory Biographical Registers, Series BO141, Box 2, New York State Archives (hereafter Elmira Reformatory Biographical Registers).

11. Last will and testament of Francis B. Palmer, August 13, 1880, in Appeal Book, *Riggs v. Palmer*, New York Court of Appeals (hereafter Appeal Book), 10–11.

12. "The Palmer Poisoning Case," *St. Lawrence Herald* [Potsdam, NY], May 6, 1882, 3; cause of Susan's death, Elmira Reformatory Biographical Registers.

13. "On Trial for His Life," *Courier and Freeman* [Potsdam, NY], November 8, 1882, 1.

14. Articles of agreement, March 16, 1882, in Appeal Book (signed by Eliza with "her X mark"), 8–10. The enumerator for the Canadian Census of 1871 checked the box in Eliza's entry identifying her as a person "au-dessus de 20 ans incapable d'écrire" (she was then 35: Census of Canada, 1871, Province of Québec, District 95 (Ottawa East), Parish of Ste.-Angélique.

15. Manuscript schedules, 1880 Federal Census of Defective, Dependent, and Delinquent Classes, Town of Stockholm, St. Lawrence County, New York; Federal Censuses of Population and Agriculture for 1880, Town of Stockholm.

16. The 1880 Census of Population recorded Martin Peck, the eighteen-year-old son of a local family, living with the Palmers and apparently playing the same role as Willis later did (his occupation was listed as "servant").

17. Where no specific sources are cited for quotations, this and the preceding paragraph and the following account of the murder and the trial are based on accounts of the testimony in the latter in five contemporary St. Lawrence County newspapers: one daily, *The Ogdensburg* [NY] *Journal*, November 1–8, 10–11, and 13, 1882, and four weeklies, the *Commercial Advertiser* (Canton, NY), November 2, 9, and 16, 1882; the *Courier and Freeman* (Potsdam, NY), November 1, 8, and 15, 1882; the *Ogdensburg* [NY] *Advance and St. Lawrence Weekly Democrat*, November 2, 9, and 16, 1882; and the *St. Lawrence Plaindealer* (Canton, NY), November 8 and 15, 1882. To guard against journalistic invention, I have only accepted statements made in more than one of these independently written accounts.

18. "The Palmer Murder Trial," *St. Lawrence Plaindealer*, November 8, 1882, 2.

19. Cheri L. Farnsworth, *Murder & Mayhem in St. Lawrence County* (Charleston, SC: The History Press, 2010), 41–48.

20. "For His Life," *Watertown* [NY] *Re-Union*, September 9, 1880, 1; "Manslaughter," ibid., September 16, 1880, 1, 3.

21. "Merrihew Murder Trial," *Lowville* [NY] *Times*, August 26, 1880, 3; "Merrihew Murder Trial," ibid., September 2, 1880, 3.

22. "On Trial for His Life," *Courier and Freeman*, November 8, 1882, 2.

23. "Death by Poison," *Ogdensburg Journal*, May 1, 1882, 3.

24. "On Trial for His Life," *Courier and Freeman*, November 8, 1882, 2.

25. "Canton," *Ogdensburg Advance and St. Lawrence Weekly Democrat*, May 18, 1882, 3.

26. "St. Lawrence County," *Ogdensburg Advance and St. Lawrence Weekly Democrat*, May 11, 1882, 3.

27. "Court Proceedings," *Ogdensburg Journal*, May 22, 1882, 3.

28. "Home Matters," *Commercial Advertiser*, June 1, 1882, 3; "Court Proceedings," *Ogdensburg Journal*, September 2, 1882, 3.

29. "The Merrihew Trial," *Journal and Republican* [Lowville, NY], September 1, 1880, 3.

30. "The Stokes Murder Trial," *Watertown* [NY] *Daily Times*, June 13, 1882, 3.

31. "The Trial of Elmer Palmer," *Commercial Advertiser*, November 9, 1882, 3.

32. "The Palmer Murder Trial," *St. Lawrence Plaindealer*, November 8, 1882, 2.

33. "The Palmer Murder Trial," *Ogdensburg Journal*, November 3, 1882, 3.

34. Charles E. Rosenberg, *The Trial of the Assassin Guiteau* (Chicago: University of Chicago Press, 1968), 170, 187.

35. "The Palmer Murder Trial," *Ogdensburg Journal*, November 2, 1882, 3.

36. "The Palmer Murder Trial," *St. Lawrence Plaindealer*, November 15, 1882, 1. The reporter acknowledged having made some corrections to the prose of both letters.

37. "On Trial for His Life," *Courier and Freeman*, November 8, 1882, 2.

38. "On Trial for His Life," *Courier and Freeman*, November 8, 1882, 2.

39. Elmira Reformatory Biographical Registers.

40. "The Trial of Elmer Palmer," *Commercial Advertiser*, November 9, 1882, 3.

41. "The Trial of Elmer Palmer," *Commercial Advertiser*, November 9, 1882, 3.

42. *New York Laws 1869*, ch. 678, §1. The provision was carried over into the comprehensive Code of Criminal Procedure adopted shortly before the Palmer trial: *The Code of Criminal Procedure of the State of New York: Being Chapter 442 of the Laws of Eighteen Hundred and Eight-One* (Albany: Weed, Parsons and Company, 1881), §393.

43. What Lang said was no less objectionable for being realistic. As one contemporary analyst put it, laws allowing a criminal defendant to testify "in reality force him to take the stand to protect himself from the inference of guilt which is almost certain to be drawn against him," even though the jury had been explicitly cautioned otherwise: William L. Maury, "Validity of Statutes Authorizing the Accused to Testify," *American Law Review* 14 (November 1880): 762–3. In 1884, a unanimous New York Court of Appeals upheld the constitutionality of such laws against the claim that they amounted to compelled self-incrimination. It observed that "while it may be difficult for a jury in many cases to exclude the inference of guilt from an omission of a defendant to be sworn, we cannot say that it may not be done. The statute assumes it to be possible, and we cannot

say, judicially, that such assumption is unfounded": *People v. Courtney*, 94 N.Y. 490, 494 (1884) (Andrews, J.).

44. The key New York cases defining the unacceptability of such statements at the time of the Palmer trial were *People v. McMahon*, 15 N.Y. 384 (1857), *Teachout v. People*, 41 N.Y. 7 (1869), and *People v. Phillips*, 42 N.Y. 200 (1870), stating rules formalized in the 1881 Code of Criminal Procedure, §395, and applied in *People v. Mondon*, 103 N.Y. 211 (1886) (overturning a conviction for first-degree murder), and *People v. McCallam*, 103 N.Y. 587 (1886). On American law around the time of the Palmer trial, see Simon Greenleaf, *A Treatise on the Law of Evidence*, 14th edition, vol. 1 (Boston: Little, Brown and Company, 1883), 281–3. A decade and a half later, the United States Supreme Court, citing a heavy preponderance of state-court decisions, would take a similarly hard line against the introduction of any testimony possibly tainted by threats or promises, in this case ones much more nebulous and less objectionable than what Lang reportedly said to or in front of Elmer: *Bram v. United States*, 168 U.S. 532 (1897). Indeed, the three justices in the minority argued, not that a statement elicited by threats was admissible, but that nothing that could be called a threat had been made, and also that the defense attorney had not objected on that point at the trial: ibid., at 569–73 (Brewer, J., dissenting).

45. "Murder in the Second Degree," *Ogdensburg Advance and St. Lawrence Weekly Democrat*, November 16, 1882, 3.

46. Unlike the statement Lang had obtained from Elmer by a menacing misstatement of the law, the trick played on Elmer and Willis did not, by contemporary standards, fatally taint the evidence it elicited: e.g., *Commonwealth v. Hanlon*, 3 Brewst. [Philadelphia] 416, 498–500 (1870). For a later overview of cases reaching similar conclusions, see John Henry Wigmore, *A Treatise on the System of Evidence in Trials at Common Law*, vol. 1 (Boston: Little, Brown and Company, 1904), 957.

47. "The Palmer Murder Trial," *Ogdensburg Journal*, November 10, 1882, 2.

48. "Murder in the Second Degree," *Ogdensburg Advance and St. Lawrence Weekly Democrat*, November 16, 1882, 3.

49. "Murder in the Second Degree," *Ogdensburg Advance and St. Lawrence Weekly Democrat*, November 16, 1882, 3.

50. "The Palmer Murder Trial," *Ogdensburg Journal*, November 11, 1882, 2.

51. *The Penal Code of the State of New York, in Force May 1, 1882*, §22.

52. *People v. Eastwood*, 14 N.Y. 562, 565 (1856).

53. *Roberts v. People*, 19 Mich. 401, 416–7, 419 (1870); *Willis v. Commonwealth*, 73 Va. 929, 936 (1879); *State v. Robinson*, 20 W. Va. 713, 741 (1882); *Cline v. State*, 43 Ohio St. 332, 334 (1885). See also Francis Wharton, *A Treatise on Criminal Law*, 8th edition, vol. 1 (Philadelphia: Kay and Brother, 1880), 80–81, 84.

54. Wharton, *A Treatise on Criminal Law*, 376.

55. Quoted in *Public Papers of Theodore Roosevelt, Governor, 1899* (Albany, NY: Brandow Printing Company, 1899), 237. Juries frequently used second-degree murder convictions in this way, and the courts permitted them to do so: Wharton, *A Treatise on Criminal Law*, 389.

56. "The Murder Trial Ended," *Watertown* [NY] *Daily Times*, July 3, 1882, 3; "The Stokes Decision," ibid., September 2, 1882, 3; "Circuit Court," *Watertown* [NY] *Re-Union*, June 20, 1883, 7.

57. "The Palmer Murder Trial," *Ogdensburg Journal*, November 13, 1882, 2.

58. *The Statute Law of the State of New York: Comprising the Revised Statutes and All Other Laws of General Interest, in Force January 1, 1881*, vol. 1 (New York: George S. Diossy, 1881), 297.

59. *The Penal Code of the State of New York, in Force May 1, 1882*, §192.

60. *The Statute Law of the State of New York*, 296.

61. L. Crampton, "The Palmer Jury," *Ogdensburg Journal*, November 15, 1882, 3. The earlier report appeared in "The Palmer Murder Trial," *Ogdensburg Journal*, November 13, 1882, 2.

62. "Arguments in Capital Cases," *New York Times*, May 2, 1882, 1.

63. *Public Papers of Alonzo B. Cornell, Governor of the State of New York, 1882* (Albany, NY: E. H. Bender, 1882), 76–77.

64. *Albany Law Journal* 25 (May 13, 1882): 363.

65. "Comparative Statement, Showing the Number of Applications for Executive Clemency, Also the Number Granted in Each Year, from 1865 to December 31, 1894, Inclusive," in *Public Papers of Roswell P. Flower, Governor, 1894* (Albany, NY: The Argus Company, 1895), 766; Carolyn Strange, *Discretionary Justice: Pardon and Parole in New York from the Revolution to the Depression* (New York: New York University Press, 2016).

66. "The Palmer Murder Trial," *St. Lawrence Plaindealer*, November 15, 1882, 3.

67. Less than a decade earlier, the US Supreme Court Justice Ward Hunt, sitting on circuit duty, had incurred a storm of criticism when he directed the jury to find the suffragist Susan B. Anthony guilty of illegally voting in a federal election. Even opponents of women's enfranchisement joined in condemning his action, and in 1882 another decision in the federal courts explicitly acknowledged its erroneousness: N. E. H. Hull, *The Woman Who Dared to Vote: The Trial of Susan B. Anthony* (Lawrence, KS: University Press of Kansas, 2012), 179–85.

68. In American law, a conviction for manslaughter automatically acquitted the defendant of murder, whether in the first or the second degree: Francis Wharton, *A Treatise on the Law of Homicide in the United States* (Philadelphia: Kay and Brother, 1875), 169, 676–7, 690. Consequently, Judge Potter's refusal to accept the first verdict ran afoul of the 1881 New York Code of Criminal Procedure, §447, which stated, following earlier precedent, that: "When there is a verdict of conviction, in which it appears to the court that the jury may have mistaken the law, the court may explain the reason for that opinion, and direct

the jury to reconsider their verdict; and if, after the reconsideration, they return the same verdict, it must be entered. But where there is a verdict of acquittal, the court cannot require the jury to reconsider it."

69. The New York courts, like those of the American states generally, fully recognized an implied acquittal whenever a defendant was convicted only of some counts in an indictment or of a lesser degree of the crime charged. For some statements from this period, see *Dowling v. People*, 84 N.Y. 478, 483 (1881) and *People v. Cignarale*, 110 N.Y. 23, 30–31 (1888).

70. Alexander W. Pisciotta, *Benevolent Repression: Social Control and the American Reformatory-Prison Movement* (New York: New York University Press, 1994), ch. 1.

71. *New York Laws, 1870*, ch. 427, §9, 10; *New York Laws, 1877*, ch. 173, §2, 5, 8, 10.

72. "The Palmer Murder Trial," *Ogdensburg Journal*, November 13, 1882, 2.

73. "End of the Palmer Murder Trial," *Courier and Freeman*, November 15, 1882, 2.

74. In 1876, a jury in neighboring Jefferson County found Frank Ruttan, an orphan and a local native, at an age a year or so less than Elmer's, guilty of second- rather than first-degree murder in the brutal killing of a ten-year-old girl, though the seeming leniency of the verdict caused some controversy: "The Trial of Frank Ruttan," *Watertown Daily Times*, May 6, 1876, 3; "Frank Ruttan" and "The Trial and Verdict," *The Re-Union* [Watertown, NY], May 11, 1876, 4. According to Victor L. Streib, *Death Penalty for Juveniles* (Bloomington, IN: Indiana University Press, 1987), 83, Edward A. Deacons was executed in upstate New York in 1888 for a first-degree murder committed at the age of sixteen, but the source he cited (a newspaper account from another state) erred; the evidence given at the trial indicates that Deacons was fully eighteen at the time of the crime: *People v. Edward A. Deacons*, Record and Briefs, New York Court of Appeals, 1888, 461.

75. "The Palmer Murder Trial." *St. Lawrence Plaindealer*, November 15, 3.

76. "The Palmer Murder Trial," *Gouverneur* [NY] *Free Press*, November 14, 1882, 2"; The Palmer Murder Trial," *Ogdensburg Journal*, November 13, 1882, 2; "End of the Palmer Trial," *Norwood* [NY] *News*, November 14, 1882, 2; "Elmira State Reformatory," *Courier and Freeman*, November 15, 1882, 2.

77. Wharton, *A Treatise on the Law of Homicide*, 676–7, 690.

78. "City and Vicinity," *Watertown* [NY] *Daily Times*, November 27, 1882, 3.

79. Elmira Reformatory Biographical Registers; comparisons calculated from statistics in annual reports, Board of Managers of the State Reformatory at Elmira, *New York Senate Documents*, 1882–1887.

80. Pisciotta, *Benevolent Repression*; Nicole Hahn Rafter, *Creating Born Criminals* (Urbana, IL: University of Illinois Press, 1997).

81. Calculated from statistics in annual reports, Board of Managers of the State Reformatory at Elmira, *New York Senate Documents*, 1882–1887.

82. Rafter, *Creating Born Criminals*, 108n32.

83. Pisciotta, *Benevolent Repression*, 17–27; Rafter, *Creating Born Criminals*, 96–100.

84. Elmira Reformatory Biographical Registers.

85. Untitled story, *St. Lawrence Herald* [Potsdam, NY], October 31, 1884, 3.

86. Calculated from statistics in annual reports, Board of Managers of the State Reformatory at Elmira, *New York Senate Documents*, 1882–1887.

87. Elmira Reformatory Biographical Registers.

88. Elmira Reformatory Biographical Registers.

89. "No Inheritance by Murder," *The Sun* [New York, NY] November 8, 1889, 5.

90. Leslie W. Russell, "The Spirit v. the Letter of the Statute: Can Legislation Legalize Murder?," *Proceedings of the New York State Bar Association, Held at the City of Albany, January 18–19, 1898* (Albany: James B. Lyon, 1898), 98.

91. Registrations of Marriages, Archives of Ontario, County of Middlesex, City of London, 1887, MS 932. The manuscript schedules of the 1911 and 1921 Canadian censuses identified Elmer's year of immigration to Canada as 1886 and 1887, respectively: Manuscript schedules, Census of Canada, 1911, Province of Ontario, District 96, Sub-District 5, City of London; Manuscript schedules, Census of Canada, 1921, Province of Ontario, District 101, Sub-District 41, City of London. Both recorded his year of naturalization as 1889.

92. *The London City and Middlesex County Directory 1887* (London, ON: R. L. Polk & Co., 1887), 221.

93. Surrogate's Court, St. Lawrence County, Probate of the last will and testament of Francis B. Palmer, late of Hopkinton, deceased, November 20, 1882.

Chapter 2

1. "Death of C. E. Sanford," *Potsdam* [NY] *Herald-Recorder*, September 10, 1915, 1.

2. In the Supreme Court: *Cecelia G. M. Preston et al., Appellants, v. Elmer E. Palmer et al.*, Respondents, in Appeal Book, 4–15.

3. Appeal Book, 16.

4. "St. Lawrence Circuit of Supreme Court," *Courier and Freeman* [Potsdam, NY], April 16, 1874, 3.

5. "Judge William H. Sawyer," *Ogdensburg* [NY] *Journal*, February 20, 1888, 2; "Judge Sawyer Dead," *Commercial Advertiser* [Canton, NY], February 22, 1888, 3; "The Democratic State Convention," ibid., October 3, 1878, 2; "The Trial of Oscar Brown," *Ogdensburg Journal*, August 16, 1872, 2.

6. "Paine's Miserly Ways," *New York Times*, December 15, 1886, 10; "Arguing for Paine's Heirs," ibid., April 27, 1887, 8; "Judge Hilton's Denials," ibid., June 5, 1887, 9.

7. *Ninety-Third Annual Report of the Regents of the University of the State of New York* (Albany, NY: Weed, Parsons and Company, 1880), 152.

8. Appeal Book, 17–19.

9. Appeal Book, 19–20.

10. "Legal Intelligence," *The Argus* [Albany, NY], November 25, 1886, 6.

11. *New York Mutual Life Insurance Co. v. Armstrong*, 117 U.S. 591, 600 (1886), 600 (Field, J.).

12. *Preston v. Palmer*, 49 N.Y. Sup. Ct. 388, 390, 391 (1887) (Landon, J.).

13. "Cecelia G (Palmer) Preston 1843–1886," at https://wikitree (visited August 11, 2021).

14. Appeal Book, 50–61.

15. "Legal Intelligence," *The Argus*, June 22, 1889, 6.

16. Brief for Appellants, *Riggs v. Palmer*, Court of Appeals (quotations from 4, 8, 18, 19).

17. Brief for Respondents, *Riggs v. Palmer*, Court of Appeals, 5. As if anticipating the point, Russell and Sanford asked rhetorically: "And was it necessary for Francis B. Palmer, in order to prevent such a result, to say in his will, 'this bequest and devise to Elmer E. Palmer is on the condition that he does not murder me'?": *Brief for Appellants, 7.*

18. Brief for Respondents, Riggs v. Palmer, Court of Appeals, 9.

19. *Owens v. Owens*, 100 N.C. 240 (1888). Either unaware of this case, or having no reply to make to it, Russell and Sanford did not mention it in their brief for the appellants.

20. *Riggs v. Palmer*, 115 N.Y. 506 (1889).

21. *Riggs v. Palmer*, 115 N.Y. 506, 509, 510, 511 (1889) (Earl, J.).

22. Brian Leiter, "Explaining Theoretical Disagreement," *University of Chicago Law Review* 76, no. 3 (Summer 2009): 1233. A "shotgun" approach deploying mutually inconsistent arguments in the hope that one or another will be accepted, he observed, is a common one in advocates' briefs, but is one that judges' opinions are supposed to eschew.

23. *Riggs v. Palmer*, 115 N.Y. 506, 511, 512, 513 (1889) (Earl, J.).

24. *Riggs v. Palmer*, 115 N.Y. 506, 513 (1889) (Earl, J.).

25. *Riggs v. Palmer*, 115 N.Y. 506, 512, 514 (1889) (Earl, J.).

26. *Riggs v. Palmer*, 115 N.Y. 506, 514–5 (1889) (Earl, J.).

27. *Riggs v. Palmer*, 115 N.Y. 506, 519 (1889) (Gray, J., dissenting).

28. *Riggs v. Palmer*, 115 N.Y. 506, 515–6, 517 (1889) (Gray, J., dissenting).

29. *Riggs v. Palmer*, 115 N.Y. 506, 516–7 (1889) (Gray, J., dissenting).

30. *Riggs v. Palmer*, 115 N.Y. 506, 517 (1889) (Gray, J., dissenting).

31. *Riggs v. Palmer*, 115 N.Y. 506, 519–20 (1889) (Gray, J., dissenting).

32. "Which Courts Exert the Greatest Influence on Our Jurisprudence? An Examination of Cases Cited," *West Publishing Company Docket* 1 (1910): 233; Lawrence M. Friedman, Robert A. Kagan, Bliss Cartwright, and Stanton Wheeler,

"State Supreme Courts: A Century of Style and Citation," *Stanford Law Review* 33, no. 5 (May 1981): 804–5.

33. "On Trial for Life," *Daily Nebraska State Journal* [Lincoln, NE], June 17, 1887, 8; "Shellenberger's Lynching," ibid., July 26, 1887, 1; "District Court," *Daily State Democrat* [Lincoln, NE], November 19, 1887, 3.

34. "A Question of Law," *Daily Nebraska State Journal*, March 25, 1888, 1.

35. *Shellenberger v. Ransom*, 31 Neb. 61 (1891).

36. *Shellenberger v. Ransom*, 41 Neb. 631 (1894).

37. Kerry Seagrave, *Parricide in the United States, 1840–1899* (Jefferson, NC: McFarland & Company, 2009), 81–83.

38. "A Murderer's Money," *Hamilton* [OH] *Evening Journal*, October 24, 1892, 3.

39. *Deem v. Risinger*, 27 Ohio Dec. 492 (Preble Common Pleas 1892).

40. *Deem v. Millikin*, 53 Ohio St. 668 (1895), affirming *Deem v. Millikin*, 6 Ohio C. C. 357 (1892).

41. "Foul Murder," *Juniata Sentinel & Republican* [Mifflintown, PA], December 20, 1893, 2; "Court Proceedings," ibid., May 2, 1894, 3; "Hung," ibid., June 13, 1894, 2.

42. "An Echo of the Carpenter Murder," *Juniata Sentinel & Republican*, February 27, 1895, 3.

43. In re Carpenter's Estate, 170 Pa. St. 203 (1895). One justice dissented in part from the decision.

44. "Sarah Kuhn Convicted," *Des Moines* [IA] *Sunday Leader*, December 23, 1900, 1; *State v. Kuhn*, 117 Iowa 216 (1902).

45. *Kuhn v. Kuhn*, 125 Iowa 449 (1904).

46. "A Terrible Tragedy," *The Western Advocate* [Mankato, KS], March 20, 1903, 4; "Murder in the First Degree," ibid., July 17, 1903, 4.

47. Untitled editorial, *The Western Advocate*, August 28, 1903, 4; "Husband Killed Her," *Topeka* [KS] *Daily Capital*, August 12, 1903, 1; "Difficult Question for Court," ibid., October 6, 1905, 7; *McAllister v. Fair*, 72 Kan. 533 (1906).

48. *De Graffenreid v. Iowa Land and Trust Company*, 20 Okla. 687 (1908), affirmed in *Holloway v. McCormick*, 41 Okla. 1 (1913); *Hill v. Noland*, 149 S.W. 288 (Tex. Civ. App. 1912).

49. *Wellner v. Eckstein*, 105 Minn. 444 (1908).

50. *Gollnik v. Mengel*, 112 Minn. 349 (1910).

51. Beth Lane, *Lies Told under Oath: The Puzzling Story of the Pfanschmidt Murders and the Surviving Son—Victim or Villain?* (Bloomington, IN: iUniverse, 2012).

52. *Wall v. Pfanschmidt*, 265 Ill. 180 (1914).

53. *Perry v. Strawbridge*, 209 Mo. 621 (1908).

54. *Box v. Lanier*, 112 Tenn. 393, 407 (1904) (Beard, C. J.).

55. *Eversole v. Eversole*, 169 Ky. 793 (1916); *Hagan v. Cone*, 21 Ga. App. 416 (1917); *Johnston v. Metropolitan Life Insurance Co.*, 85 W. Va. 70 (1919).

56. In re the Estate of Mertes, 181 Ind. 478 (1914).

57. *Murchison v. Murchison*, 203 S.W. 423 (Tex. App. 1918).

58. *Harrison v. Moncravie*, 264 F. 776 (1920).

59. *Owens v. Owens*, 100 N.C. 240, 242 (1888) (Smith, C. J.).

60. R. Michael Wilson, "Rough on Rats and Siblings," *Wild West*, August 2015, 51–56.

61. "Murderer's Heirs Profit by His Crime," *San Francisco* [CA] *Call*, November 26, 1898, 3.

62. "Belew May Appeal," *San Francisco Call*, December 15, 1898, 2.

63. Lewis J. Swindle, *The Story and Trials of Adolph Julius Weber* (Victoria, BC: Trafford Publishing, 2002).

64. "Weber Injunction Suit Is Dismissed," *San Francisco Call*, November 30, 1905, 2; "Weber's Fortune for Defense," ibid., October 9, 1906, 1.

65. "New England News Items: Eastern Massachusetts," *Springfield* [MA] *Weekly Republican*, January 2, 1869, 2. On the details of the case, see Charles G. Davis, ed., *Report of the Trial of Samuel M. Andrews, Indicted for the Murder of Cornelius Holmes, before the Supreme Judicial Court of Massachusetts, December 11, 1868* (New York: Hurd and Houghton, 1869), and Leslie Margolin, "Madman in the Closet: 'Homosexual Panic' in Nineteenth Century New England," *Journal of Homosexuality* 68, no. 9 (2021): 1471–88.

66. "Their First Move," *Wheeling* [WV] *Register*, August 29, 1890, 1; "Murdered Women's Money," *Wheeling* [WV] *Daily Intelligencer*, February 3, 1892, 5.

67. "Dale's Property Right," *Indianapolis* [IN] *Journal*, September 8, 1900, 5; "Thrown Out of Court," ibid., October 3, 1900, 1; "The Dale Case Dismissed," *Indianapolis* [IN] *News*, December 20, 1900, 9.

68. *Hedger v. State*, 144 Wis. 279 (1911); Arthur E. Lenicheck, "Homicide as Affecting the Devolution of Property," *Marquette Law Review* 4, no. 1 (1919): 42; "Jessie Root Jenkins' Property," *Colorado Statesman* [Denver, CO], November 21, 1914, 2; "Woman's Property Goes to Mother of Man Who Slew Her," *Omaha* [NE] *Daily Bee*, January 11, 1915, 1.

69. *Civil Code of the State of Louisiana; Preceded by the Treaty of Cession with France, the Constitution of the United States and of the State* (n.p. 1825), Article 960, §1, p. 243; Article 1547, §1, p. 355.

70. Alan G. Gauthreaux and D. G. Hippensteel, *Dark Bayou: Infamous Louisiana Homicides* (Jefferson, NC: McFarland & Company, 2016), 40–51.

71. "For the State," *Daily Picayune* [New Orleans, LA], June 30, 1886, 6.

72. Brief for Appellants, *Riggs v. Palmer*, Court of Appeals, 14.

73. *Laws and Resolutions of the State of North Carolina Passed by the General Assembly at Its Session of 1889*, Ch. 499.

74. *Tennessee Laws 1905*, ch. 11; *Kansas Laws 1907*, ch. 193; *Wyoming Laws 1915*, ch. 95; "No More Money for Murder in Wyoming," *Billings* [MT] *Gazette*, March 1, 1915, 6.

75. *Annotated Code of the State of Iowa, 1897*, §3386 (referred to in *Kuhn v. Kuhn*, 125 Iowa 449, 450–51, 453 [1904]); *Oregon Laws 1917*, ch. 270.

76. F. F. Thomas Jr., "Public Policy as Affecting Property Rights Accruing to a Party as a Result of Wrongful Acts," *California Law Review* 1, no. 5 (July 1913): 407–8.

77. Nebraska Laws 1913, ch. 162; Raymond M. Remick, *The Statutory Law of Decedents' Estates in Pennsylvania* (Philadelphia: Geo. T. Bisel Co., 1922), 157, 246.

78. Henry M. Hart Jr. and Albert M. Sacks, *The Legal Process: Basic Problems in the Making and Application of Law*, edited by William N. Eskridge Jr. and Philip P. Frickey (Westbury, NY: The Foundation Press, 1994), 98; Wade, "Acquisition of Property," 715n1. It is thus an exaggeration to say that "whenever state courts understood state law to let murderous heirs or beneficiaries receive property by will or intestate succession, state legislatures almost universally reacted by enacting a slayer statute": Caleb Nelson, *Statutory Interpretation* (New York: Foundation Press 2011), 25.

79. Remick, *Statutory Law*, 127, 157, 202, 246.

80. John W. Wade, "Acquisition of Property by Willfully Killing Another: A Statutory Solution," *Harvard Law Review* 49, no. 5 (March 1936): 715.

81. Wade, "Acquisition of Property," 724n37.

82. Anne-Marie Rhodes, "Consequences of Heirs' Misconduct: Moving from Rules to Discretion," *Ohio Northwestern University Law Review* 33, no. 3 (2007): 979–80.

Chapter 3

1. Karl Llewellyn, *The Bramble Bush* (Dobbs Ferry, NY: Oceana Publications, 1960), 158.

2. Grant Gilmore, *The Ages of American Law* (New Haven, CT: Yale University Press, 1977), 56.

3. The same can be said of the proto-realist Roscoe Pound's disparagement of "mechanical jurisprudence" as involving "a jurisprudence of conceptions": "Mechanical Jurisprudence," *Columbia Law Review* 8, no. 8 (December 1908): 605–23.

4. Karl Llewellyn, *The Common Law Tradition: Deciding Appeals* (Boston: Little, Brown, 1960). Similarly, H. L. A. Hart defined formalism as a mindset that "both seeks to disguise and to minimize" the need for judges sometimes to make choices: *The Concept of Law* (Oxford: Clarendon Press, 1961), 129.

5. Thomas M. Cooley, *A Treatise on the Constitutional Limitations Which Rest upon the Legislative Power of the States of the American Union*, 2nd edition (Boston: Little, Brown, and Company, 1871), 60n.

6. *United States v. Fisher*, 6 U.S. 358, 399 (1805) (Marshall, C. J.).

7. *Northern Securities v. United States*, 193 U.S. 197, 401 (1904) (Holmes, J., dissenting).

8. William S. Blatt, "The History of Statutory Interpretation: A Study in Form and Substance," *Cardozo Law Review* 6, no. 4 (Summer 1985): 799–845; William D. Popkin, *Statutes in Court: The History and Theory of Statutory Interpretation* (Durham, NC: Duke University Press, 1999), ch. 3. An American legal scholar writing in the early twentieth century referred to "the general repudiation of the doctrine of equitable interpretation or construction": W. H. Loyd, "The Equity of a Statute," *University of Pennsylvania Law Review* 58, no. 2 (1909): 76.

9. Theodore Sedgwick and John Norton Pomeroy, *A Treatise on the Rules Which Govern the Interpretation and Construction of Statutory and Constitutional Law*, 2nd edition (New York: Baker, Voorhis & Co., 1874), 194.

10. J. G. Sutherland, *Statutes and Statutory Construction* (Chicago: Callaghan and Company, 1891), 310.

11. *Shellenberger v. Ransom*, 41 Neb. 631, 642 (1894) (Ryan, C.); *McAllister v. Fair*, 72 Kan. 533, 536 (1906) (Johnston, C. J.).

12. *Deem v. Millikin*, 6 Ohio C.C. 357 (1892) (Shauck, J.).

13. *Owens v. Owens*, 100 N.C. 240, 242 (1888) (Smith, C. J.).

14. *Gollnik v. Mengel*, 112 Minn. 349, 351 (1910) (O'Brien, J.).

15. *Hill v. Noland*, 149 S.W. 288, 289 (Tex. Civ. App. 1912) (Levy, J.).

16. *McAllister v. Fair*, 72 Kan. 533, 535 (1906) (Johnston, C. J.).

17. *Shellenberger v. Ransom*, 41 Neb. 631, 644 (1894) (Ryan, C.).

18. *Deem v. Millikin*, 6 Ohio C.C. 357 (1892) (Shauck, J.).

19. *Kuhn v. Kuhn*, 125 Iowa 449, 453 (1904) (Sherwin, J.).

20. *Wall v. Pfanschmidt*, 265 Ill. 180, 190–1 (1914) (Carter, J.).

21. *Shellenberger v. Ransom*, 41 Neb. 631, 644 (1894) (Ryan, C.).

22. *Gollnik v. Mengel*, 112 Minn. 349, 351 (1910) (O'Brien, J.).

23. *Deem v. Millikin*, 6 Ohio C.C. 357 (1892) (Shauck, J.).

24. *McAllister v. Fair*, 72 Kan. 533, 536 (1906) (Johnston, C. J.).

25. "Murderer's Heirs Profit by His Crime," *San Francisco* [CA] *Call*, November 26, 1898, 3.

26. *United States v. Wiltberger*, 28 F. Cas. 727, 3 Wash. C. C. 515 (1819).

27. *United States v. Wiltberger*, 18 U.S. 76 (1820).

28. *United States v. Wiltberger*, 18 U.S, 76, 95–96, 105 (1820) (Marshall, C. J.).

29. *Riggs v. Palmer*, 115 N.Y. 506, 517 (1889) (Gray, J., dissenting).

30. "Murderer's Heirs Profit by His Crime," *San Francisco Call*, November 26, 1898, 3.

31. During the decade following *Riggs*, the courts of New York and the United States upheld the application of a state statute withholding a physician's license from anyone convicted of a felony to such a conviction occurring prior to the act's passage. They justified it not as an added punishment, in which case it would have fallen afoul of the ex post facto prohibition, but solely as involving a proper qualification for the right to practice medicine. Even so, at no stage of the litigation was the plaintiff's argument rejected unanimously (the United States Supreme Court divided 6–3 on the issue): *People v. Hawker*, 43 N.Y.S. 516 (1897); *People v. Hawker*, 152 N.Y. 234 (1897); *Hawker v. People of New York*, 170 U.S. 189 (1898).

32. *Kuhn v. Kuhn*, 125 Iowa 449, 451 (1904) (Sherwin, J.)

33. In re Estate of Emerson, 191 Iowa 900, 906 (1921) (De Graff, J.); *Harrison v. Moncravie*, 264 F. 776, 784 (1920) (Sanborn, J.).

34. *Blanks v. Jiggetts*, 192 Va. 337, 342 (1951) (Whittle, J.).

35. Wade, "Acquisition of Property," 750–1.

36. Sutherland, *Statutes and Statutory Construction*, 439–40.

37. K. J. Kesselring, "Felons' Effects and the Effects of Felony in Nineteenth-Century England," *Law and History Review* 28, no. 1 (February 2010): 111–39; Kim Lane Scheppele, "Facing Facts in Legal Interpretation," *Representations* no. 30 (Spring 1990): 50–53.

38. *The Penal Code of the State of New York: In Force May 31, 1882* (New York: Banks and Brothers, 1881), §710.

39. Joel Prentiss Bishop, *Commentaries on the Law of Criminal Procedure*, 2nd edition, vol. 1 (Boston: Little, Brown and Company, 1872), 55.

40. *Preston v. Palmer*, 49 N.Y. Sup. Ct. 388, 391 (1887) (Landon, J.).

41. *Wall v. Pfanschmidt*, 265 Ill. 180, 193 (1914) (Carter, J.).

42. *Holloway v. McCormick*, 41 Okla. 1, 7 (1913) (Galbraith, C. J.); *Johnston v. Metropolitan Life Insurance Company*, 85 W. Va. 70, 74 (1919) (Ritz., J.); "A Question of Law," *Daily Nebraska State Journal* [Lincoln, NE], March 25, 1888, 1.

43. In re Carpenter's Estate, 170 Pa. St. 203, 207–8 (1895) (Green, J.).

44. *Hamblin v. Marchant*, 103 Kan. 508 (1918); Wade, "Acquisition of Property," 721.

45. *Crumley v. Hall*, 202 Ga. 588, 591 (1947) (Atkinson, J.).

46. As noted by Caleb Nelson, *Statutory Interpretation* (New York: Foundation Press, 2011), 17.

47. *Deem v. Millikin*, 6 Ohio C.C. 357 (1892) (Shauck, J.).

48. *Riggs v. Palmer*, 115 N.Y. 506, 511 (1889) (Earl, J.).

49. *United States v. Wiltberger*, 18 U.S. 76, 91–93 (1820).

50. *United States v. Wiltberger*, 18 U.S. 76, 105 (1820) (Marshall, C. J.).

51. Veronica M. Dougherty, "Absurdity and the Limits of Literalism: Defining the Absurd Result Principle in Statutory Interpretation," *American University*

Law Review 44, no. 1 (October 1994): 127–66: John F. Manning, "The Absurdity Doctrine," *Harvard Law Review* 116, no. 8 (June 2005): 2387–486.

52. *United States v. Kirby*, 74 U.S. 482 (1868).

53. David Achtenberg, "With Malice towards Some: *United States v. Kirby*, Malicious Prosecution, and the Fourteenth Amendment," *Rutgers Law Journal* 26, no. 2 (Winter 1995): 273–342.

54. *Church of the Holy Trinity v. United States*, 143 U.S. 457 (1892).

55. Ernst Freund, "Interpretation of Statutes," *University of Pennsylvania Law Review* 65, no. 3 (January 1917): 223–24.

56. *Riggs v. Palmer*, 115 N.Y. 506, 513 (1889) (Earl, J.).

57. In re Carpenter's Estate, 170 Pa. St. 203, 208–209 (1895) (Green, J.).

58. *Kuhn v. Kuhn*, 125 Iowa 449, 453 (1904) (Sherwin, J.).

59. Brief for the Appellants, *Riggs v. Palmer*, Court of Appeals, 8; Herbert Broom, *A Selection of Legal Maxims, Classified and Illustrated* (Philadelphia: T. and J. W. Johnston, 1845), 205.

60. Broom, *A Selection*, 31, 40.

61. William J. Novak, *The People's Welfare: Law and Regulation in Nineteenth-Century America* (Chapel Hill, NC: University of North Carolina Press, 1996), traces some of this history, with an emphasis on the use and the decay of two maxims, *Salus populi suprema lex est* and *Sic utero tuo ut alienum non laedas*, in American law.

62. *Gollnik v. Mengel*, 112 Minn. 349, 351 (1910) (O'Brien, J.).

63. Ward E. Lattin, "Legal Maxims," *Georgetown Law Journal* 29, no. 1 (November 1937): 4, 10.

64. *Shellenberger v. Ransom*, 41 Neb. 631, 645–6 (1894) (Ryan, C.).

65. Ames, "Can a Murderer," 227, 229.

66. Roscoe Pound, "Spurious Interpretation," *Columbia Law Review* 7, no. 6 (June 1907): 379–86 (quotations from 382, 383).

67. Freund, "Interpretation of Statutes," 223.

68. James D. Livingston, *Arsenic and Clam Chowder: Murder in Gilded Age New York* (Albany, NY: State University of New York Press, 2010).

69. In re Fleming, 16 Misc. 442 (1896).

70. In re Fleming, 5 A.D. 190, 191, 193 (1896) (Barrett, J.).

71. Livingston, *Arsenic and Clam Chowder*.

72. Beth Lane, *Lies Told under Oath: The Puzzling Story of the Pfanschmidt Murders and the Surviving Son—Victim or Villain?* (Bloomington, IN: iUniverse, 2012).

73. "Literally Roasted to Death," *Daily Inter Ocean* [Chicago, IL], June 26, 1888, 8; "Criminal Court Matters," ibid., September 27, 1888, 7; "Zehn Jahre Zuchthaussstrafe," *Illinois Staats-Zeitung*, October 1, 1888, 8. Schreiner was pardoned by Governor Joseph W. Fifer in November, 1891: "Stadt Chicago: Begnadigt," ibid., November 30, 1891, 7.

74. "A Murderer Can Not Profit by the Death of His Victim," *Chicago Legal News* 22 (November 23, 1889): 96.

75. *Schreiner v. Catholic Order of Foresters*, 35 Ill. App. 381 (1890). The case, moreover, involved the law of contract, a common-law domain, not one governed by statute, as inheritance was in New York.

76. *Gollnik v. Mengel*, 112 Minn. 349, 351 (O'Brien, J.), 352 (Lewis, J., concurring) (1910).

77. Nicola Peart, "Reforming the Forfeiture Rule: Comparing New Zealand, England and Australia," *Common Law World Review* 31, no. 1 (2002): 1–34 (quotation from 1).

78. *Riggs v. Palmer*, 115 N.Y. 506, 519 (1889) (Gray, J., dissenting).

79. *Box v. Lanier*, 112 Tenn. 393, 425 (1904) (Wilkes, J., dissenting).

80. Peart, "Reforming the Forfeiture Rule," 15.

81. "A Question of Law," *Nebraska State Journal* [Lincoln, NE], March 25, 1888, 1.

82. Scheppele, "Facing Facts in Legal Interpretation," 49.

83. Ames, "Can a Murderer," 226.

84. Daniel A. Farber, "Courts, Statutes, and Public Policy: The Case of the Murderous Heir," *S.M.U. Law Review* 31, no. 1 (Winter 2000): 33.

85. Scheppele, "Facing Facts in Legal Interpretation."

86. *Bowles v. Habermann*, 95 N.Y. 246, 251 (1884) (Earl, J.).

87. *Preston v. Palmer*, 49 N.Y. Sup. Ct. 388, 391 (1887) (Landon, J.).

88. Most emphatically, William M. McGovern, Jr., "Homicide and Succession to Property," *Michigan Law Review* 68, no. 1 (November 1969): 65–67.

89. Wade, "Acquisition of Property," 717n9; the case was *Carter v. Montgomery*, 2 Tenn. Ch. R. 216 (1875).

90. *Shellenberger v. Ransom*, 31 Neb. 61, 62 (1891).

91. "State News," *Charlotte* [NC] *Home-Democrat*, December 24, 1886, 2.

Chapter 4

1. James Parker Hall, "The Selection, Tenure and Retirement of Judges," *Proceedings of the Ohio State Bar Association* 37 (1916): 142–51.

2. Peter Karsten, *Heart versus Head: Judge-Made Law in Nineteenth-Century America* (Chapel Hill, NC: University of North Carolina Press, 1997), 306–12.

3. "The Palmer Will Case," *Courier and Freeman* [Potsdam, NY], October 16, 1889, 2.

4. Bryan A. Garner, *Garner's Dictionary of Legal Usage*, 3rd edition (New York: Oxford University Press, 2011), 403.

5. *United States v. Wiltberger*, 18 U.S. 76, 96 (1820) (Marshall, C. J.).

6. *Northern Securities Co. v. United States*, 193 U.S. 197, 400–1 (1904) (Holmes, J., dissenting).

7. Frederick Schauer, "Do Cases Make Bad Law?," *University of Chicago Law Review* 73, no. 3 (Summer 2006): 883–918 (quotation from 903).

8. This discussion is based on Marianne Wesson, " 'Particular Intentions': The Hillmon Case and the Supreme Court," *Law and Literature* 18, no. 3 (Fall 2006): 343–402; and " 'Remarkable Stratagems and Conspiracies': How Unscrupulous Lawyers and Credulous Judges Created an Exception to the Hearsay Rule," *Fordham Law Review* 76, no. 3 (December 2007): 1675–1706. See also the same author's *A Death at Cripple Creek: The Case of the Cowboy, the Cigarmaker, and the Love Letter* (New York: NYU Press, 2013).

9. Wesson, "Remarkable Stratagems and Conspiracies," 1695.

10. Andrew J. Wistrich, Jeffrey J. Rachlinski, and Chris Guthrie, "Heart versus Head: Do Judges Follow the Law or Follow Their Feelings?," *Texas Law Review* 93, no. 4 (March 2015): 855–923.

11. "No Inheritance by Murder," *The Sun* [New York, NY], November 8, 1889, 5.

12. *Riggs v. Palmer*, 115 N.Y. 506, 519 (1889) (Gray, J., dissenting).

13. Brief for Appellants, *Riggs v. Palmer*, Court of Appeals, 19.

14. *Shellenberger v. Ransom* (1894), 634; *Deem v. Millikin* (1892), 358; In re Carpenter's Estate, 204; *McAllister v. Fair*, 533; *Wall v. Pfanschmidt*, 181; on the effective abolition of executions in Kansas, see Sara M. Benson, *The Prison of Democracy: Race, Leavenworth, and the Culture of Law* (Berkeley: University of California Press, 2019), 152n125.

15. *Owens v. Owens*, 241; *State v. Kuhn*, 117 Iowa 216 (1902); *De Graffenreid v. Iowa Land and Trust Company*, 690; *Wellner v. Eckstein*, 445; *Gollnik v. Mengel*, 349.

16. "May Continue the Patton Case," *Marshall* [TX] *Messenger*, October 18, 1912, 1; *General Accident, Fire & Life Assurance Corporation v. Stedman*, 153 S.W. 692 (Texas Civ. App.) (1912).

17. See the sources cited on these cases in Chapter 2.

18. "No Inheritance by Murder," *The Sun* [New York, NY], November 8, 1889, 5.

19. *Riggs v. Palmer*, 115 N.Y. 506, 525 (1889) (Gray, J., dissenting).

20. "Mrs. Kuhn Must Serve," *Ottumwa* [IA] *Tri-Weekly Courier*, April 12, 1904, 2.

21. *Ellerson v. Westcott*, 95 N.Y. Sup. Ct. 389, 391 (1895) (Merwin, J.).

22. *Ellerson v. Westcott*, 148 N.Y. 149, 154 (1896) (Andrews, C. J.).

23. On the basic doctrines and procedures of equity in the nineteenth-century United States, see Gary L. McDowell, *Equity and the Constitution: The Supreme Court, Equitable Relief, and Public Policy* (Chicago: University of Chicago Press, 1982), chapters 1 and 2; Peter Charles Hoffer, *The Law's Conscience: Equitable Constitutionalism in America* (Chapel Hill, NC: University of North Carolina Press, 1990); and the standard contemporary work by John Norton Pomeroy, *A Treatise on Equity Jurisprudence, as Administered in the United States of America*, 3 vols. (San Francisco: Bancroft-Whitney Co., 1886–1887).

24. On the merger of law and equity in New York State, see Kellen Funk, "Equity without Chancery: The Fusion of Law and Equity in the Field Code of Civil Procedure, New York, 1846–1876," *Journal of Legal History* 36, no. 2 (2015): 152–91 and Amalia D. Kessler, *Inventing American Exceptionalism: The Origins of American Adversarial Legal Culture, 1800–1877* (New Haven, CT: Yale University Press, 2017), chapters 1–4.

25. Pomeroy, *A Treatise on Equity Jurisprudence*, vol. 1, 136–8; vol. 2, 626–9.

26. *Newton v. Porter*, 69 N.Y. 133 (1877).

27. [James Barr Ames], "Can a Murderer Acquire Title by His Crime?," *Harvard Law Review* 4, no. 8 (March 1891): 394–5.

28. James Barr Ames, "Can a Murderer Acquire Title by His Crime and Keep It?," *American Law Register and Review* 45, no. 4 (1897): 225–38 (quotation from 229). "Good faith" assumes a belief that a murderer could legally inherit, but that, as I have argued, was the belief that prevailed both before *Riggs* and after it.

29. An anonymous author in 1895 asserted that *Riggs* itself had been an equitable and not a legal decision, and the same claim was made, presumably independently and with no reference to the earlier discussion, a century and a quarter later: "Murder, the Law of Inheritance and Wills," *Weekly Law Bulletin and Ohio Law Journal* 33, no. 1 (January 14, 1895): 14–18; John C. P. Goldberg and Benjamin C. Zipursky, "From *Riggs v. Palmer* to *Shelley v. Kraemer*: Judicial Power and the Law-Equity Distinction," in Dennis Klimchuk, Irit Samet, and Henry E. Smith, eds., *Philosophical Foundations of the Law of Equity* (Oxford: Oxford University Press, 2020), 291–312. But even the earlier writer frankly confessed (pp. 15–16) to be reconstructing Judge Earl's opinion according to a logic not clearly stated in it, and the more recent authors acknowledged that they were presenting "a charitable reading of *Riggs*," the opinions in which, they admitted, "are not as clear as they might have been" (pp. 298, 298n15). For a more accurate characterization of Earl's opinion—as stating as law what would more defensibly have been framed as equity—see Kenneth Henley, "Abstract Principles, Mid-Level Principles, and the Rule of Law," *Law and Philosophy*, vol. 12, no. 1 (February 1993), 128–30. Inasmuch as the vast majority of readers, past and present, have taken Earl to have been asserting legal and not equitable grounds, and interpreting a statute, the 1895 and 2020 discussions themselves are best understood as arguing that equity, as employed in *Ellerson*, would have been a sounder basis for the result it reached.

30. *Wellner v. Eckstein*, 105 Minn. 444, 461–7 (1908) (Elliott, J., dissenting).

31. [Ames], "Can a Murderer Acquire Title by His Crime?," 395.

32. Roscoe Pound, "The Decadence of Equity," *Columbia Law Review* 5, no. 1 (January 1905): 32, 34–35. For another strong endorsement of the device in such cases, see Alvah C. Hough, "A New Use for the Constructive Trust," *The Green Bag* 21, no. 7 (July 1909): 335–9.

33. "A Striking Omission in the New York Statute of Devolution," *Fiduciary Law Chronicle* 2, #3 (March 1931): 36.

34. Alison Reppy, "The Slayer's Bounty—in New York," *New York University Law Quarterly Review* 20, no. 3 (July 1945): 270.

35. Judicial decisions applying New York's slayer rule express "divergent views" that leave many matters "wildly uncertain": Ilene S. Cooper and Jaclene D'Agostino, "Forfeiture and New York's 'Slayer Rule,'" *New York State Bar Association Journal*, March–April 2015, 33; see also Julie J. Olenn, "'Til Death Do Us Part: New York's Slayer Rule and In re Estates of Covert," *Buffalo Law Review* 49, no. 3 (Fall 2001): 1341–78 and C. Raymond Radigan and Peter K. Kelly, "Need for Slayer Statute to Determine Effect of Homicide on Property Rights," *New York Law Journal* 249, no. 9 (January 14, 2013): 3.

36. Francis Bergan, *The History of the New York Court of Appeals, 1847–1932* (New York: Columbia University Press, 1985), ch. 5, "The Pressure of Calendar Problems," 120–44.

37. For example, Thomas O. Main, "Traditional Equity and Contemporary Procedure," *Washington Law Review* 78, no. 2 (May 2003): 429–514; and many of the chapters in Klimchuk, Samet, and Smith, eds., *Philosophical Foundations of the Law of Equity*. One equity remedy, the injunction, certainly has thrived and proliferated (with its origins sometimes forgotten), but most have not.

38. The rule of bipartisan renomination was strictly followed from the creation of the court in its new form in 1869 through the end of the century: *Albany Law Journal* 64 (April 1902): 105–7.

39. Such as *People ex rel. Sherwood v. Board of Canvassers* 129 N.Y. 360 (1891); *People ex rel. Nichols v. Board of Canvassers*, 129 N.Y. 395 (1891); and *People ex rel. Carter v. Rice*, 135 N.Y. 473 (1892). On the other hand, a unanimous and bipartisan Court in the same year as *Riggs* issued a rebuke to the state's Republican boss by finding him ineligible to hold an office to which he had been appointed: *People v. Platt*, 117 N.Y. 159 (1889).

40. *People v. King*, 110 N.Y. 245 (1888); *People ex rel. King v. Gallagher*, 93 N.Y. 438 (1883).

41. Albert M. Rosenblatt, ed., *The Judges of the New York Court of Appeals: A Biographical History* (New York: Fordham University Press, 2007).

42. "Justice of the Supreme Court," *Ogdensburg* [NY] *Journal*, October 6, 1873, 2; George Baker Anderson, *Our County and Its People: A Descriptive and Biographical Record of Saratoga County, New York* (The Boston History Company, 1899), 513–14; "Obituary: Judge William L. Learned," *The Argus* [Albany, NY], September 21, 1904, 6.

43. Rosenblatt, *The Judges of the New York Court of Appeals.*

44. Brian Leiter, "Explaining Theoretical Disagreement," *University of Chicago Law Review* 76, no. 3 (Summer 2009): 1232–46. What he suggested tentatively

in this article, he ten years later treated as having been conclusively established: Brian Leiter, "Theoretical Disagreements in Law: Another Look," in David Plunkett, Scott J. Shapiro, and Kevin Toh, eds., *Dimensions of Normativity: New Essays on Metaethics and Jurisprudence* (New York: Oxford University Press, 2019), 250–1.

45. "Buffalo Curious over Robed Judges," *The Argus*, June 6, 1901, 6; Frank H. Hiscock, "The Court of Appeals of New York: Some Features of Its Organization and Work," *Cornell Law Quarterly* 14, no. 3 (1929): 138.

46. Leiter, "Explaining Theoretical Disagreement," 1242–4 (quotation from 1243).

47. *Haynes v. Sherman*, 117 N.Y. 433, 437, 438 (1889) (Earl, J.).

48. *People ex rel. Bockes v. Wemple*, 115 N.Y. 302, 308, 311 (1889) (Gray, J.).

49. Leither, "Explaining Theoretical Disagreement," 1246.

50. *People v. Budd*, 117 N.Y. 1 (1889).

51. *People v. Budd*, 117 N.Y. 1, 30–34 (1889) (Gray, J., dissenting).

52. In re Jacobs, 98 N.Y. 98 (1885); William E. Forbath, *Law and the Shaping of the American Labor Movement* (Cambridge, MA: Harvard University Press, 1991); Mary O. Furner, "Defining the Public Good in the U.S. Gilded Age, 1885–1898," *Journal of the Gilded Age and Progressive Era* 17, no. 2 (April 2018): 241.

53. *People v. Budd*, 117 N.Y. 1, 71 (1889) (Peckham, J., dissenting).

54. *People ex rel. Nechamcus v. Warden of the City Prison*, 144 N.Y. 529 (1895).

55. *People ex rel. Nechamcus v. Warden of the City Prison*, 144 N.Y. 529, 542 (1895) (Peckham, J., dissenting).

56. *People v. Lochner*, 177 N.Y. 145, 165 (1904) (Gray, J., concurring); *Lochner v. New York*, 198 U.S. 45 (1905).

57. Leiter, "Explaining Theoretical Disagreement," 1246.

58. Leiter, "Explaining Theoretical Disagreement," 1241–2.

59. Stanley E. Fish, "Normal Circumstances, Literal Language, Direct Speech Acts, the Ordinary, the Everyday, the Obvious, What Goes without Saying, and Other Special Cases," *Critical Inquiry* 4, no. 4 (Summer 1978): 632–4.

60. *Records, Constitution, By-Laws and List of Members of the Century Association for the Year 1916* (New York: The Knickerbocker Press, 1916), 29; see also "Hon. John Clinton Gray," *Frank Leslie's Illustrated Newspaper*, February 4, 1888, 413.

61. *Bonnell v. Griswold*, 80 N.Y. 128 (1880); *People ex rel. Bush v. Thornton*, 25 Hun [N.Y.] 456 (1881).

62. *Bonnell v. Griswold*, 80 N.Y. 128, 135 (1880) (Danforth, J.).

63. Rosenblatt, *The Judges of the New York Court of Appeals*.

64. On Ruger: "William C. Ruger," in Dwight H. Bruce, ed., *Onondaga's Centennial: Gleanings of a Century*, vol. 2 (n.p.: The Boston History Publishing Company, 1896), 182–3. On Andrews: "Andrews, Charles," in Charles Elliott Fitch, *Encyclopedia of Biography of New York*, vol. 4 (Boston: American Historical Society, 1916), 116–17, and Francis J. McConnell, *Edward Gayer Andrews: A Bishop of*

the Methodist Episcopal Church (New York: Eaton & Mains, 1909), 5. Francis M. Finch's home town, Ithaca, was a village for most of his life and received a city charter only in 1888. Its population in 1890 was about 11,000.

65. Geo. W. Smith, "Life History of Robert Earl," in Arthur T. Smith, compiler, *Papers Read before the Herkimer County Historical Society for the Years 1899, 1900, 1901, and to July 1, 1902, and a Memorial of the Late Robert Earl* (Herkimer, NY: Citizen Publishing Company, 1902), 432–9.

66. Oliver Wendell Holmes to Felix Frankfurter, March 28, 1922, in Robert M. Mennel and Christine L. Compston, eds., *Holmes and Frankfurter: Their Correspondence, 1912–1934* (Hanover, NH: University Press of New England, 1996), 138.

67. Richard Skolnik, "Rufus Peckham, 1838–1909," in Leon Friedman and Fred L. Israel, eds., *The Justices of the United States Supreme Court, 1789–1969* (New York: Chelsea House Publishers, 1969), vol. 3, 1687, 1700–1701.

Chapter 5

1. The fullest biography is Andrew L. Kaufman, *Cardozo* (Cambridge, MA: Harvard University Press, 1998); chapter 12, pp. 199–212, deals with Cardozo's Storrs Lectures and the book that resulted from them.

2. Benjamin N. Cardozo, *The Nature of the Judicial Process* (New Haven, CT: Yale University Press, 1921), Lecture I, "Introduction. The Method of Philosophy," 9–50.

3. Cardozo, *The Nature*, 40–43.

4. Cardozo, *The Nature*, 71.

5. Cardozo, *The Nature*, 14.

6. Cardozo, *The Nature*, 42.

7. Cardozo, *The Nature*, 43.

8. Kaufman, *Cardozo*, chapter 13, 223–42; H. Jefferson Powell, "Cardozo's Foot: The Chancellor's Conscience and Constructive Trusts," *Law and Contemporary Problems* 56, #3 (1993): 7–27.

9. *Beatty v. Guggenheim Exploration Co.*, 225 N.Y. 380, 386, 389 (1919) (Cardozo, J.).

10. Kaufman, *Cardozo*, 363.

11. He has been aptly described as "[a] genius at making the law appear changeless as he changed it": Edward A. Purcell, Jr., *Brandeis and the Progressive Constitution* (New Haven, CT: Yale University Press, 2000), 133.

12. Most notably John T. Noonan Jr., "The Passengers of *Palsgraf*," in *Persons and Masks of the Law: Cardozo, Holmes, Jefferson, and Wythe as Makers of the Masks* (Berkeley: University of California Press, 1976), 111–51, and Richard Polenberg, *The World of Benjamin Cardozo: Personal Values and the Judicial Process* (Cambridge, MA: Harvard University Press, 1997). For other examples, see William

Powers Jr., "Reputology," *Cardozo Law Review* 12, no. 6 (June 1991): 1941–54; Dan Simon, "On the Double-Consciousness of Judging: The Problematic Legacy of Cardozo," *Oregon Law Review* 79, no. 4 (Winter 2000): 1033–80; Michael D. Green and Ashley DiMuzio, "Cardozo and the Civil Jury," *Touro Law Review* 34, no. 1 (2018): 183–235; and Steven L. Winter, "Cardozo's Freudian Slips," *Touro Law Review* 34, no. 1 (2018): 359–76.

13. *Slocum v. Metropolitan Life Insurance Co.*, 245 Mass. 565 (1923); In re Tyler's Estate, 140 Wn. 679 (1926) (over two dissenting opinions); In re Wilkins's Estate, 192 Wis. 111 (1927); *Garwols v. Bankers Trust Co.*, 251 Mich. 421 (1930); *Smith v. Todd*, 155 S.C. 323 (1930); *De Zotell v. Mutual Life Insurance*, 60 S.D. 532 (1932); *Price v. Hitaffer*, 164 Md. 505 (1933).

14. *Wilson v. Randolph*, 50 Nev. 371 (1927); see also *Wilson v. Randolph*, 50 Nev. 440 (1928).

15. *Bryant v. Bryant*, 193 N.C. 372 (1927); *Sherman v. Weber*, 113 N.J. Eq. 451 (1933).

16. Matter of Sparks, 172 Misc. 642 (N.Y. Surr. Ct. 1939), discussed in detail by Alison Reppy, "The Slayer's Bounty—in New York," *New York University Law Quarterly Review* 20, no. 3 (July 1945): 270–311.

17. On the two authors, the course, and the textbook, see the excellent and detailed essay by William N. Eskridge, Jr. and Philip P. Frickey, "An Historical and Critical Introduction to *The Legal Process*," li–cxxxvi, in Henry M. Hart Jr. and Albert M. Sacks, *The Legal Process: Basic Problems in the Making and Application of Law*, edited by William N. Eskridge Jr. and Philip P. Frickey (Westbury, NY: The Foundation Press, 1994). On the *Legal Process* school of thought, see G. Edward White, "The Evolution of Reasoned Elaboration: Jurisprudential Criticism and Social Change," *Virginia Law Review* 59, no. 2 (February 1973): 279–302; Vincent A. Wellman, "Dworkin and the Legal Process Tradition: The Legacy of Hart and Sacks," *Arizona Law Review* 29, no. 3 (1987): 413–74; and Neil Duxbury, "Faith in Reason: The Process Tradition," *Cardozo Law Review* 15, no. 3 (December 1993): 601–705.

18. Duxbury, "Faith in Reason," 661.

19. "Problem No. 2: An Introduction to the Differences between Enacted and Decisional Law: The Case of the Murdering Heir," in Hart and Sacks, *The Legal Process*, 68–102.

20. Such slanting is not unavoidable, as witness the genuinely probing and open-minded exploration of *Riggs*, though also based chiefly on the conventional legal sources, in another textbook: Caleb Nelson, *Statutory Interpretation* (New York: Foundation Press, 2011), 5–26.

21. Hart and Sacks, *The Legal Process*, 98.

22. Hart and Sacks, *The Legal Process*, 68–71.

23. Hart and Sacks, *The Legal Process*, 68.

24. Hart and Sacks, *The Legal Process*, 68.

25. Hart and Sacks, *The Legal Process*, 93–94.

26. Hart and Sacks, *The Legal Process*, 89.

27. Hart and Sacks, *The Legal Process*, 88–90.

28. Hart and Sacks, *The Legal Process*, 92.

29. Though, again, only because of a detail in their invented case, the jury's indefensibly lenient verdict.

30. On the same clear though rarely explicit preference in Hart's other writings for law made by judges rather than by legislatures, see Purcell, *Brandeis and the Progressive Constitution*, chapter 9.

31. Hart and Sacks, *The Legal Process*, 97.

32. Hart and Sacks, *The Legal Process*, 97.

33. Hart and Sacks, *The Legal Process*, 91.

34. Hart and Sacks, *The Legal Process*, 1198–205 (quotation from 1198–9); see also 492.

35. Hart and Sacks, *The Legal Process*, 482–96.

36. Hart and Sacks, *The Legal Process*, 496.

37. Ronald M. Dworkin, "The Model of Rules," *University of Chicago Law Review* 35, no. 1 (Autumn 1967): 14–46; *Taking Rights Seriously* (Cambridge, MA: Harvard University Press, 1977).

38. H. L. A. Hart, *The Concept of Law* (Oxford: Clarendon Press, 1961), especially chapters 6 and 7.

39. Dworkin, *Taking Rights Seriously*, 40–41.

40. Dworkin, *Taking Rights Seriously*, 39, 41.

41. Dworkin, *Taking Rights Seriously*, 58.

42. Dworkin, *Taking Rights Seriously*, 118–23.

43. Dworkin, *Taking Rights Seriously*, 41–42.

44. Ronald Dworkin, *Law's Empire* (Cambridge, MA: Belknap Press of Harvard University Press, 1986).

45. Dworkin, *Law's Empire*, 130–131.

46. Dworkin, *Law's Empire*, 39.

47. Dworkin, *Law's Empire*, 20, 38, 39.

48. Dworkin, *Law's Empire*, 36, 38.

49. Dworkin, *Law's Empire*, 17, 137.

50. Dworkin, "The Model of Rules," 23.

51. Dworkin, *Law's Empire*, 354.

52. Brian Leiter, "Explaining Theoretical Disagreement," *University of Chicago Law Review* 76, no. 3 (Summer 2009): 1215–50.

53. Leiter, "Explaining Theoretical Disagreement," 1244–6.

54. Brian Leiter, *Naturalizing Jurisprudence: Essays on American Legal Realism and Naturalism in Legal Philosophy* (New York: Oxford University Press, 2007).

55. Dworkin, *Taking Rights Seriously*, 42.

56. *Riggs v. Palmer*, 115 N.Y. 506, 511–12 (1889) (Earl, J.).

57. Jamal Greene, "The Anticanon," *Harvard Law Review* 125, no. 2 (December 2011): 379–475.

58. For illustrations, see Paul Finkelman, "*Scott v. Sandford*: The Court's Most Dreadful Case and How It Changed History," *Chicago-Kent Law Review* 3, no. 1 (2007): 5–10.

59. Stewart F. Hancock, Jr., "Meeting the Needs: Fairness, Morality, Creativity and Common Sense," *Albany Law Review* 68, no. 1 (2004): 87.

60. Jeremy Waldron, *"Partly Laws Common to All Mankind": Foreign Law in American Courts* (New Haven, CT: Yale University Press, 2012).

61. Waldron, *"Partly Laws,"* 63, 66–67.

62. Waldron, *"Partly Laws,"* 24; see also 50–51.

63. Recall, too, that Earl deliberately excluded one supporting precedent from a jurisdiction foreign to New York and deeply influenced by French law, Louisiana, that would have blunted his claim that the matter could not be left to legislative action.

64. P. B. Olney, "John Clinton Gray," *Harvard Graduates' Magazine* 24, no. 94 (December 1915): 387.

65. R. H. Helmholz, *Natural Law in Court: A History of Legal Theory in Practice* (Cambridge, MA: Harvard University Press, 2015), 165–8 (quotation from 165).

66. Adrian Vermeule, *Common-Good Constitutionalism: Recovering the Classical Legal Tradition* (Malden, MA: Polity Press, 2022).

67. Richard A. Posner, *Cardozo: A Study in Reputation* (Chicago: University of Chicago Press, 1990), 24–26; *The Problems of Jurisprudence* (Cambridge, MA: Harvard University Press, 1990), 106; *The Problematics of Moral and Legal Theory* (Cambridge, MA: Belknap Press of Harvard University Press, 1999), 140–141.

68. Posner, *The Problematics*, 140.

69. *International Union, Aerospace & Agricultural Implement Workers v. Johnson Controls, Inc.* 886 F.2d 871, 903 (7th Cir. 1989) (Posner, J., dissenting). For extended praise of *Riggs* by another leading legal pragmatist, see Daniel A. Farber, "Courts, Statutes, and Public Policy: The Case of the Murderous Heir," *S.M.U. Law Review* 53, no. 1 (Winter 2000): 31–47.

70. The two, however, can be and sometimes are combined, for example in the argument that judges should honestly recognize the role of extralegal factors in their thinking and rely chiefly on the ones (different for different realists) that would best guide their decisions.

71. Leiter, "Explaining Theoretical Disagreement," 1244–6.

72. Dennis W. Patterson, "Theoretical Disagreement, Legal Positivism, and Interpretation," *Ratio Juris* 31, no. 3 (September 2018): 260–75 (quotations from 271–2, 273).

73. Antonin Scalia and Bryan A. Garner, *Reading Law: The Interpretation of Legal Texts* (St. Paul, MN: Thomson/West, 2012), 99–100.

74. Antonin Scalia, *A Matter of Interpretation: The Federal Courts and the Law: An Essay* (Princeton, NJ: Princeton University Press, 1997).

75. Antonin Scalia, "The Rule of Law as a Law of Rules," *University of Chicago Law Review* 56, no. 4 (Autumn 1989): 1175–88.

76. That a law of rules and a set of equitable remedies departing from them to achieve justice in the situation of a particular case are complementary rather than opposed is a longstanding theme, argued by, for example, Lawrence B. Solum, "Equity and the Rule of Law," *Nomos* 36 (1994): 120–147.

77. *Grupo Mexicano de Desarrollo, S.A. v. Alliance Bond Fund, Inc.*, 527 U.S. 308 (1999).

78. For example, Frederick Schauer, "The Generality of Law," *West Virginia Law Review* 107, no. 1 (Fall 2004): 227 and "The Limited Domain of the Law," *Virginia Law Review* 90, no. 7 (November 2004): 1937–8.

79. Paula R. Backscheider, *Reflections on Biography* (New York: Oxford University Press, 1999), 175.

Chapter 6

1. Sarah E. Hamill, "Review of Legal History," *Social & Legal Studies* 28, no. 4 (August 2019): 538–59.

2. Richard A. Posner, *The Problems of Jurisprudence* (Cambridge, MA: Harvard University Press, 1990), 210.

3. Paul A. Lombardo, "Legal Archaeology: Recovering the Stories behind the Cases," *Journal of Law, Medicine & Ethics* 36, no. 3 (Fall 2008): 589.

4. Karl Llewellyn, *The Bramble Bush* (Dobbs Ferry, NY: Oceana Publications, 1960), 39.

5. Joan Vogel, "Cases in Context: Lake Champlain Wars, Gentrification and *Ploof v. Putnam*," *St. Louis University Law Journal* 45, no. 3 (Summer 2001): 791–815.

6. Debora L. Threedy, "A Fish Story: *Alaska Packers' Association v. Domenico*," *Utah Law Review* 2000, no. 2: 185–222.

7. A. W. Brian Simpson, *Leading Cases in the Common Law* (Oxford: Clarendon Press, 1995), 11.

8. For a view of legal archaeology as pedagogically counterproductive in more than small doses, see Patricia D. White, "Afterword and Response: What Digging Does and Does Not Do," *Utah Law Review* 2000, no. 2: 301–3.

9. Jerome Frank, "A Plea for Lawyer-Schools," *Yale Law Journal* 56, no. 8 (September 1947): 1311.

10. Judith Resnik, "Constructing the Canon," *Yale Journal of Law & the Humanities* 2, no. 1 (Winter 1990), 226.

11. David Achtenberg, "With Malice towards Some: *United States v. Kirby*, Malicious Prosecution, and the Fourteenth Amendment," *Rutgers Law Journal* 26, no. 2 (Winter 1995): 273–342.

12. Angela Fernandez, "An Object Lesson in Speculation: Multiple Views of the Cathedral in *Leaf v. International Galleries*," *University of Toronto Law Journal* 58, no. 4 (Fall 2008): 481–519.

13. William R. Casto and Val D. Ricks, " 'Dear Sister Antillico': The Story of *Kirksey v. Kirksey*," *Georgetown Law Journal* 94, no. 2 (January 2006): 321–97 (quotation from 326).

14. Judith L. Maute, "*Peevyhouse v. Garland Coal & Mining Co.* Revisited: The Ballad of Willie and Lucille," *Northwestern University Law Review* 89, no. 4 (1995): 1346.

15. John Hasmas, "The Myth of the Rule of Law," *Wisconsin Law Review* 1995, no. 1: 214; Waldron, "*Partly Laws*," 63; Claire Finkelstein, "Hobbesian Legal Reasoning and the Problem of Wicked Laws," in S. A. Lloyd, ed., *Hobbes Today: Insights for the 21st Century* (Cambridge: Cambridge University Press, 2013), 67; and Frederick Schauer, "Second-Order Vagueness in Law," in Geert Keil and Ralf Poscher, eds., *Vagueness and Law: Philosophical and Legal Perspectives* (Oxford: Oxford University Press, 2016), 180. See also Wikipedia, "*Riggs v. Palmer*" (visited August 11, 2021): "his grandfather's large estate."

16. *Riggs v. Palmer*, 115 N.Y. 506, 508 (1889) (Earl, J.).

17. *Preston v. Palmer*, 42 Hun 388, 389 (1887).

18. For example, Stanley E. Fish, "Normal Circumstances, Literal Language, Direct Speech Acts, the Ordinary, the Everyday, the Obvious, What Goes without Saying, and Other Special Cases," *Critical Inquiry* 4, no. 4 (Summer 1978): 632; Allan C. Hutchinson and John N. Wakefield, "A Hard Look at 'Hard Cases': The Nightmare of a Noble Dreamer," *Oxford Journal of Legal Studies* 2, no. 1 (Spring 1982): 95; Charles Silver, "Elmer's Case: A Legal Positivist Replies to Dworkin," *Law and Philosophy* 6, no. 3 (December 1987): 383; Mitchell C. Newton-Matza, "*Riggs v. Palmer*," in Peter Eisenstadt, ed., *The Encyclopedia of New York State* (Syracuse, NY: Syracuse University Press, 2005), 1305–06. The list could easily be made much longer.

19. *Riggs v. Palmer*, 115 N.Y. 506, 508–9 (1889) (Earl, J.).

20. *Riggs v. Palmer*, 115 N.Y. 506, 508 (1889) (Earl, J.).

21. "End of the Palmer Murder Trial," *Courier and Freeman* [Potsdam, NY], November 15, 1882, 2.

22. "End of the Palmer Murder Trial," *Courier and Freeman* [Potsdam, NY], November 15, 1882, 2.

23. Appeal Book, 6.

24. Carl Becker, "The Reviewing of Historical Books," *Annual Report of the American Historical Association for the Year 1912* (Washington, DC: American Historical Association, 1914), 133.

25. Kim Lane Scheppele, "Facing Facts in Legal Interpretation," *Representations* no. 30 (Spring 1990): 73n49; Frederick Schauer, *Thinking Like a Lawyer: A New Introduction to Legal Reasoning* (Cambridge, MA: Harvard University Press, 2009), 33; A. W. Brian Simpson, *Reflections on "The Concept of Law"* (Oxford: Oxford University Press, 2011), 211; Brian Leiter, "Explaining Theoretical Disagreement," *University of Chicago Law Review* 76, no. 3 (Summer 2009): 1235; R. H. Helmholz, *Natural Law in Court: A History of Legal Theory in Practice* (Cambridge, MA: Harvard University Press, 2015), 166; Hadley Arkes, review of Helmholz, *Natural Law in Court*, *First Things* #261 (2016): 49.

26. The Court's classic statement of the need for genuinely adverse interests in a case is *Lord v. Veazie*, 49 U.S. 251 (1850).

27. Maute, "Peevyhouse."

28. The similarly fortuitous involvement of a legal heavyweight (in this instance, Nathan Sanford, a future chancellor of New York State) likewise had much to do with transforming a minor local squabble into the leading property case of *Pierson v. Post*: Angela Fernandez, *Pierson v. Post, the Hunt for the Fox: Law and Professionalization in American Legal Culture* (New York: Cambridge University Press, 2018).

29. Lindsay G. Robertson, *Conquest by Law: How the Discovery of America Dispossessed Indigenous Peoples of Their Lands* (New York: Oxford University Press, 2005).

30. Robertson, *Conquest by Law*, xii. For an argument that another important decision of Marshall's, the last of his career, was crucially shaped by strategic political considerations of the moment, see William Davenport Mercer, *Diminishing the Bill of Rights: Barron v. Baltimore and the Foundations of American Liberty* (Norman, OK: University of Oklahoma Press, 2017).

31. Robertson, *Conquest by Law*, 116.

32. Robertson, *Conquest by Law*, ch. 6.

33. Sally Greene, "*State v. Mann* Exhumed," *North Carolina Law Review* 87, no. 3 (March 2009): 701–55.

34. A. W. B. Simpson, "Legal Liability for Bursting Reservoirs: The Historical Context of *Rylands v. Fletcher*," *Journal of Legal Studies* 13, no. 2 (June 1984): 209–64 (quotation from 249).

35. Jed Handelsman Shugerman, "The Floodgates of Strict Liability: Bursting Reservoirs and the Adoption of *Rylands v. Fletcher* in the Gilded Age," *Yale Law Journal* 110, no. 2 (November 2000): 333–78; see also the same author's "The Twist of Long Terms: Judicial Elections, Role Fidelity, and American Tort Law," *Georgetown Law Journal* 98, no. 5 (June 2010): 1349–413.

36. Blake A. Watson, *Buying American from the Indians: Johnson v. McIntosh and the History of Native Land Rights* (Norman, OK: University of Oklahoma Press, 2012), 406–7n53.

37. Ilan Wurman, "Law Historians' Fallacies," *North Dakota Law Review* 91, no. 1 (2015): 206.

38. David L. Faigman, *Constitutional Fictions: A Unified Theory of Constitutional Facts* (New York: Oxford University Press, 2008), 90–91.

39. Charles L. Barzun, "Impeaching Precedent," *University of Chicago Law Review* 80, no. 4 (Fall 2013): 1626, 1627.

40. Barzun, "Impeaching Precedent," 1629–30.

41. *Mitchell v. Helms*, 530 U.S. 793, 826, 828 (2000) (Thomas, J.).

42. Seminole Tribe of *Florida v. Florida*, 517 U.S. 44, 116–22 (1996) (Souter, J., dissenting).

43. On the same discrepancy, see also Edward A. Purcell Jr., "The Particularly Dubious Case of *Hans v. Louisiana*: An Essay on Law, Race, History, and Federal Courts," *North Carolina Law Review* 81, no. 5 (June 2003): 2058.

44. Barzun, "Impeaching Precedent," 1654, 1675.

45. Barzun, "Impeaching Precedent," 1676.

46. Paul A. Lombardo, *Three Generations, No Imbeciles: Eugenics, the Supreme Court, and Buck v. Bell* (Baltimore, MD: Johns Hopkins University Press, 2008).

47. Timothy Messer-Kruse, *The Trial of the Haymarket Anarchists: Terrorism and Justice in the Gilded Age* (New York: Palgrave Macmillan, 2011).

48. *United States v. Wiltberger*, 18 U.S. 76, 96 (1820) (Marshall, C. J.); *Northern Securities Co. v. United States*, 193 U.S. 197, 400 (1904) (Holmes, J., dissenting).

49. Richard Danzig, "*Hadley v. Baxendale*: A Study in the Industrialization of the Law," *Journal of Legal Studies* 4, no. 2 (June 1975): 249–84.

50. Danzig, "*Hadley v. Baxendale*," 250.

51. Danzig, "*Hadley v. Baxendale*," 284.

52. 310 U.S. 534 (1940).

53. William D. Popkin, *Statutes in Court: The History and Theory of Statutory Interpretation* (Durham, NC: Duke University Press, 1999), 204–6 (quotation from 204).

54. Leonard W. Levy, *A License to Steal: The Forfeiture of Property* (Chapel Hill, NC: University of North Carolina Press, 1996).

55. *Bouie v. City of Columbia*, 378 U.S. 347, 352 (1964) (Brennan, J.).

56. Robert Kaatz, "Is There an Ex Post Facto Prohibition on Judicial Decisions that Retroactively Enlarge Criminal Punishment?" *Wayne Law Review* 47, no. 4 (Winter/Spring 2001–2002): 1367–84.

57. Lawrence M. Friedman, *Total Justice* (New York: Russell Sage Foundation, 1985), 120–121.

58. Keith Whittington, "The New Originalism," *Georgetown Journal of Law and Public Policy* 22, no. 2 (Summer 2004): 599–613.

59. Jack M. Balkin, "*Brown v. Board of Education*—A Critical Introduction," 1–74, in Jack M. Balkin, ed, *What Brown v. Board of Education Should Have Said* (New York: New York University Press, 2001), 14.

60. Robertson, *Conquest by Law*, xiii.

61. *Smith v. Allwright*, 321 U.S. 649, 669 (1944) (Roberts, J., dissenting).

62. Jack M. Balkin, *Constitutional Redemption: Political Faith in an Unjust World* (Cambridge, MA: Harvard University Press, 2011), 188.

63. Jamal Greene, "The Anticanon," *Harvard Law Review* 125, no. 2 (December 2011): 379–475.

64. Examples of the use of the phrase in Supreme Court opinions are Planned Parenthood of *Southeastern Pa. v. Casey*, 505 U.S. 833, 863 (1992) (O'Connor, Kennedy, and Souter, JJ.), and *Trump v. Hawaii*, 585 U.S. ___ (slip opinion, 38, Roberts, C. J.); also the equivalent wordings "not correct when it was decided" (*Lawrence v. Texas*, 539 U.S. 538, 578 [2003]) (Kennedy, J.) and "egregiously wrong when it was decided" (*Dobbs v. Jackson Women's Health Organization*, 547 U.S. ___, slip opinion, 6, see also 44, 69, Alito, J.). The term and its use are discussed by Balkin, *Constitutional Redemption*, ch. 7; Morton J. Horwitz, "Foreword: The Constitution of Change: Legal Fundamentalism without Fundamentality," *Harvard Law Review* 107, no. 1 (November 1993): 30–117; L. A. Powe Jr., "Intragenerational Constitutional Overruling," *Notre Dame Law Review* 89, no. 5 (May 2014): 2093–127; and Christopher R. Green, "Constitutional Truthmakers," *Notre Dame Journal of Law, Ethics & Public Policy* 32, no. 2 (2018): 497–525.

65. Balkin, *Constitutional Redemption*, 180.

66. R. G. Collingwood, *An Autobiography* (Oxford: Clarendon Press, 1939), 31, 33.

67. Kenneth Minogue, "Method in Intellectual History: Quentin Skinner's *Foundations*," *Philosophy* 56, no. 218 (October 1981): 544.

68. Richard A. Posner, *The Problems of Jurisprudence* (Cambridge, MA: Harvard University Press, 1990), 3.

69. Some notable examples are proposed in the chapters on Holmes and Cardozo in John T. Noonan Jr., *Persons and Masks of the Law: Cardozo, Holmes, Jefferson, and Wythe as Makers of the Masks* (Berkeley: University of California Press, 1976). Another may be the case of *Erie Railroad Co. v. Tompkins*, 304 U.S. 65 (1938), on which, see Edward A. Purcell Jr., *Brandeis and the Progressive Constitution* (New Haven, CT: Yale University Press, 2000); and Suzan Sofia McGovern, *Erie v. Tompkins: An Erie History* (New York: n.p., 2020).

Epilogue

1. "The Republican County Convention," *Ogdensburg* [NY] *Journal*, September 5, 1887, 2.

2. "Some of the Measures Introduced by Mr. Lang," *Courier and Freeman* [Potsdam, NY], March 9, 1892, 2; Will L. Lloyd, *The Red Book: An Illustrated Legislative Manual of the State* (Albany, NY: James B. Lyon, 1892), 141.

3. "Death of Lewis C. Lang," *Ogdensburg Journal*, December 11, 1893, 4.

4. "Pardon C. Williams," *New York Times*, January 19, 1925, 17; John A. Haddock, *The Growth of a Century: As Illustrated in the History of Jefferson County, New York, from 1793 to 1894* (Philadelphia: Sherman & Co., 1894), 273–5.

5. *Lawton v. Steele*, 152 U.S. 133 (1894), affirming *Lawton v. Steele*, 119 N.Y. 226 (1890). See William B. Meyer, "Class, Conservation, and the Police Power in the American Gilded Age: The Origins of *Lawton v. Steele*," *American Journal of Legal History* 62, no. 3 (September 2022): 215–36.

6. "Death of C. E. Sanford," *Potsdam* [NY] *Herald-Recorder*, September 10, 1915, 1.

7. Carlton E. Sanford, *Early History of the Town of Hopkinton* (Boston: The Bartlett Press, 1903); C. E. Sanford, *Letters, Essays and Biographical Sketches* (Saratoga Springs, NY: The Saratogian Print, 1907), 217–18.

8. "Ex-Justice Russell Dead," *New York Times*, February 4, 1903, 9.

9. Leslie W. Russell, "The Spirit v. the Letter of the Statute: Can Legislation Legalize Murder?" *Proceedings of the New York State Bar Association, Held at the City of Albany, January 18–19, 1898* (Albany: James B. Lyon, 1898), 90–99.

10. "Judge Potter Criticised," *Commercial Advertiser* [Canton, NY], September 3, 1885, 2; untitled editorial, *Ogdensburg* [NY] *Advance and Weekly St. Lawrence Democrat*, October 22, 1885, 2; "Judge Joseph Potter," *Ogdensburg Journal*, November 24, 1885, 2.

11. "Hon. Joseph Potter," *The Medico-Legal Journal* 21 (1903): 488.

12. *The National Register of Historic Places 1976* (Washington, DC: Department of the Interior, 1976), 525.

13. "Judge Sawyer Dead," *Commercial Advertiser* [Canton, NY], February 22, 1888, 3.

14. "The Retirement of Judge Landon," *Proceedings of the New York State Bar Association, Held at the City of Albany, January 21–22, 1902* (Albany: The Argus Company, 1902), 395.

15. Richard Skolnik, "Rufus Peckham, 1838–1909," in Leon Friedman and Fred L. Israel, eds., *The Justices of the United States Supreme Court, 1789–1969* (New York: Chelsea House Publishers, 1969), vol. 3, 1685–703.

16. "Judge Finch," *The Argus* [Albany, NY], February 25, 1895, 4.

17. Veronica Benigno, "Robert Earl," in Albert M. Rosenblatt, ed., *The Judges of the New York Court of Appeals* (New York: Fordham University Press, 2007), 127–33.

18. Brian Quinn, "Charles Andrews," in Rosenblatt, *The Judges of the New York Court of Appeals*, 177–84.

19. Brian Quinn, "William Shankland Andrews," in Rosenblatt, *The Judges of the New York Court of Appeals*, 433–8.

20. "A Fruitful Life Ended," Rochester [NY] *Democrat and Chronicle*, September 26, 1899, 10; Norman Kee, "George Franklin Danforth," in Rosenblatt, *The Judges of the New York Court of Appeals*, 199.

21. Margery Corbin Eddy, "John Clinton Gray," in Rosenblatt, *The Judges of the New York Court of Appeals*, 243–4; "Republicans Concede Judge Gray's Election," *New York Times*, November 7, 1902, 2.

22. United States Census of Population, 1900, Town of Stockholm, St. Lawrence County, New York; "West Stockholm," *Norwood* [NY] *News*, February 27, 1906, 8.

23. United States Census of Population, 1900, Town of Stockholm, St. Lawrence County, New York; "West Stockholm," *Potsdam* [NY] *Herald-Recorder*, December 6, 1929, 7.

24. "Willis Doud Dies at 96," *Ogdensburg* [NY] *Journal*, May 21, 1963, 7.

25. "Mrs. Philo P. Riggs," *Norwood* [NY] *News*, March 23, 1909, 8; "Philo P. Riggs Was Buried Wednesday," *Ogdensburg* [NY] *Advance and St. Lawrence Weekly Democrat*, February 19, 1920, 1.

26. "Etta May (Preston) Riggs 1878–1968" and "Leslie Ernest Riggs 1874–1943" at https://wikitree (pages maintained by Wallace Philips, visited August 11, 2021).

27. Dale J. Burnett, *Hopkinton: The Second Hundred Years* (Bloomington, IN: AuthorHouse, 2008), 234.

28. R. H. Coats and M. C. Maclean, *The American-Born in Canada: A Statistical Interpretation* (Toronto: The Ryerson Press, 1943), 23–24.

29. Manuscript schedules, Census of Canada, 1891, Province of Ontario, District 92, South Middlesex, Township of Westminster, 28; Manuscript schedules, Census of Canada, 1901, Province of Ontario, District 87, East Middlesex, Sub-District C, 3; Manuscript schedules, Census of Canada, 1911, Province of Ontario, City of London, Sub-District 5; "Local Items: Death of Mrs. Gray," *The Advertiser* [London, ON], April 8, 1908, 8; Manuscript schedules, Census of Canada, 1921, Province of Ontario, City of London, Ward 3, Sub-District 41; Archives of Ontario, Registrations of Deaths, Middlesex, 1916.

30. Certificates of Registration of Death, Archives of Ontario, MS 935, Reel 489; photograph of the gravestone in "Elmer E Palmer (1865–1934)," https://www.findagrave.com (visited August 11, 2021); Archives of Ontario, Registrations of Deaths, Middlesex, 1914.

31. "Ice Bound Isle Is Home of 600," *Detroit* [MI] *Free Press*, January 5, 1930, part 3, 15; "Brave Doctor about to Start 16th Year of Service on Isle," ibid., Jan. 23, 1939, 4; "Friend of Many," *The State Journal* [Lansing, MI], September 2, 1961, 16; Fran Martin, "Et Ceteras," *Petoskey* [MI] *News-Review*, May 11, 1973, 4; Doyle C. Fitzpatrick, "Dr. Russell E. Palmer," *Journal of Beaver Island History*, 2 (1980): 118–25.

32. Harold Frederic, *Seth's Brother's Wife: A Study of Life in the Greater New York* (New York: Charles Scribner's Sons, 1887), 388.

Index

Owens, Sarah, 87, 96, 97
Owens v. Owens: 44; New York Court of Appeals rejects as precedent, 46, 48, 49; mentioned. 53, 54, 83, 84, 86; *see also* North Carolina; Sarah Owens

Paine, James H., 40
Palmer, Byron, 13, 14
Palmer, Cecelia, *see* Preston, Cecelia
Palmer, Dorothea, 13
Palmer, Edgar, 175, 176
Palmer, Eliza: background of, 14, 179n14; at Elmer E. Palmer's trial, 21, 23, 26, 27; later life of, 174; marriage to Francis B. Palmer, 14–15, 16, 18, 22, 36; provisions for in Francis B. Palmer's will, 14–15, 37, 39; supposed change in will to favor, 146–48
Palmer, Elmer E.: arrest and imprisonment of, 17–19; and death of Francis B. Palmer, 15–16; early life of, 14–15; at Elmira Reformatory, 34–36; inheritance challenged in the courts, 37–48; light sentence as explanation of outcome in *Riggs v. Palmer*, 15, 7, 91–92, 95–98, 102, 104, 105, 113, 148, 149, 156, 169; motives for murdering Francis B. Palmer, 146–48; moves to Canada, 36–37, 184n91; not civilly dead, 85–86; trial, conviction, and sentence of, 20–34
Palmer, Francis B.: background and family of, 12, 13–14; character questioned, 24, 34; death of, 1, 8, 11, 15–16, 17–18, 19; Elmer E. Palmer's trial for murdering, 20–28; second marriage of, 14–15, 36; provisions of will of, 14, 37; supposed testamentary intentions

of, 54, 146–48; supposed wealth of, 146; mentioned, 175
Palmer, Ida, 175, 176
Palmer, Lorette, *see* Riggs, Lorette
Palmer, Mary Gray, 175
Palmer, Ona, 175
Palmer, Percy Douglas, 175
Palmer, Phoebe, 13, 14
Palmer, Russell Ethelbert, 175–76
Palmer, Suzanne Brisbois, 175–76
Palsgraf v. Long Island Railroad Co., 173
Patterson, Dennis M., 136–37
Peckham, Rufus W., Jr., 106, 109–10, 111–13, 173
Peevyhouse v. Garland Coal & Mining Co., 150
Pennsylvania, court decisions in, 50–51, 71, 75; punishment of murdering heirs in, 84, 97; slayer statute, 58–59, 126; mentioned, 28, 32, 155
People v. Budd, 108–10, 132, 173
People v. Walsh, 109–10, 173
Perry v. Strawbridge, 53, 59, 75, 90, 97, 103, 132
Pfanschmidt, Blanche, 52
Pfanschmidt, Charles, 52
Pfanschmidt, Mathilda, 52
Pfanschmidt, Ray, 52–53, 80
picra, 15, 23, 25, 27
Piltdown Man, 134
plain meaning, 64–65, 72, 107, 108, 163
Plessy v. Ferguson, 133, 167
Ploof v. Putnam, 143
poisoning: cases of in postbellum northern New York, 16–17; and definition of first-degree murder, 28–29; as means of murder, 16. *See also* strychnine
Popkin, William D., 163–64
positivism, legal, 135, 136–37

9 781438 496351